COLLEGE STUDENT DEATH

Guidance for a Caring Campus

Edited by

**Rosa Cintrón
Erin Taylor Weathers
Katherine Garlough**

College Student
Educators International

University Press of America,® Inc.
Lanham · Boulder · New York · Toronto · Plymouth, UK

Copyright © 2007 by
American College Personnel Association

University Press of America,® Inc.
4501 Forbes Boulevard
Suite 200
Lanham, Maryland 20706
UPA Acquisitions Department (301) 459-3366

Estover Road
Plymouth PL6 7PY
United Kingdom

Library of Congress Control Number: 2007922241
ISBN-13: 978-0-7618-3700-8 (paperback : alk. paper)
ISBN-10: 0-7618-3700-0 (paperback : alk. paper)

Co-published by arrangement with
the American College Personnel Association

♾™ The paper used in this publication meets the minimum
requirements of American National Standard for Information
Sciences—Permanence of Paper for Printed Library Materials,
ANSI Z39.48—1984

Dedication

For Danielito

Marlo

and

Logan

Every day you are missed.
Every day we were blessed.

Contents

Acknowledgements

The editors wish to thank the following persons for their participation in this book: Thank you to the American College Personnel Association (ACPA) for their generous support of this endeavor, especially Dr. Stan Carpenter, ACPA Media Board Editor Chair until 2002, and Dr. Nancy Evans, Media Board Editor until 2006. Media Board Editor Dr. Ellen Broido was equally consistent in her involvement with this project. We extend our gratitude to all ACPA Books and Media Board Members who served as reviewers. Our profound gratitude is extended to each of our contributors, experts and survivors alike. Many of you shared painful memories as professionals, witnesses, or family members, and these accounts greatly enriched our book. This topic has never been easy to write about, but each of you did so with dignity, eloquence, and thoughtful insight.

Rosa is indebted to Erin who walked into Rosa's office one day after having presented a paper at a regional conference on this topic. Her insistence was translated into this manuscript. Like some of my other students, she has educated me in areas in which I was unfamiliar. For her collegiality I will always be thankful.

Erin wishes to thank Jan Schultz and Nancy Welch, who are both contributors to this project, dear friends and people important in Logan's life. Their grace and humor in the midst of my sorrow reminded me I would laugh again. A profound thank you goes to my amazing parents who allowed me to share some of their most painful moments. And finally, I thank my patient husband, Ned, and three perfect children, Gwyn, Ian, and Henry—my cup runneth over.

Katherine thanks her family and friends for a love that sustains all that she does. I am thankful to Rosa Cintrón for inviting me to work on the editing team. At the very end of the manuscript's completion my dear uncle passed suddenly, reminding me that it is impossible to divorce the strong emotions that death evokes from the practical tasks one must perform while in the midst of grief and that gracefulness in crisis is a blessing.

Rosa Cintrón, Erin Taylor Weathers, and Katherine Garlough

Introduction

Death on Campus:
A Subject We Would Rather Not Imagine

Rosa Cintrón

Death, many argue, is ultimately the most painful reality of life. Dying is the final act of living, the moment where all we are culminates and slips away. However, generally university administrators, faculty, and students do not anticipate that they will face death on campus. College campuses are where dreams usually begin, not end. Colleges are often thought of as gateways to new lives, where adolescence encounters the questions and concerns of adulthood. Nevertheless, it is estimated that between 6,000 to 22,000 students die every year on college and university campuses (Iserson, 1999). The death of a college student generates strong feelings of disbelief, sadness, and questions about mortality. Death is difficult for adults, and for many, the thought of dealing with the death of a young person is overwhelming. Thus, many administrators find ways to resolve the 'crises' of student deaths by maintaining some emotional distance under the façade of 'professionalism.'

The first book on college student death, *Death and the College Student* was published in 1972. The author, Professor Shneidman of Harvard University, was surprised when his new course concerning death on campus was full the first week of class. *Death and the College Student* is a compilation of essays from students in this class. It is presently out of print. Thirteen years later, in 1985, Ellen Zinner edited *Coping with Death on Campus* published by Jossey-Bass as part of their series, New Directions for Student Services. It is also out of print. To our knowledge, no other similar book has been published since that time.

It is not clear if administrators who deal with death experience specific feelings of loss in the forms of depression or anger. When a student dies on campus it can indeed be a stressful situation. An added repercussion is the threat of legal action. The question administrators must face is: What resources do administrators need so they may navigate the aftermath of students' deaths with proaction

Rosa Cintrón is an Associate Professor at the University of Central Florida. At the beginning of this book project she was a faculty member in Adult and Higher Education and Dean of University College at the University of Oklahoma. She received her doctorate at Florida State University and her master's in Clinical Psychology from the University of Puerto Rico. Her current research interests focus on the first year experience and issues of diversity and social justice.

and compassion? To assist university administrators and staff in providing families, students, and faculty with supportive and clear guidance in cases of death, *College Student Death: Guidance for a Caring Campus* addresses the following questions: What roles do student affairs personnel assume when a college student dies? What are the distinct concerns surrounding the death of a student from a special population (e.g., international students, athletes, residents, etc.)? How does the university interact with the media? How can the institution's image be restored after a highly publicized critical incident? With which external community agencies should universities maintain close coordination in order to better prepare for traumatic campus incidents? What can administrators learn from emergency personnel? How can administrators best serve the grieving family in instances where there is perceived liability? What protocols are involved in telephone notifications to parents or community members? What types of commemoration can universities develop for grieving students and families? What lessons can be learned from other universities' procedures with student death to enhance their own critical response training?

Death of a College Student presents theoretical readings and detailed cases highlighting the working knowledge, writing, and research in the field of institutional responses to student death. The chapters provide helpful information and recommendations for those in charge of making decisions when students die on college campuses. The text is also written to serve as a training tool for new professionals in college student affairs.

The complexity of this topic certainly merits chapters that the reader may deem crucial. As editors, we needed to make difficult decisions regarding the priority of topics and the mundane reality imposed by publishing guidance, including limitations on the number of pages. The following topics are additionally of great concern to college administrators but could not be presented here: death of other members of the university community (e.g., faculty), death of a parent or other significant person during the course of a student's enrollment, counseling techniques related to grieving and bereavement, death due to natural disasters (e.g., tornados) or terrorism, the prevention of accidental deaths, or the possible threat of a serial killer on campus.

College Student Death is divided into five distinct parts: (I) Enhancing our preparedness, (II) Compassion in the midst of crisis, (III) Issues within student populations, (IV) In remembrance, and (V) Administrative concerns.

In Part I, the authors urge colleges and universities to anticipate the unexpected intrusion of death on their campuses in order to enhance organizational and human preparedness. In other words, responding effectively to a death on campus is often difficult and complex. Maybe the very nature of campus life and the university administrative structure complicate the process of providing effective responses. An effective response is almost always a team effort requiring planning and coordination. In Chapter 1, Ruth F. McCauley and John D. Powell focus on the critical need for coordination to prevent the delay, duplication, and inappropriateness of the services offered. Another efficient way to avoid disruption, and possibly, even disaster on many college campuses is to partner with surrounding community agencies in order to identify and assess purveyors of the necessary resources. Jo N. Collier and Tom Hollis propose, in Chapter 2, that the manner in which resources are garnered and plans are formulated have an impact on who and what our educational institution will be in the aftermath of a disruptive incident involving death. In Chapter 3, J. Thomas Owens, Jr. and Katherine Garlough analyze a number of policies from various colleges and universities by providing points of similarity and specificity while describing the most significant elements of a well-crafted policy document.

In Part II, the authors discuss the sudden and abrupt intrusion of death on campus. Although we may feel helpless when a student dies, truly we are not. We cannot change what has happened, but we can share with the family the information we have and the sorrow we feel. Chapter 4 points to the many ways college staff and families can come together at times of great sorrow. Author Erin Taylor Weathers argues that as professionals committed to improving the quality of students' lives we are obligated to continue serving them in their deaths. When students die, their peers grieve. However, grieving, especially its spiritual components, is unfamiliar territory for most young adults. Chapter 5 provides a telephone notification chart provides a sound foundation for the announcement to the deceased's family members. In Chapter 6, Barbara and Tom Boyd define spiritual as the "most fundamental concerns related to life-meaning." The authors argue that when a student dies there is an opportunity for universities to become spiritual caregivers, for if the institutional response to the needs of students is to be adequate, it must include this dimension of human life. In Chapter 7, Tara M. Nielsen confronts the reader with a difficult theme, funeral arrangements. While it is best to make a decision about a funeral home, crematorial, cemetery, and related issues, before death, few people do. In other words, while parents usually make health insurance provision for their children it is safe to say that most do not plan mortuary arrangements for a child attending college. Unfortunately, survivors may need to make this type of decision quickly. This is one area where professional staff could provide brief information on the general services of a funeral director or funeral home. Chapter 8 offers personal perspectives that provide administrators and policy makers with specific examples detailing emotional contexts that families and universities have encountered. These perspectives relate the emotions that arose during a tragedy and help readers see a moment of crisis from the perspective of those more personally involved. Among the vignettes is the case of a Seton Hall resident advisor speaking of his struggle with the media after a residence hall fire killed three students. Through his narrative, we hear how a campus balances protecting its grieving students while dialoguing with national news agencies. In order to provide real examples of student crises that mandate institutional responses, we also hear the voice of a campus police chief speaking of his experience on the day after the Texas A&M bonfire collapse. The authors are grateful to those who shared these intensely personal experiences and believe their narratives are critical to our knowledge and understanding of the needs of students' loved ones and university communities.

Part III, death associated with specific student populations and settings, begins with Wayne D. Griffin, author of Chapter 9, who focuses on how loss affects students living on-campus and how institutional interventions can facilitate individual and community bereavement. Kelly A. Norton and Shaun R. Harper in Chapter 10 offer a guide to administrators for creating or modifying existing protocols for dealing with the death of a student athlete. With international students on US campuses and American students studying abroad, one of the responsibilities of international education administrators is to effectively manage losing students to death. In Chapter 11, Connie Shoemaker balances ways of dealing with death at the same time as issues such as transportation of the body, international laws, and cultural differences frame crucial considerations. In Chapter 12, Nancy Crist Welch offers recommendations on ways the university community can respond sensitively and responsibly when a student completes a suicide.

Part IV begins with Sylvia Grider's description of the Bonfire Memorabilia Project, suggesting the importance of gathering and preserving memorabilia in an 'archive of grief' for future generation of students. In the days and weeks following the bonfire accident at Texas A&M, a fence became the locus of a vast spontaneous shrine composed of thousands of grief offerings brought to the campus by students and the extended Aggie family. Those in university development and in student affairs are probably aware of instances in which contributions were accepted for particular purposes that were not sufficiently clarified between the donor and the receiving institution, creating confusion and resentment as a result of misunderstandings. In Chapter 14, Jerome C. Weber and Katherine Garlough address options of memorials and bequests, including the role of development directors, by presenting to the reader a series of important questions to consider when a family inquires about these options. Chapter 15

In Part V, the authors share with the reader one of the most excruciating developmental tasks of any professional; that is, what he or she has learned at the end of a painful experience. In Chapter 16, Lee E. Bird, Suzanne Burks, and Cindy Washington retell the events and aftermath of the Oklahoma State University 2001 plane crash that killed several basketball players, coaching staff, and members of the press. The OSU story is bound to instruct student affairs staff on the value of a well-trained crisis response team. In Chapter 17, Joseph Beckham, Douglas Person, and K. B. Melear highlight the most prominent legal cases clarifying the boundaries between institutional and individual responsibility. In Chapter 18, Kathleen Donohue Rennie posits that the media coverage of higher education has become more investigative, aggressive, and similar to coverage of corporations, politicians, and the entertainment industry. She explains the process involved in restoring a university's integrity and honor among the members of its own community and the collective psyche of higher education. Chapter 19 includes training scenarios with specific questions to teach student affairs personnel detailed strategies to help them as they aid students in times of crisis.

This book has taken a long time to become a reality. During this time the pendulum of life and death consistently moved on our campuses. Although most parents and students will start and complete the journey of higher education with a sense of joy and accomplishment, a few will remember our colleges and universities with sadness and pain. It is for the reality of death in the lives of those few that we need to prepare. It is only on a caring campus where life, even in death, thrives.

Reference

Iserson, K. (1999). *Grave words: Notifying survivors about sudden, unexpected deaths*. Tucson, AZ: Galen Press.

Part I

Enhancing Our Preparedness

1

Campus Response Teams:
The Need for Coordination

Ruth F. McCauley and John D. Powell

An effective and well-planned response to a student death can not only be a meaningful intervention for students and others in the campus community affected by a death, but can also be a gratifying personal and professional experience for staff members who provide services. The organized resources of the administrative staff can address the intense needs of personnel and students in a powerful, meaningful way through the Emergency Dean.

Responding effectively to students following a death on the college campus is often a complicated process. In addition to the psychological distress that must be addressed, there are often a variety of administrative decisions that need to be made on behalf of students. Responding to the many levels of need in a timely way requires collaboration.

A death on the college campus presents some distinct challenges given the age and developmental concerns of the student population. In addition to the immediate shock and emotional aftermath, the death of a student can create some existential crises as well for those who survive (Powell, 1998). For example, experiencing the death of a college friend may call into question students' meaning and motivation for academics. They may question their values and relationships. Many lose their sense of purpose when thinking of career plans. For many students, the death of a college friend is their first close experience with death and with their own mortality at a time when life, for the most part, holds a

Ruth F. McCauley is Associate Dean of Students at the University of Illinois at Urbana-Champaign. John D. Powell is a licensed psychologist and a Clinical Counselor at the Counseling Center at the University of Illinois at Urbana-Champaign.

great deal of promise and possibility. In addition, many students are more vulnerable to emotional distress because for them the college experience is a time of great stress and rapid change, and many students are less connected to family and other familiar emotional supports. This turmoil compounds the normal, intense emotional reactions to the death of someone close.

At a time of loss, it is important for those affected by the death to be engaged in a grief process that includes stepping back and taking time to experience the loss, making the necessary adjustments in life, and slowly reengaging in life activities. However, the university setting and the nature of the academic endeavor often do not allow such emotional luxuries. Academic programs and departments are often limited by how much flexibility they can offer a student who is grieving the loss of a friend. Often, it is the student who has self-expectations to get back to work and forge ahead. Thus, the student is left with a great deal of emotional work to do but feels pushed from within and without to put her emotional work aside and catch up with the academic work she may have already missed.

Finally, the nature of campus life and the university administrative structure can complicate the process of providing effective responses. Because students are often connected to the campus community in multiple ways, a student's death may have a far-reaching impact on many groups and individuals. It is not unusual for a student's death to impact many in the living unit, in an academic department, in a social and/or service organization, at a workplace, and within the student's own informal social network. Identifying these many connections and providing services to each can be a daunting task for administrators.

Because of these and many other possible factors, the grief process is almost always complicated and painful for students impacted by a death on campus. Providing an effective response for the emotional, academic, and administrative needs of those who must continue with life at the university is crucial.

An effective response is almost always a team effort requiring planning and coordination. Swenson and Ginsberg (1996) described many difficulties that can arise due to poor coordination, such as delays in services, duplication of services, inappropriate services offered, dissemination of inaccurate information, and failure to provide services to at-risk students. In addition to being a team effort, effective responses are typically a process rather than an event. This process will vary greatly depending on a number of variables, such as the nature of the death, the interpersonal connections of the student or students who died, the interest of the media, and the cooperation of academic and administrative units. In order to provide thoughtful and effective services, it is important to have a core team of people who can be notified at the time of a student's death to begin the process of responding. It is also important to have a protocol in place to guide the planning and coordinating of services.

Because of their professional expertise with grief, trauma, and responding to psychological distress, many universities rely on counseling center staff to provide both the coordination and response services to students affected by a death on campus. Many counseling centers have developed systematic plans and have trained staff for such responses. The collaboration described in this chapter is unique in that the primary initiative and coordination takes place in the Office of the Dean of Students rather than in the Counseling Center.

At the University of Illinois at Urbana-Champaign (UIUC), two units, the Emergency Dean program and the Counseling Center Trauma Response Team, work closely together and are frequently involved in the process of planning and carrying out responses to student death. The collaboration of these two units provides a unique approach that combines important administrative functions of the Office of the Dean of Students and the therapeutic services of the Counseling Center.

The success of the coordinated approach presented here may lie in some part in its administrative location in the Office of the Dean of Students, a broad-based services and programs office with responsibilities for the care, well-being, and success of students both individually and collectively in the larger institutional environment. Units with specific tasks of care-giving and problem-solving, such as the Counseling Center and the underrepresented student population support services, report to the Associate Vice Chancellor/Dean of Students. This arrangement provides both a breadth of vision and an agreement on the approach to crisis intervention. While the Counseling Center focuses on the emotional and psychological well-being of students, the Office of the Dean of Students is concerned about the full range of developmental issues and challenges.

The Emergency Dean Program

The Emergency Dean (E-Dean) program is most often the gateway to activating the institutional response to the death of a student. This program was implemented by the university in 1970 as a way to assist students and their families during times of trauma or crisis. The simple premise of the program is to extend the helping services of the Office of the Dean of Students into the evening and weekend hours when students, family members, and care providers in the community (including police and fire services, as well as hospital staff) seek help from the university. Over the years, the Emergency Dean program has come to serve as the receiving center for information concerning all varieties of emergencies, including student deaths, serious illnesses, accidents, sexual assaults, mental health crises, and other traumatic events involving students or their families. The program also serves as the primary information conduit among the individuals and units involved in the responses.

The Emergency Dean staff is made up of 16-20 staff members from various units in the division of student affairs. Student affairs staff may volunteer to serve with the program, or they may be recruited. The Dean of Students selects E-Deans from candidates recommended by the Coordinator. Successful E-Deans demonstrate maturity, sound judgment, and a solid working knowledge of university and community resources. A caring attitude and concern for the students they serve are also valued attributes of staff serving as deans. At a minimum, E-Deans must have a graduate level degree in some area of student personnel services or social work. Because it is crucial that they know the University system and local community resources, they are required to have worked at the University of Illinois for at least two years before being considered for the program. Emergency Deans are given a zero-time, zero-pay appointment in the Office of the Dean of Students. As compensation, they are extended 2.5 additional vacation days per week of duty served as a token of gratitude by the university. Serving as an Emergency Dean has become a source of pride for many of the professional staff selected for the program.

At various times in the 33-year history of the program, staffing issues have arisen—specifically the voluntary nature of the assignment, the lack of monetary compensation, and the waxing and waning pool of potential deans who are able and willing to serve and who meet expectations of professionalism and sound judgment. One of the alternative staffing arrangements considered is "professionalization" of the position of Emergency Dean by hiring a full-time staff member or graduate assistant to serve during the hours the office is closed. This approach is similar to the "advisory nurse" programs many student health centers and area hospitals provide for evening and weekend access. Many staffing and accountability issues are eliminated or minimized with this approach. However, the cost increases substantially, particularly if it is determined that more than one person is needed in the position to facilitate proper use of vacation and sick leave and to keep the staff member alert. The total hours of service to be provided each week would be a daunting 128 hours, requiring three or more full-time staff members.

Training involves a four-hour seminar in which procedures and policies are reviewed, reporting systems explained, and protocols specific to emergencies and crisis events are introduced. There are protocols for dealing with such events as student death, notification of a missing student, life-threatening illness or injury, fire, and suicide attempts. These protocols are not intended to be prescriptive or to be followed rigidly. Rather, they provide guidance and structure to the Emergency Dean on duty for responding to the individual circumstances of each traumatic event. Hence training is on-going, as major events and E-Dean responses are continually and informally debriefed in order to fine tune responses and protocols. The coordinator of the Emergency Dean program is a senior staff member in the Office of the Dean of Students. This person also coordinates the professional staffs in the Dean of Students Office who provide daily assistance to students, their families, and other members of the university community during business hours. In this way, there is always a "dean on duty" during business hours to meet with students, to take calls or emails, to take action on their behalf, to refer them to other programs or services, or to provide advocacy in other campus units, as appropriate. When the Office of the Dean of Students is closed, the Emergency Dean for the week comes on duty.

A crucial part of the E-Dean program is "The Bag." The E-Dean bag is a lockable brief case that contains a variety of resources, including the emergency protocols, the code of policies and regulations affecting all students, class time-tables, listings of housing staff members and their home numbers, sorority and fraternity contact numbers, home contact information for representatives of each college, maps of the campus and surrounding area, contact information for all campus and community emergency services, etc. A significant piece of equip-ment included in "The Bag" is the cellular telephone through which the Emer-gency Dean is contacted when the office is closed. The E-Dean is expected to have "The Bag" available at all times during the week of duty.

Emergency Deans typically serve one week each semester. The procedures by which they operate are detailed below:

- E-Dean duty for the week begins at 5 p.m. Friday when the Office of the Dean of Students closes for the weekend.
- The E-Dean receives the E-Dean bag.
- The E-Dean is on-call around the clock until the Office re-opens on Monday at 8:30 a.m.
- Duty resumes Monday at 5 p.m. and so on until 8:30 a.m. the following Friday.
- When there is a change in Emergency Dean, the out-going dean returns the E-Dean bag to the Office of the Dean of Students after 8:30 a.m. Friday for the next dean to retrieve before 5 p.m. that same day.

Several universities appear to have some variation of an "emergency dean" service to provide assistance to students and families outside of institutional business hours, including Duke University, Colby College, the University of Florida in Gainesville, and the University of Louisiana at Lafayette. The degree to which these programs resemble the UIUC program varies widely, as do their relationships with counseling center services, crisis intervention teams, and other emergency services on their campuses and in their larger communities.

The Emergency Dean telephone number is widely published and the duty roster is distributed among University housing units, the three area police agen-cies, the two hospitals and the two fire fighting agencies, and other campus enti-ties. The main student assistance telephone number in the Office of the Dean of Students is transferred to a "mailbox" each evening when the office closes. The mailbox features both an out-going message and a message-taking function. When the office is closed, the recording indicates that the Emergency Dean is on duty, and callers are given the cellular telephone number to call to reach the dean. Callers may leave messages on the main office telephone line and are told the office will respond to their messages when it reopens, but that if they need immediate assistance for an urgent and pressing matter, the Emergency Dean should be called on the cell phone. The recording also refers callers to the University Police Department's non-emergency telephone number should they for some reason be unable to reach the Emergency Dean on duty on the cell phone. The University Police have the dean on duty roster and are able to call the E-Dean at a private home number in the event that there is a problem with the cell phone.

On average, the Emergency Dean Program's after-hours service receives 700 calls a year. The volume of calls may not be surprising given that UIUC has 39,000 students, the majority of whom are traditional aged and 14,000 of whom reside in University housing. Of those calls each year, about 8-10 concern the death of a student, and many more concern attempted or threatened suicide, serious accident or illness, hospitalization locally or at home for mental health crisis, sexual assault, death in the family, or other serious events. About 50% of these calls come from students or their parents, about 35% come from housing staff members, and the remaining calls come from fire, police, or hospital staff.

When the E-Dean receives such a call, it becomes his or her responsibility to determine what other campus units or individuals need to be notified. These individuals and campus units are called into action depending on the nature and circumstances surrounding the student's death and the people involved. One such unit frequently involved is the Counseling Center's Trauma Response Team.

The Trauma Response Team

The Trauma Response Team (TRT) is composed of professional staff members of the university's Counseling Center whose task it is to be available to provide a range of easily accessible, timely, and professional services to students who are affected by a death or other traumatic incident and/or psychological emergency. While the E-Dean is often the information conduit among units and handles many of the logistical concerns of responses, the services provided by the TRT most often address the emotional and psychological needs of those affected by the death.

The TRT is chaired by one Counseling Center staff member who has the responsibility of recruiting and training other staff members, maintaining regular contact with the Emergency Dean Coordinator, overseeing the rotating roster (described below), and developing and maintaining printed resources used in responding.

A roster of TRT members, along with procedures for contacting them, is distributed to E-Deans, housing staff, and others who are likely to be reporting deaths or other traumas. Personnel who make up this roster are members of the clinical staff of the Counseling Center who have expressed a willingness to be available to receive calls and provide needed responses. Because many of the skills needed for responding to such calls are consistent with their clinical training and experience, additional training involves introducing models of grief and trauma, reviewing how therapeutic skills can be adapted to trauma response intervention, and introducing the procedures for collaborating with the E-Dean. Counselors on the roster do not receive contract time for this service, but they are compensated for each response by being relieved of one initial assessment (intake) within the next week. The roster, usually consisting of 5 or 6 names, operates on a rotating basis. That is, a person's name is at the top of the list for one month and rotates to the bottom of the list as other names move up. In this way, each person is at the top of the list to receive calls no more than once each semester.

Often, the TRT member whose name is at the top of the list that month is called by the E-Dean who has received the initial call, though sometimes housing staff will call the TRT member directly. If that person cannot be reached, the procedures are to call down the list until someone is contacted and given the information. It then becomes the responsibility of the TRT member who gets the call to make the response. In the event that the team member is unable to respond, that team member assumes the responsibility for calling down the list until someone is committed to providing a response.

The primary purpose of the roster is to make sure someone is designated to provide a timely response in the case of a trauma. In the unlikely event that no one on the roster can be reached or can make the needed response, other Counseling Center staff members are contacted.

The TRT provides timely, on-the-scene intervention and support services to those directly affected by an emergency situation and/or those in positions of making decisions and providing care after the trauma, such as housing staff, deans, Greek house officers, etc. However, prior to any services being offered, there is typically some necessary consultation and planning that take place.

Developing a Collaborative and Comprehensive Response

The collaborative efforts of the Office of the Dean of Students Emergency Dean's program and the Counseling Center's Trauma Response Team are one small part of the larger campus Critical Incident Team (CIT). The CIT meets regularly to plan for a variety of larger disaster possibilities, such as natural disasters, terrorism, or other traumas that might affect large segments of the campus population. The Dean of Students and Counseling Center Director are each members of the CIT. The Emergency Dean program and the Trauma Response Team coordinate efforts and call in alternate resources when an event such as a student death does not reach the numeric threshold for a response from the CIT.

Another way of understanding the institutional response to crisis events is to view such events on a continuum: The Emergency Dean program sits on one end of the continuum dealing with "individual care" events, engaging other units as needed in responding to the emergency. The CIT sits on the other end of the continuum, addressing issues of "mass care" for larger populations affected by trauma or disaster.

The decision to involve other units or to contain a response to a student's death is initially made by an Office of the Dean of Students-Trauma Response Team collaboration, fueled by the principle that the "Office of the Dean/E-Dean does what others can't, and the Counseling Center/TRT does what others don't want to do." A valuable safeguard in this decision-making process is the firm commitment not to make decisions in isolation: The E-Dean on duty consults the E-Dean Coordinator who consults the Dean of Students who consults the Vice Chancellor for Student Affairs, and so on. Along the consultation path, which mirrors the administrative hierarchy, others are consulted (such as police, hospital staff, housing staff, etc.).

When the death of a student is reported, either to the Office of the Dean of Students or to the Emergency Dean on duty, an assessment is made of the degree of need for immediate intervention and the desirability of apprising other campus units, such as academic departments, housing units, athletic team coaches, or the university public affairs office. The E-Dean who receives that initial call then contacts the Coordinator of the E-Dean program.

During the first telephone conversation between the E-Dean on duty and the Coordinator, an initial plan of action is made from answering a series of questions: (a) What information is still needed, and from whom might it be obtained? and (b) Which of the two staff members will make such calls, and when will they report the outcomes of those calls to one another? Frequently the initial information is sketchy, and follow-up calls to hospital staff, police officers, housing staff, or the coroner are helpful in filling in details. These sources of information are also frequently able to report "on-site," to give information about friends, roommates, significant others, or family members who are present on the scene and for whom E-Dean and Trauma Response Team support services are sought. The University Police Department is able to access limited student records through the University database, to give accurate information regarding the student's enrollment status, college and degree program, and year in school, as well as local, permanent, and emergency addresses and telephone numbers. University Police also interface with the two local community police agencies and will often have more detailed information to share about the timing, location, and nature of the incident that resulted in a student's death.

After information is gathered, the Coordinator and the E-Dean together determine which of them will call the Trauma Response Team into action and who will notify University administrators. There is an automatic "call out" system implemented by University Police to notify administrators of major campus events, such as deaths, power outage, fire, etc. However, the Coordinator and the E-Dean program's protocols call for information-sharing as well, so there may be some duplication of effort. It has been a positive practice which assures that the right staff members are aware of an incident, even if notified twice. Some of the staff members typically called by the E-Dean or the Coordinator in the event of a student death are the Dean of Students and Associate Vice Chancellor for

Student Affairs, the Vice Chancellor for Student Affairs, dean of the student's college, the residence hall director or living unit director if the student is a resident, and the Director for Public Affairs.

The Coordinator and the E-Dean will determine which of them will go to the appropriate site. If the police and coroner's office staff are still on-site at an apartment or residence hall and roommates or other students are still present, the Coordinator and/or the E-Dean will go to that location immediately. Sometimes the scene has shifted to the hospital where the waiting rooms and special "family lounges" are the scene of some commotion, if family and concerned students have gathered either prior or subsequent to the death and transfer of the ill, injured, or deceased student. The Trauma Response Team will be kept apprised of the locus of operation so that TRT members respond to the right place as needed. Sometimes the TRT members will go to work with students at a residence hall or apartment or fraternity/sorority house, while the E-Dean goes to the hospital or police station to make initial contact with family members and other loved ones. Family members themselves are often the most helpful suppliers of information about the student and the death. Likewise, the E-Dean's presence and the information E-Deans provide to the family about the University and its support services is almost always a source of comfort to the family.

After the initial intervention by the E-Dean and/or the TRT, the Coordinator, the E-Dean on duty, TRT members, and others (such as housing staff and the Dean of Students) consult about continuing TRT efforts directed toward identified populations and about what role the Emergency Dean will play in those follow-up activities and meetings. A key role played by the Emergency Dean or the Coordinator in subsequent interventions is providing accurate and detailed information about the incident as well as communicating–when and where appropriate–the wishes and plans of the student's family. These plans may include organ donation, religious or memorial services to which University community members are invited, plans for memorial scholarships programs, and family members' desires to participate in or help shape campus memorial programs of some sort.

A final issue to consider when developing a collaborative and comprehensive response to student death is that of confidentiality. In addition to the variable degrees to which staff members are held to strict confidentiality depending on licensure restrictions or state law, all staff members at all institutions are bound by provisions of the Family Educational Rights and Privacy Act of 1974 (FERPA), and by the recently enacted Health Insurance Portability and Accountability Act of 1996 (HIPAA). These two pieces of federal legislation are intended to protect individuals' privacy and confidentiality rights related to education and to health care.

Under FERPA, "directory information" which has not been suppressed by the student may be given to third parties. Directory information falls into two categories: personal information (name, addresses, telephone numbers, date of birth), and academic information (name, college, curriculum and major field of study, class level, dates of attendance, full- or part-time status, etc.). And while FERPA rights of a student cease when the student dies, institutions have the latitude to determine what information will be shared with third parties about the deceased student. Frequently, the media are interested in obtaining a photograph of the student for their coverage, assuming that most institutions provide picture identification cards for enrolled students. It is entirely a matter of institutional policy whether the ID photograph is considered directory information, either personal or academic, and shareable with third parties while the student lives; likewise, it is an institutional decision about release of photographs upon the death of a student.

While FERPA pertains to the release of information from universities and colleges to third parties, HIPAA concerns the release of information from third parties–namely hospitals and other health care providers–to universities and colleges. It remains to be seen what ultimate impact there is on the reasonable exchange of information currently enjoyed between the UIUC Emergency Dean program and the two local hospitals, but to date, when hospitals need the E-Dean's assistance, they contact him or her. Likewise, when the E-Dean is aware of a student incident, hospital staff have sought the student's permission to speak with the E-Dean on duty and shared information in order to help the student. The relationship which has evolved over 30 years between the hospitals and the Emergency Dean program has contributed to the desire to care for the student community.

Important Components of the Response

One thing that E-Deans and members of the Trauma Response Team have learned over the years is that every situation calls for something different. Because of unique features of every death or trauma, it is crucial to consider a number of important factors when developing an immediate response and aftercare. Identifying those factors begins with one or more consultation meetings. In rare situations, the consultation meeting may be as brief as a particular phone call from the E-Dean to the TRT chair several years ago, following a student suicide: "We need someone over there right now." A one-minute phone call in that situation provided all the information needed to begin the response. More often the consultation meeting–held as soon after the incident as possible–involves several people putting together a planful response that often includes other meetings with distinct purposes (Powell, 1998).

The primary purposes of the consultation meeting include: convening the people who can identify those most directly affected by the death, providing accurate information about the circumstances of the death, determining what interventions are needed first, and making the necessary logistical arrangements for the interventions. With these purposes in mind, the initial consultation meeting usually includes: (a) someone who can address administrative and academic decisions and coordinate information dissemination between individuals and offices (often the E-Dean Coordinator), (b) someone who can facilitate debriefing meetings if needed (often the TRT member), and (c) one or more people representing the living unit, academic department, and other institutional or social structures impacted by the death. Depending on the situation, it may be necessary to have subsequent consultation meetings as new information is revealed and as the needs of students and staff are assessed further. Because of the E-Dean Coordinator's involvement in gathering information and notifying others, s/he frequently coordinates the scheduling of these meetings. A frequent outcome of the consultation meeting is the planning of one or more debriefing meetings. While the most visible and often impacting service is the at-the-scene debriefing meeting, (described below), the consultation meetings that take place prior to the debriefing are of utmost importance and often determine whether or not the debriefing will be effective.

It is important to offer some kind of service to students who have been directly involved with or affected by the event as soon as possible. A debriefing meeting or series of meetings is often that first intervention with students. These meetings generally focus on disseminating accurate information, helping people report and attend to the shock and immediate physical and emotional response to trauma, communicating appropriate information about the grief process, and providing referral information. The debriefing meeting format is loosely based on the Critical Incident Debriefing Process (Mitchell, 1983), which outlines a clear progression of experiences to help participants experience and express their reactions. Mitchell's model was specifically designed to help those who have experienced the shock of being on the scene of a traumatic event, and sometimes this is the case in a campus death situation. For example, a debriefing meeting might include people who were present and witnessed an alcohol poisoning in which the student could not be resuscitated. Often, such meetings are conducted with those who may not have been involved in the death incident but who knew the deceased and are engaged in their first stages of grief and coping. A meeting might be conducted for those who were very close to the deceased by virtue of friendships, living arrangements, or academic affiliation. It is important for the meeting facilitator to adapt the meeting format to the particular group needs.

The E-Dean Coordinator, in collaboration with the TRT member and others in the consultation meeting, must identify several important factors in planning debriefing meetings in order to increase the likelihood of their effectiveness. The authors have learned valuable, and often painful, lessons from conducting debriefing meetings that took place without sufficient information or planning. Some suggestions for planning the debriefing meeting are:
- Determine likely attendance.
- Secure a setting for the meeting that is private, comfortable, and will allow interaction among the participants.

- Acquire as much information about the group and individuals as possible.
- Identify individuals who are likely to be particularly affected by the trauma (roommates, closest friends, etc.).
- Secure information about the event and designate an information person to share that information at the outset of the meeting (often the E-Dean Coordinator).
- Brainstorm support networks and individuals.
- The TRT member assumes primary responsibility for facilitating the meeting. Have a second TRT member available who can provide backup facilitation or who can talk with individuals as needed.
- Go into the meeting with a flexible plan, but do not improvise. Frequently, the debriefing meetings will reveal other responses needed or will identify at risk students that may need special attention.
- Plan a follow-up meeting as needed.

A follow-up meeting may be held a few days or weeks after the death with the same group that met for the debriefing. Often this meeting is scheduled at the conclusion of the debriefing meeting. The goal of this gathering is to assist individuals and the group with the ongoing tasks of grieving by providing an opportunity for individuals to talk openly about the feelings, thoughts, and concerns that have come up since the death of the student. This follow-up contact can also provide the E-Dean Coordinator or TRT member with information about those who continue to struggle and might need special attention or services. This is also an opportunity for the group to develop a plan for memorializing the individual who has died.

It is often the case that because of the interconnectedness of a college campus, the death of one or more students may have an impact on many who did not know the deceased, but are nonetheless affected by the event. Informational meetings can be used to address the needs of those people. For example, if the death was highly publicized, was of a violent nature, or the circumstances of the death remain unknown, many on campus may be fearful or confused about safety concerns. An instructor might be concerned about reactions of students following the death of someone in the department. Such a meeting may be useful in providing emotional and physical safety information, can help identify resources, and educate others about normal grief reactions. These meetings are generally coordinated by the E-Dean Coordinator and the TRT.

Of course, these meetings typically do not fall neatly into one category or another. The different types of meetings are generally determined by the timing of the meeting relative to the death. However, the types of interventions offered are determined by the needs of those who attend. Therefore, determining the purpose of each meeting and the group being served is important and requires consultation and collaboration among the many parties involved, highlighting the importance of liberal exchanges of information among the E-Dean program, the TRT member, and others involved in planning the interventions.

Part of the debriefing meeting or follow-up meetings with groups is to talk about what would constitute a meaningful tribute to the person who has died and then help with those arrangements as needed. Often students or staff request that a memorial service take place. Universities have different approaches to this. At the University of Florida, for example, one of the members of the response team is closely connected to the network of campus clergy and often helps facilitate such services by recruiting a clergy member and helping with needed arrangements. At the University of Illinois, because many of the campus clergy are adjunct members of the Dean of Students Office, the Emergency Dean, who is involved and knowledgeable about the campus clergy, often works with groups to facilitate these services. Some campuses, such as Purdue University, hold annual memorial services to recognize and remember all the students who have died during the academic year. Others have developed their own rituals for giving students the opportunity to express their grief. For example, several schools report having a memorial wall where students can write personal sentiments. Others have tree plantings or other ways of providing an enduring symbol.

A look at two different cases at UIUC might illustrate how the E-Dean and TRT collaboration plays out in practice and offer insight into how the program works well and when mistakes have been made and lessons learned.

Case 1: "Collapsed in the parking lot and died"

Classes had been in session for the spring semester for several weeks the Saturday afternoon Emergency Dean on duty Ralph Jones took a call from a UIUC student reporting the death of popular African-American sophomore Jack Smith. The student calling had very little information about what had happened, but he did know which local hospital was involved. E-Dean Jones called the hospital's emergency room, a long-standing practice used by the E-Dean to follow up on reports of student hospitalizations. Amidst the background noise of a busy ER, a harassed-sounding nurse who answered the phone on the tenth ring was able to confirm that student Jack Smith had "collapsed in the parking lot and died." She did not have time to give E-Dean Jones any details.

After consulting with the E-Dean Coordinator, E-Dean Jones called to notify housing staff about the death, and the Coordinator notified the Dean of Students and the Vice Chancellor for Student Affairs. The Trauma Response Team was put on alert and asked to stand by. Housing staff were asked to help assess the urgency of the need for TRT intervention and to arrange times and locations for debriefing and follow-up meetings. A debriefing meeting was held that night in a large public lounge in the residence hall. This was not an optimal location for the meeting as it did not provide much privacy, but it was the best space available on short notice. Immediately prior to the meeting, two TRT members and two housing staff met to discuss procedures. It was decided that one of the housing staff would provide the group with the information available and one TRT member would facilitate the meeting. There were approximately 40 distressed students in attendance.

The designated housing staff member presented the information available, restating the nurse's comments that Jack Smith "had collapsed in the parking lot of the hospital and died." There was an immediate uproar among the students, some of whom had been at the hospital with Smith. These students stated adamantly that this was not what had happened. In a short time, there were several different versions of the events surrounding the death and more than a little suspicion on the part of the students about why the meeting facilitators had reported erroneous information. Because there were so many conflicting views of what happened and such a paucity of actual information from the hospital, another session was scheduled for a few days later.

From the less-than-successful first attempt at a debriefing meeting, the Emergency Dean Coordinator sought the assistance of the Dean of Students who was able to speak directly with Jack's attending physician. It was learned that Jack had undergone an intrusive lung procedure which he had not tolerated well that Friday afternoon, and he left the hospital against his doctor's recommendation. Friends had picked him up in the hospital parking lot, driven around the block, and returned to the ER entrance when Jack collapsed in the car. Jack subsequently underwent several hours of lung surgery during which physicians attempted to remove numerous emboli in each lung. Ultimately, Jack was taken to the ICU where he died a few hours later early Saturday afternoon.

In response to this new information, the leaders of the second debriefing session asked for several new participants. In addition to Trauma Response Team members (one of whom was a well-known, much-beloved clinical counselor who proved invaluable in gaining the confidence of the students) and the E-Dean Coordinator, also present were the Dean of Students and Jack's attending physician. The physician was remarkably forthcoming and candid in describing Jack's physical condition and the efforts hospital staff made to save his life. Approximately 20 students attended the second debriefing session. The meeting began with some expressed suspicion and anger, but by the end of the 90-minute meeting, sadness and sorrow came to the fore. Subsequent follow-up meetings were scheduled to continue to share information about the grieving process and resources available to students coping with their loss.

Several lessons were learned during this incident; the most obvious lesson was that one must be very clear about incident details and even more careful about how and when those details are communicated. A tragic situation was exacerbated through the unwitting words of people trying to do a good job under adverse conditions. A fall-out from this incident was an immediate change in E-Dean protocol. No longer does the E-Dean call that hospital's emergency room. Now the calls are made to the "House Officer" at the hospital who serves as liaison between the ER staff and the Emergency Dean. Initially, there were concerns that this new protocol would have a chilling effect on what information was shared by hospital staff with the E-Dean. However, that has not proven to be the case, and more often than not, the House Officer gives the E-Dean a patient's status report and then transfers the call directly to the doctor or nurse working with the student. The protocol for contacting the other area hospital remains calling emergency (ER).

Another lesson learned was that it is extraordinarily important to go to the scene of the incident. When the E-Dean or the Coordinator goes to the hospital or to the residence hall and is present on-site to gather information directly, the potential for gathering accurate and detailed information about the incident is enhanced.

Case 2: Murder and Suicide

The Emergency Dean Coordinator had just come on duty that Friday evening and was gearing up for what promised to be a busy weekend. It was a holiday weekend in which alcoholic excesses and the behavior that inevitably follows would likely require visits to ERs or to police stations, or both. Even so, she was surprised that the first call came at 5:20 p.m. that Friday, and even more surprised that it was the county coroner calling.

He wanted to report that Adam Wright, an older undergraduate student from Canada, had been struck by a train and killed outright an hour or so earlier. The accident had occurred on the main north-south railroad tracks that bound the university area on the west side of campus. The coroner did not know yet if alcohol or drugs played a role in the incident but promised to call back if and when he had more information.

A few years earlier, a student lost both an arm and a leg when he fell off a slow-moving freight train on that same track. He and several buddies had discovered that train-hopping was a fun way to get back to campus after a night of drinking at one of the more popular downtown taverns. However, the coroner did not think that was the situation with Adam—it was too early in the evening for that kind of thing, he thought. Conversations with the coroner and police during the course of the early evening yielded new information: The engineer of the train reported that the student had stood resolutely on the tracks, heedless of the train whistle warning of its approach. Speculation was that Adam had committed suicide, but that official finding would not be announced until several weeks later during the county coroner's inquest.

About an hour later the E-Dean was called by police and coroner's staff and informed of the discovery of the body of a 40-year-old university employee. She appeared to have been forcibly taken to a remote room in an academic building where she was bound, gagged, and strangled to death some time that afternoon.

Because this death involved a university staff member who was not a student, the Emergency Dean would not necessarily have been contacted. However, because of the contacts already being made about the student death and because of the collegial relationship the Coordinator had developed over the years with various police officers and the coroner, information about the staff member's murder was freely, though confidentially, shared. Institutional protocols related to the staff member's death call for the University Police Department to activate "call-outs" to a wide variety of administrators, including the Dean of Students and the Vice Chancellor for Student Affairs. It was probable that if the E-Dean had not already been informed of the murder, the Dean of Students would have notified her of the incident. As it was, there had already been numerous telephone conversations during the course of the night and the weekend during which information was sought and shared freely about both deaths.

It was more than a week before the suicide of the undergraduate student and the murder of the staff member were officially linked by evidence and confirmed by police authorities, though many members of the campus and wider community thought it highly improbable that the University would experience two such heinous events within hours of each other that were not somehow related. Before the link between the two deaths was made, though, the possibility that a killer was stalking the campus created a climate on campus and in the two surrounding cities of extreme fearfulness and anxiety.

The student had resided in a small house off campus with two other male students. They did not know him well, and the configuration of the house lent itself well to Adam's reclusive ways. His housemates rarely saw him, let alone interacted with him. While they were shocked about his death, the housemates told the E-Dean that they had no need for Trauma Response Team or Emergency Dean interventions, and they both went home for the remainder of the weekend. They were given information about Counseling Center services and assistance with missed classes, should they determine later that help was wanted.

There was no immediate action to take with identified friends or roommates on campus. Adam's family in Canada had been notified of his death by the local county coroner as is the practice. Under no circumstances is that task assigned to the E-Dean or the Coordinator. The family members were making plans to come to town within the next days, and by the time they arrived, the Coordinator had spoken to them by phone a few times and arranged to meet them at the police station. By that time, there was emerging evidence being cautiously released by the police to the public that Adam and the staff member knew each other casually. However, physical evidence linking the murder and suicide were not released to the public for more than a week while the investigation continued. The intervening days were challenging for the University and community.

Because the events and subsequent anxieties affected so much of the campus community, much of the coordination of services came from the Chancellor's office. For example, the Chancellor convened daily crisis management meetings to coordinate institutional response and support for the entire community of faculty, staff, and students. The E-Dean program and the Office of the

Dean of Students staff, and the Trauma Response Team and the Counseling Center staff, along with housing staff, police, and others planned a variety of debriefing and informational meetings. Over the course of 10 days, more than a dozen such meetings were convened in residence halls, sorority houses, academic departments, classrooms, and public forums, responding to any and every request for their services.

Since the family developed a close and comfortable relationship with a University police officer who helped in their debriefing at the police station, the officer helped the family pack up Adam's room. This task often falls to the Emergency Dean. However, one family member maintained close telephone contact with the Emergency Dean in the months that followed the incident, asking for copies of local newspaper accounts of police findings and the result of the coroner's inquest. Both of these tasks were out of the ordinary or taken on by persons who do not normally play such roles, but the expressed needs of the participants was met by the most natural helper on the scene for persons seeking the help.

Ten days after the two deaths, the local district attorney held a well-attended press conference, confirming the speculations that the student, Adam Wright, had abducted and killed the university employee and then willfully killed himself by standing in the path of an on-coming freight train.

Conclusion

Among the lessons learned during this incident were the following: (a) the strength of the relationships built among the TRT and Emergency Dean program with hospital staff, police agencies, and the coroner was an invaluable tool in providing the best information and support all units could provide to a hurting community; (b) some incidents become more complicated and involve more elements, and to some degree, control in determining the kinds of institutional responses to be implemented is to be assumed by leaders higher in the university organization; and (c) because of the complex nature of some cases, helping staff will be asked to step outside their accustomed roles in order to meet individuals' needs more effectively.

Clearly, not all responses will involve so many units or will have these types of challenges. A majority of responses involve a consultation meeting with targeted staff to identify groups likely to need services and to arrange for debriefing meetings with specific groups of students, follow-up meeting as needed, and specific services offered to at-risk students.

An effective and well-planned response to a death can not only be a meaningful intervention for students and others in the campus community affected by a death, but it can also be a gratifying personal and professional experience for staff members who provide services. When the resources of one person can be matched with the intense needs of others, the results can be powerful. This is often the case with a team response to death on campus.

References

Mitchell, J. T. (1983). When disaster strikes: The critical incident stress debriefing process. *Journal of Emergency Medical Services, 8*, 36-39.

Powell, J. D. (1998). Responding to death in the residence hall or family housing. *Talking Stick 16*, 16-17.

Swenson, D. X., and Ginsberg, M. H. (1996). A comprehensive model for campus death postvention. *Journal of College Student Development, 37*, 543-549.

2

Alliances with Law Enforcement: Garnering Your Community's Resources

Jo N. Collier and Tom Hollis

The ways in which university administrators and law enforcement respond to death in the university community reflects not only how they value individual people, but a respect for the larger community itself. Their responses to the legal, policy, regulation, and jurisdiction questions that arise in crisis can reflect a commitment to garnering the community's resources. University administrators therefore prepare for student death with a firm understanding of the legal issues when caring for their community to support the mission of the institutions represented.

Death will visit campus. The vehicle that delivers it may be murder, suicide, accident, catastrophe, disease, or natural disaster. It will come, and regardless of how it appears, it will demand action. Any member of a campus community may be called upon to respond. Some administrators may believe that when death does come to their campus, the responsibility for the ramifications of such an incident will not be theirs to confront. These are conscientious, learned administrators who doubt that any circumstance could result in a threat to the standing of their college or university. There is danger, however, in these assumptions. When the ivy on the hallowed walls begins to shake, the administra-

Jo N. Collier is the Director of Student Support Services at Rogers State University, the former Director of the Oklahoma Regional Community Policing Institute, a partnership of the U.S. Department of Justice and the University of Oklahoma. She is presently pursuing a Ph.D. in Educational Foundations. Tom Hollis, Ph.D., is the Director of Graduate Studies in Education at Southwest Baptist University, and he writes on ethics and standards of excellence in educational administration.

tion's refuge will be found in carefully marshaled resources. Resources will be found among those who have the most at stake: the members of the administrative community.

Protecting the students and defending the university involves preparedness. Part of this preparation includes learning the responsibility of each governmental level and gaining familiarity with their roles before, during, and after an event involving the death of a student.

When an incident of death involves potential criminal acts, alliances with local law enforcement are essential. Jim Cox, Executive Director of the Oklahoma Association of Chiefs of Police, stressed the importance of advance preparation by having memorandums of understanding (MOU), mutual aid pacts, and cooperative agreements with local governmental authorities to establish jurisdiction. Cox (personal communication, April 12, 2001) pointed out that the time for knowing who has authority is not at the time of a crisis. Most competent officials know where their duties begin. To be most effective, officials need to have clear knowledge, in advance, of where their responsibilities begin and end.

Too often, during times of heightened emotion, appropriate abdication of authority is difficult. Cox (personal communication, April 12, 2001) noted that his experience with direct involvement in several disasters, including the Murrah Federal Building bombing, confirmed that people do not always want to step back and let others do the job. Being able to relinquish control is vital because arguing about whom should give and take orders wastes valuable response time and squanders resources. It can even cost lives. Agreements well designed and solidified in writing will serve the campus administration favorably.

The academic community, as a corporal component of the surrounding community, will generally fall within the geographic jurisdiction of one or more local police forces. The circumstances under which local police or other law enforcement authorities come onto campus, and their authority once they are on campus, should be a major concern for key administrators to resolve where appropriate mutual aid agreements or proper memorandum of understanding do not exist.

The authority and jurisdiction of local police and each level of jurisdiction of governmental authority have different characteristics and requirements. Therefore, local laws or ordinances have necessarily been drafted with the individual needs of the community in mind. Guidance or provisions can be obtained from other jurisdictions, but local response must meet local needs. Those closest to the community know the unique features of the community, where something is most likely to go wrong, where special complexities exist, and where sources of support may most readily be found. The jurisdictions, spheres of influence, and implied and legitimate authority of others in the university community will impact an institution's stability and will affect its ability to recover from all kinds of crises in countless ways.

The nature of tragedy often reveals the true symbiotic nature of the campus to other community institutions and the need to be prepared to help each other. Gallaudet University, a premier institution bringing together deaf, hearing-impaired, and hearing students and faculty, is a campus community with strengths and some special needs. In September of 2001, Gallaudet freshman Benjamin Varner was found murdered in his fourth floor residence hall room. This, the second murder in the same residence hall in a four month period, caused a wave of fear and pain that was difficult to express, and even more difficult to investigate. In his February 5, 2001 interview with ABC News, Police Chief Charles Ramsey explained that because nearly all of the university's inhabitants are deaf, police required the use of sign language interpreters when interviewing witnesses. The sheer number of witnesses and the difficulty in conducting those interviews in a timely fashion was exacerbated by the need to interpret, thereby slowing down the investigative process (Yang, 2001).

Should Gallaudet campus authorities and local law enforcement have been able to anticipate the tragic circumstances that so sadly affected their campus? It is indeed a grave challenge to try to anticipate the needs of every community member. The Gallaudet experience illustrates the vital importance of involving local resources in planning for response to such critical incidents as student death on campus. On every campus, as with Gallaudet, the need is human, personal, and particular to the specific needs of the people involved.

The campus community may find that networking can bring immediate, perhaps serendipitous rewards in areas of community relations, problem solving, and conflict resolution. Campus and municipal law enforcement, local government entities, civic organizations, faith-based organizations, and various media outlets are visible, obvious professionals in the business of community engagement. Alliances formed with these entities can nurture a cache of resources that will, at some point, be a treasure trove of resources. If university personnel have nurtured their friendship and support, the people in these organizations can come to the institution's aid by curtailing the spread of misinformation, helping to defend the university's position, providing credibility, and saving staff time and energy. Civic organizations, law enforcement, faith-based organizations, and media outlets are experts at down to earth, pragmatic problem solving.

Death as a result of homicide will require an especially thoughtful approach for restoring normalcy. Partnering with law enforcement officials to reestablish a sense of security is critical. There will need to be increased security efforts in the weeks and months afterward. Campus law enforcement or security and local police officials will necessarily be very visible. This visibility may bring emotions and reactions to light that will need to be managed. If a campus or university has its own uniformed security officers, administrators must decide what working relationships these officers will have with local police. This decision will depend partially on the extent of the officer's authority, especially regarding arrests, searches, seizures, or any traffic enforcement that may be necessary.

This authority is carefully delineated and administrators should know well in advance of an emergency situation the difference in campus disciplinary proceedings and the realities of arrest and prosecution through local courts (Kaplin & Lee, 1995). Administration officials should not hesitate to consult counsel concerning any questions that may arise with regard to the authority of local police on campus and partnerships with other authorities.

Case: A Community College

Located just at the four corners of the heartland of America, a community college had an experience that one official identified as "a teachable moment." The death of an international student in a traffic accident brought some things sharply into focus for the administration and for local law enforcement. First, patrol level municipal police officers had not been made aware that a significant number of international students lived in the community. Second, neither the international students, nor the police, knew what behaviors to expect from each other. One officer put it this way: "I was pretty used to dealing with freshmen, away from home for the first time, apprehensive about being questioned by a police officer, but the pure fear I saw on the faces of these international students gave me a real wake up call." Students visiting the United States from other countries and even various ethnic and cultural groups from other regions of the United States have often had very different and varying experiences with law enforcement. The result of these experiences may lead to reactions and interactions that confound, confuse, and frustrate everyone involved.

The heartland community college and local civic leaders responded quickly. They began with outreach programs. They invited everyone involved to identify their fears and their concerns. Local officials initiated a series of informal student gatherings where people could talk face to face. "The students are learning a great deal, but we are learning, too, about American civics and about ourselves." The Mayor boasted that he has a new appreciation for the rights of the citizen. A series of articles in the student newspaper now addresses questions with responses posed in non-threatening ways from appropriate leadership. One article spelled out the basic expectations people should have about a traffic stop. One officer summed up the sentiments of many in the heartland community when he said, "It is just such a personal regret of mine that we didn't anticipate the needs before the crisis. The death of this student was horrible, but the fear students had of the police really just made things so much worse. This was a sad situation, but we can now say that some good, positive things will eventually come from it."

Conclusion

University law enforcement officers and other first responders often set the tone for recovery. Senior law enforcement officers remind us that the first response can strongly influence potential witnesses' subsequent participation in investigation and prosecution if crime is involved. Administrators will need to be familiar with the responsibilities of law enforcement officials. This is another reason for advance planning and a thorough understanding of the nuances of local authority and jurisdiction. Administration should be ready to yield authority and appropriately facilitate the role of law enforcement.

Many law enforcement and campus security departments are prepared to take the lead in the development of practical exercises and drills that can potentially mean the difference between student life and death. Campuses that have experienced catastrophic incidents involving multiple deaths have often cited the benefits of such preparation. It is equally important to remember that, while the focus of law enforcement is on investigation and evidence gathering for prosecution of a crime involving death, as well as establishing order, the focus of campus administration will more than likely be to concentrate on their efforts to resume the normal operations of the campus.

References

Kaplin, W., & Lee, B. (1995). *The law of higher education* (3rd ed.). San Francisco: Jossey-Bass.

Yang, C. (2001). *Silent fear*. ABCNEWS.com. Retrieved February 5, 2001. Available: http://moreabcnews.go.com/sections/us/dailynews/ gallaudet-murder010205.html.

3

College Student Death Policies

J. Thomas Owens, Jr. and Katherine Garlough

In the wake of a college student's death, university professionals need policy and procedures in place that are clear and concise to support the grieving family and university community.

There are few occasions that demand a greater empathic response or are a more solemn endeavor for university professionals than the death of a student. Considering the emotional tableau of the moment of death, it may be prudent for university administration to establish a policy, thereby creating a way for the institution to proceed without the pitfalls that emerge with a process of trial and error. "The death of a student, faculty member, or staff person impacts the entire campus community...guidelines have been established to provide an orderly, effective, and caring response" (Western Oregon University, 2006, ¶ 1). The institutional challenges of college student death could be minimized through a comprehensive structure of considerate solutions and policies reflecting the more human side of bureaucracy. The intent of this chapter is to provide an exploration of current policy and procedures from on-line policies currently available. For institutions with a student death policy, adaptation is possible. Policies should be tailored to the culture, mission, and needs of each particular campus. Demographic or particular characteristics of institutions discussed in this chapter are not relevant, since bureaucratic idiosyncrasies exist across type.

J. Thomas Owens, Jr., Ph.D., is a faculty member in the College of Education at the University of Central Florida. His research interests include education and national development, social justice, and policy analysis. Katherine Garlough, Ph.D., is the executive director of International Development for Enterprise and Autonomy, has authored several international grants, and teaches at Oklahoma City Community College.

Review of the content and context of student death policies offers a continuum of policy from compassionate to clerical. While there are as many variations in the policies that address student death as there are institutional locations, purposes, and characteristics, a few common elements exist. Brelsford (2000) listed questions that university administrators ask when student deaths occur: what staff, faculty, and administrators should be contacted? Who will be the coordinator regarding information and tasks? Who will contact the parents? Who will deal with law enforcement? Who will contact secondary survivors? What will be the university's role in providing services to the survivors? These questions reflect considerations of what should be included in a policy statement, yet many policies answer few of these important questions. Additionally, there is a paucity of academic literature that might guide the author of a policy on college student death. Of the few articles available, Wrenn (2002) and Swenson and Ginsberg (1996) detailed models for developing policies and procedures for addressing the difficult task of responding to student death.

Many universities make their policy statements publicly accessible on the internet for the convenience of university administrative staff who often need to access information and support material promptly. These public documents are important sources of data and have certain advantages such as cost-free and trouble-free accessibility and the possibility of yielding a greater quality and quantity of data (Merriam, 1998). Public documents are widely available and can include college web sites found in the public domain. These must be evaluated by the staff for particular relevance and need. In this discussion, web pages and college catalogues are considered as primary sources of data. While document authenticity is a possible limitation and must be considered in the review and possible use of most material, the web pages of institutions of higher education can be assumed to be authentic material for policy discussion.

Many universities have publicly posted student death policies on the web, and our model will rely upon a composite of several documents reviewed for explanation and structure. Over 30 policies were reviewed from a wide variety of institutions: public and private; research, comprehensive, and community colleges; and those with large and relatively small student populations. However, it is noted that the University of California, Berkeley's online policy statement (Berkeley, 2002a) provides, in our consideration, the most exemplary online model for response to student death. The following are a synthesis of elements included in student death policies to varying degrees: a) a focused introduction, b) a clearly defined purpose section, c) defined leadership positions, d) family notification, e) a crisis response team, f) notification of administrators, g) campus community support, h) media involvement, i) memorials, and j) debriefing. These categories will be used to organize the description of policy and procedure for college student death. Each will be described with the aim to provide practical and useful information in drafting a policy.

A focused introduction generally includes a statement of commitment to the safety and well-being of students or an affirmation of the tragic nature of student death. For example, the following introduction offers a balm to the emotional distress of students, family, and staff. "As a campus, one of our goals is to make this a caring, human place. This means not only do we strive to celebrate each other's accomplishments, but we are supportive and compassionate during difficult times" (University of California, Berkeley, 2002b, ¶ 1). Some institutions use the introduction to explain the history of the policy or to whom the policy applies, while others merely state who is in charge. Introductions are clear and often sympathetic while providing a public orientation to the policy.

A clearly defined purpose section assists in response coordination, provides for accurate communication, and supports those impacted by death. While there was tremendous variation in the manner in which purpose was stated, most policies were a logical follow-up to the introduction. Typically these can be described as response priorities, indicative of the control of communication and guidelines to the manner in which responders proceed. For example, a purpose section might immediately follow the introduction directing the user to a reference list of the role or position the deceased member of the university community held. The positions indicate to the site user the path with which to proceed for the lost member of the university community. Clicking on one of the positions, "Academic/Faculty, Emeriti and Retirees, Graduate Student, Staff, Undergraduate Student, Visiting Scholar or Postdoc, Visitor to Campus" immediately takes the user to a specific list of procedures. There are many approaches to introductions and purpose sections of policies. Some policies define a scope of application as their purpose and included definitions, such as on-campus or off-campus. Additionally, some policies state response priorities, life safety issues and population welfare, post-event assessments, and additional resources. A purpose section sets the appropriate tone, must be easily readable and able to be used as a quick reference guide, and must highlight specific components in a clear and succinct manner.

Defined leadership provides clear lines of responsibility and states the individual in charge to coordinate the administrative and support process. "The coordinator acts as a compassionate link between the family and the campus community and facilitates the business aspects of the guidelines" (University of California, Berkeley, 2006, ¶ 1). Perusal of online policies indicated that there is no consistency on who will be responsible. That is, the assigned responsibility rests within the particular administrative and bureaucratic structure of the college. The responsibility may rest with the Registrar, the Chief Officer of Student Affairs, the state police, the Dean of Student Development, the Supervisor of Enrollment, the Vice President for Business and Finance, the Vice President for Educational Services, or the Vice Chancellor for Student Affairs. Other policies were ambiguous regarding leadership, a situation that could lead to overlapping, mixed support, and conflicted approaches to the administrative procedures of crisis situations.

Family notification is a section of the policy stating responsibility and procedure for telling the family of the student's death. Most policies called for notification to be done by the attending physician, the coroner, or campus police. Some institutions relied on the local police in the student's hometown to notify the family. A clause in one policy directed the coordinating administrator to contact the Registrar to ascertain if there were other students with the same last name. Some institutions have separate notification procedures for on and off-campus fatalities (University of North Carolina, Charlotte, 2006). Most often, the notification is required to be done by campus police, the coroner, or the hospital staff. While rarely will a university official be asked to make the first call to the family, unusual circumstances may occur.

Establishing a crisis response team is a section of the policy that determines staff involvement. The crisis response team is the primary coordinating entity for all responses. Team composition varies by institution. For example, in one institution the team was made up of the academic affairs vice president, student affairs director, and legal counsel while other institutions included personnel from counseling, housing, and even physical plant. Most often, the crisis response team had a detailed plan for many contingencies.

The section on the notification of administrators addresses the business concerns and the official university response detailing units or departments that are to be notified. Most of the on-line policies reviewed require that all senior administrators be notified in a timely manner and one senior administrator officially represents the institution in offering condolences to the family. Appropriate university representatives may wish to attend the student's funeral or wake when possible (University of Wisconsin, La Crosse, 2006). Some policies called for the notification to run through a calling chain while others opted to have a blanket e-mail to all personnel that needed to know. Commonly, these offices are notified: the Registrar, Enrollment and Admissions, the President/Chancellor's office, Human Resources, Financial Aid for loans and scholarship, Office of Student Life, Student Affairs, Public Affairs, Business Affairs, General Counsel, Residential Life, Risk Management, Campus Police, and Health Services.

Campus community support entails the support of level one and level two survivors (Glendale Community College, 2006). Level one survivors include students and staff who were personally acquainted with the deceased, such as classmates, instructors, roommates, teammates, and members of study groups, and are most likely to be directly affected by the death. Many institutions make provisions for a counselor to contact instructors whose classes the student is enrolled in and provides as much information as is known at the time about the death, memorial services, and family wishes. The counselor may offer assistance with class discussions, bereavement materials, referrals for individual grief counseling, and special support groups outside the classroom setting. Additionally, the counselor may talk with staffs who knew the student, such as coaches, heads of special services or programs, club advisors and so forth. Level two survivors include students and university employees who share a common identification and empathy with the deceased through their connection to the university, regardless of being personally acquainted with the deceased. Some institutions provide a campus community notice of the death through the campus newspaper or campus-wide e-mail.

Media involvement necessitate an institutional contact person be designated. To provide consistency, most institutions place one person in charge of all media requests. In the event of student death there will inevitably be many rumors, and the institution's ability to provide support will be diminished if multiple versions of the event abound. The Office of Public Relations or Public Affairs may be trained to deal with delicate situations and often becomes the official spokesperson for all public communication regarding the incident. "It is important that no university official speculate as to the cause of death or make statements assigning responsibility for the cause of death to any individual or group" (Western Oregon University, 2006). In all cases of student deaths, the name of a student should not be released to the press without the coroner's permission and not until the parents or next of kin have been notified.

While universities generally will not send memorial flowers or gifts, the President or Chancellor may elect such condolences, and more often the student's college will respond with condolences. A statement of sympathy may be written in the form of a letter and sent to the student's next of kin by the Dean of the student's college (University of California, Berkeley, 2006). One policy reviewed asked the campus minister send a letter to the family. The memorial section of the policy may designate the university official who will attend the funeral. At some institutions flags are flown at half-mast.

Debriefing is a section of policy that details assessment: what we did right and what we did wrong. The appropriate personnel meet with the coordinating administrator to review the university's response and to discuss future policy implications. This section may also suggest that after an initial period of shock and the funeral, further contact with the family may be made offering assistance with any other university matters. Designated staff members may be assigned to pack the belongings of the student who resided in campus housing, if a relative is unable.

The March 31, 2003, edition of *The Spectator* displayed an article illustrating a case of policy changes at the University of Wisconsin-Eau Claire. Professors and students had become alarmed at the university's slow response to providing campus-wide notification of a student's death. Because the death passed without official notification from the university, many staff and students experienced conflicting information and personal distress. The Associate Dean, Bob Shaw, commented that indeed, "he received questions regarding the university's death policy from a couple of [the deceased's] friends, prompting a reexamination of the protocol for such situations." The problem was that Shaw was not prepared to respond to the situation that had arisen in a manner that was timely and appropriate.

A word about urban legends: The plot of the 1998 movie *Dead Man on Campus* portrays a myth regarding university policies of college student death (Gale, Hurd, Malina, & Toffler, 1998). The story involves two freshmen who have demonstrated poor academic performance and decide to seek the demise of an unstable co-dweller who is teetering on the brink of desperation. The strategy is based on the students' unwarranted belief that institutional policy states that students will be awarded straight A's if a roommate dies. Suffice to say, no policy on student death we found mentioned academic compensation in the form of straight A's for the roommate's demise. However, some colleges do offer the consideration of course load reductions, incompletes, alternative course completions, or withdrawals for personal leave (Duke University, 2006). Indeed, in reviewing institutional policy responding to student death, roommates are more often the forgotten survivors.

Student deaths are a tragic reality experienced by members of the college community. Although the number of students who die each year is relatively small in comparison to the overall student population, it is important to have identifiable procedures that recognize loss and convey sensitivity and understanding to survivors, the deceased's family, instructors, classmates and friends, and the campus community (Glendale Community College, 2006). Therefore, when tragedy does occur, it is the responsibility of the university to respond in a sensitive and sympathetic manner (University of North Carolina, Charlotte, 2006). While campus death protocol can be comprehensive, "...each death is unique and requires judgment to ensure a compassionate and supportive response for the campus" (University of California, Berkeley, 2006a, ¶ 5). The policies and procedures for college student death assist those involved in order to facilitate the most humane and considerate response possible while supporting the family and the academic community (West Virginia University, 2006).

References

Brelsford, G. (2000). Developing a sudden death policy. *Residence Life Executive*. Retrieved May 3, 2002. Available from http://www.paperclip.com/student_affairs/oct2000/student_affairs4.htm

Duke University. Death in the family: Bereavement Policy. Retrieved April 16, 2006. Available from http://www.aas.duke.edu/trinity/t-reqs/bereavement.html.

Gale, D., Hurd, G. A., Malina, M., & Toffler, V. (Producers). Cohn, A. (Director). Abrams, A. Broder, A. L., Traeger, M., & White, M. (Writers). (1998). *Dead man on campus*. [Motion Picture]. United States: Paramount Pictures.

Glendale Community College: Responding to the death of a student at Glendale Community College. Retrieved April 16, 2006. Available from http://www.gc.maricopa.edu/facultystaffhandbook/index.cfm?id=1253.html

Merriam, S. (1998). *Qualitative research and case study application in education*. San Francisco: Jossey-Bass.

Swenson, D. X. & Ginsberg, M. (1996). An administrative model for postvention in campus death. *Journal of College Student Development, 37*, 543-548.

University of California, Berkeley. (2002a). UC Berkeley: Guidelines for responding to death. Coordinator. Retrieved April 16, 2006. Available from http://death-response.chance.berkeley.edu/all/coordinator.html.

University of California, Berkeley. (2002b). UC Berkeley: Guidelines for responding to death. Introduction. Retrieved April 16, 2006. Available from http://death-response.chance. berkeley.edu/introduction.html

University of Wisconsin, La Crosse. Procedures to be followed in the event of life-threatening emergencies or of the death of a University of Wisconsin-La Crosse student. Retrieved April 16, 2006. Available from http://www.uwlax.edu/police/ appendix _1.htm

West Virginia University. Operating procedures for emergencies involving students. Retrieved April 16, 2006. Available from http://www.studentlife.wvu.edu/emergency_procedures_2005. pdf.

Western Oregon University. Issuing department: Student Affairs, Subject: Death of student, faculty, or staff person: Policy. Retrieved April 16, 2006. Available from http://ww2. wou.edu:7777/pls/wou2/policy.publicview. policy_detail?policy_to_display=64.

Wrenn, R. (2002). Bereavement Management and Counseling at the University Level. (ERIC Document Reproduction Service No. ED 469 355).

Part II

Compassion in the Midst of Crisis

4

Assisting the Grieving Family:
The Worst That Can Happen,
The Best That We Can Do

Erin Taylor Weathers

Student affairs professionals have the opportunity and obligation to respond to student death compassionately. Crisis response training should include exposure to grief educators as well as family survivors. Thorough and recurrent training minimizes fear and encourages student affairs personnel to consider what is needed by the devastated family and university community. Recommendations for meaningful responses may appear to be minor, but in fact, offer a professionally-relevant compassionate response.

American culture views death as a taboo subject, with admonitions to grieve quietly. Rarely do discussions occur about what happens to our bodies, spirits, and legacy when we die. But because more than 6,000 college students die annually (Iserson, 1999), we must acknowledge that student affairs personnel will have to navigate the aftermath of students' deaths.

In 2000, my sister Logan was a sophomore at the University of Saint Thomas in Houston. She died suddenly from a medical complication that December. My family lived overseas, and Logan was my only sibling. Despite my background in student affairs, this chapter is written primarily from my experiences o the first days after Logan's death.

Erin Taylor Weathers completed her Ph.D. in Adult and Higher Education at the University of Oklahoma in 2006. She has served in numerous student affairs capacities working with adult students, universities abroad, and marginalized female populations.

Families' Expressions of Shock and Loss

Grief counselors agree there is no death as devastating as that of a child. This loss is rarely "overcome," and family members struggle with their sorrows for the rest of their lives. While the death of anyone's child is horrific, the death of a college student marks the abrupt end to a parent-child relationship that is in a transitional stage. Parents often feel anguish that they nurtured their child to young adulthood, only to lose her or him before the child's personal and career goals could be realized. Furthermore, because most college student deaths are accidents or suicides, families are devastated by the unexpectedness of the death (this in no way diminishes the grief caused when a child's death is anticipated, as in terminal illness).

Unfortunately, our society imposes beliefs about what is appropriate and inappropriate grieving, including a timeline by which survivors of the deceased should "be over it." It is critical that we remember we are witnessing a family in their most tragic days. It would be presumptuous for us to say we know what the family is feeling, even if we have survived our own family deaths. Different members of the same family will react differently to the news of their loved one's death. Some become almost robotic in their efficiency, some confrontational, and many become incapacitated by their sadness. These are all normal expressions of people in shock. Finkbeiner (1996) noted, "Shock is probably the body's kindness, the time to realize the facts slowly, to ease into the pain" (p. 4). Student affairs professionals should be cognizant of the physical symptoms of shock, which include an inability to focus, forgetfulness, physical pain, fatigue, insomnia, dizziness, loss of appetite, and disorientation. Temporary memory loss associated with shock emphasizes the need for communication to be repeated and in a written format.

Receiving the news that a son or daughter has died is often too much to bear. A parent may seem incapable of absorbing the facts. However, denial is not always an unhealthy reaction. It can serve as a buffer, providing protection from overwhelming emotional trauma. Family members may manifest their shock and initial grief by providing support for other family members or taking on the unpleasant bureaucratic tasks when a person dies. Parents and family members also react with anger. Gilliand and James (1997) explained this feeling, writing, "It is a desperate attempt to gain attention, to demand respect and understanding, and to establish some small sense of control" (p. 420). Support staff can enhance their assistance to grieving persons by looking for these emotional cues. As trying as this situation may become, staff must practice patience. Families often find it difficult to maintain patience when they are in desperate need of answers. Remaining calm, empathetic, and repeating information can be proactive for both parties.

Initial Encounters with the Grieving Family

Student affairs personnel are often the first "in person" contact the family has after learning about their child's death. Naturally, this is an unimaginably painful professional task. While the family may appear shocked to the point of numbness, it is unlikely they will forget how they were treated on your campus.

There are crucial considerations to be made before speaking to the family. Student affairs personnel should reflect upon the student's social and personal situation: (a) Was this an international or first generation student? (b) What was her or his living situation? (c) What information did the institution have about this student's home and campus life? (d) Who from the student's family will the staff be meeting with? Personnel must be sensitive to the fact that they may be dealing with divorced, widowed, or single parents, and blended families. Siblings, grandparents, spouses, and children of the deceased may also be involved. Surviving siblings can feel left out in the proceedings. As noted by Elder (1999), surviving siblings may believe their feelings are discounted. Student affairs personnel should be sensitive to the complications deaths have in multiple member family situations.

Student affairs personnel should "practice" what to say to the family beforehand, as another staff member can consider how it might be received (Iserson, 1999). It is helpful to prepare a private room in the residence hall for families. All phones and pagers should be silenced, and supplies such as water, tissues, pens, and paper should be available. Only one staff member should be allowed to enter the room in the case of a necessary interruption. Another staff person should help organize and respond to incoming students. Student peers often want to extend condolences, but it should be noted that this is difficult for the family in the immediate hours after their child's death. Personnel may want to consider a "team approach" where two or three staff members sit with the family and serve as liaisons. Business cards of university support services and staff and other contact information should be made available to every adult member.

There is no perfect protocol for this moment. Staff should introduce themselves, their position, and any relationships they had to the deceased student and then acknowledge the family's shock and grief. Expressed sorrow and memories of the student do not create additional pain. Rather, they help to assure the family that the student was cherished and important to the wider community of friends, professors, and mentors.

While there is no blueprint for what student affairs representatives should say to the family, there are phrases to avoid. Relay the events as you know them and expect that you will need to retell portions of it. If you are asked about events that you are unsure of, instruct a staff member to locate this information as soon as possible. Provide an overview of the roles campus police, local law enforcement, medical staff, coroners, residence hall, and student life staff will play. Kenneth Iserson, a veteran emergency room doctor, suggested you speak directly to the adult who seems to be best handling the news (Iserson, 1999). If young children are present, ask the parents if they would like a staff member to sit with them in an adjacent space, offering the children snacks and some distraction. Staff may only have to offer that there are no words to express the sadness and that it is difficult to imagine the family's shock. At times, gentle honesty provides a suitable form of condolence. For example, "I am sorry for your loss" neither identifies who was "lost" nor what they were "lost" to. "I am sorry Gretchen died" is both more honest and personal. When we hesitate to use words such as "died" or "killed" and replace them with more vague terms such as "lost" or "passed," we inadvertently discredit what the surviving family finds all too terribly real. However, the term "passed" is often used among African-American families as the preferred, respectful term. Phrases to avoid include:

1. You will/have to get over this.
2. We need to find some closure.
3. Your son is in a better place.
4. At least you had 18, 20, 25 years with her.
5. Luckily, you have other children.
6. God never gives you more than you can bear.
7. Were you aware your son struggled with drugs?
8. Remember your child is an angel in heaven now.
9. You need to be strong for your wife, your father, etc.

The surviving family may incorporate these statements as comforts or realizations *at a later time*, as they progress through their grieving, but they are not useful in the immediate aftermath of death.

There will come a time when it seems appropriate to talk with the family about the student's life. This discussion does not need to be saved for memorial events. Compassionate humor and positive memories about the student's time at your campus demonstrate how much he or she will be missed and that he or she enjoyed happy and fruitful times.

Immediate Assistance

This section focuses on specific tasks your staff can do for the family in the first days after the student's death. While some of these suggestions may seem minor, the family often remembers them as acts of kindness and professionalism. Remembering the family is probably still in shock, establishing trust provides a "safe place" for parents to express their preliminary grief. This trust is built by listening, providing accurate information, offering condolences, and helping in every way possible. The following are ways to ease the transition for the visiting family:

1. If the family is arriving by plane, can a staff member meet them at the airport? Arrange for a rental car and hotel. The family may want an on-campus private room to make and receive phone calls.
2. Offer sodas, juice, coffee, or meals.

3. Know where the student's physical body is located at all times. It can be very distressing for the family to hear that officials are unclear where their child is at the moment.

4. Ascertain where the student's personal possessions are—their wallets, jewelry, car, etc.

5. Do not assume the family knows its way around the campus or community or how things operate on a college campus.

6. Ask the family if they would like to meet with a counselor or member of the clergy. It is advisable that you also retain a physician on call while the family is on campus.

7. If students have begun leaving memorial items at some location, invite the family to see these.

8. Offer a contact sheet to every adult family member with all necessary phone numbers and campus and city maps.

9. Walk the family to their car after the conclusion of each meeting. If possible, ensure families have access to convenient parking on your campus by issuing them a special permit.

If you have seen the student's body and the family asks you directly about their loved one's appearance, be honest without making the situation more nightmarish than it already is. Families may also ask for the sequence of events leading up to the death. While we want to protect grievers from details that may connote their child suffered, parents often imagine this suffering anyway. If we can say that "The police say she died instantly," or that "Juan's hospital room was filled with his friends in those last moments," we effectively extend some solace. "The harder the details are for parents and siblings to acquire, the more they feel 'victims' of circumstances and procedures beyond their control" (Riches & Dawson, 2000, p. 155).

Some student affairs staff worry that what they say could be used in a potential lawsuit on the deceased student's behalf. Since we live in a litigious society, campuses are naturally concerned they may be held liable (justifiably or not) in the student's death. Our professionalism should override these potentialities, making our obligation to the mourning family first and foremost. Harper stressed, "We don't want to avoid the family because we feel we might have some liability in the death" (personal communication). It can be argued that the withholding of information and access to relevant officials inadvertently persuades the family to seek legal recourse. In writing on the development of a trauma response team Scott, Fukuyama, Dunkel, and Griffin (1992) theorized: "Administrators may need to deal with the institutional liability and fear of a lawsuit. It is generally felt that institutions reduce the probability of a lawsuit by sharing information with the family rather than withholding" (p. 232). The grieving family needs accurate information, and this should be met by sharing observations and official documentation, not by speculation.

The Week after the Death

There is no standard for how long a family will need daily interaction with the campus. Our best efforts are a combination of not rushing the family through the process while not prolonging the wait for information. Once the initial shock has passed, most family members realize certain tasks need to be accomplished but struggle with prioritizing these. Families may also feel it will be left to them to remove their child's possessions, settle any university bills, and retrieve academic records. At this juncture, student affairs staff should convey to family members what tasks a staff member can do for them and which can wait for a later time.

Families should not be sent to various campus offices to take care of "closing details." Student affairs personnel should call the relevant department in advance and escort the family to these appointments or directly handle these matters so the family need not do so. The bursar, parking office, financial aid office, and other revenue collecting programs should be notified immediately of the student's death. The deceased student's professors and student organizations in which he or she was involved also need immediate notification. It is likely that students and families will want to come together in both an informal setting and a memorial event. Student affairs, a local religious community, or students might organize these opportunities.

One of the most difficult tasks facing the family is the removal of their child's possessions from his or her residence. Student affairs personnel should establish a time when they can remove the belongings, but be careful not to pressure the family to do so immediately. Many universities offer storage of a deceased student's possessions for the remainder of the year. Sometimes residence life staff offers to pack up a student's residence hall. At this time, it is advisable for the roommate as well as a residence life staff member to be present or nearby. Another simple thing student affairs can do is to provide decent boxes, bubble wrap, and markers for the family. While we should certainly ask fellow students to respect the family's privacy at this time, we also can solicit student volunteers to move boxes out of the residence.

Eventually the time will come for the family to return home, which can be both a relief and wrenching experience for the survivors and attending student affairs staff. Student personnel staff should assure the family they will maintain contact with them for any concerns that arise and provide them with necessary phone contacts as well as mementos from campus memorial events. This is also the time to ascertain the morale of the staff. Setting aside debriefing needs, those university persons directly involved in the death of a student need their own time to grieve and emotionally regroup.

Cultural Sensitivity

Just as no two people grieve the same, different cultures maintain unique mourning practices. Notions of death, dying, belief in an afterlife, funerary processes, and bereavement vary widely among ethnic and religious communities. Within the United States there is considerable diversity in grieving habits. "Appropriate" mourning is both individually expressed and culturally sanctioned.

Any generalization about a culture is just that—a stereotype that may or may not be applicable to the individual survivors. The key is to listen closely to what the survivor says, take a lead from the key survivor, and whenever possible include a member of that culture on the notification team (e.g., staff member, neighbor, friend, minister) (Iserson, 1999, p. 45).

In the event of a student's death, the university's goal is to inform, assist, and offer sympathies in a fashion that is most respectful to the family's beliefs, situation, and heritage. Any student's death is traumatic, but the crisis situation is even more difficult when international student status, language barriers, and cultures with which you are unfamiliar play roles in the process.

When an international student dies and the family resides overseas, most universities contact that country's consulate, asking that they complete the death notification process. It may take some time for the consulate to accomplish this. Therefore, it is critical to ask students from the same country not to call their own families with the news until the deceased student's family has been notified.

Families from abroad may be unfamiliar with U.S. laws, medical practices, transportation options, and American college lifestyles. Some families may not want to or may be unable to come to the United States. In addition, language barriers between staff and the student's family can damage an already strained situation. If the deceased student's family is not proficient in English, a foreign language instructor or fellow international student can serve as an interpreter. An interpreter should speak directly to the family, maintaining eye contact with them. If complicated medical issues need to be discussed, they should be referred to the attending hospital that often employs interpreters proficient in medical terminology. A foreign language instructor can additionally assist in the composing of a condolence letter.

The same instructors and international students are instrumental in educating staff on ethnically and religiously appropriate memorial traditions. Harper (personal communication) provided an illustration of this as she recalled the death of a Japanese student. Student peers informed Student Life that Japanese mourners wear much more formal attire to funerals than the common business attire found at western services. Imagine the message inadvertently sent to the mourning family if Student Life had not known this. The family may want to include something from their faith or homeland in a campus memorial.

The matter of returning an international student's belongings can be complicated, especially if the family does not come to the United States. Critical and personal belongings such as passports, death certificates, jewelry, and photographs need to be returned as soon as possible. International mail is not the most secure way to do this. Another option is to air express the items via an international courier service. After this is done, discuss with the family what they would like to see happen with the student's other belongings. Student affairs personnel should make it clear that the campus is more than willing to securely store these items for an extended period. Do not forget the student may own a car.

Circumstances Surrounding the Death

An unfortunate reality of young adults dying is that the majority die violently as a result of accidents, suicides, and homicides. The grieving survivors' imaginations can be relentless with graphic images and thoughts of suffering. Supporting persons want to offer solace, but in light of these circumstances, they may feel helpless. In some cases, an illness or choice plays a role in a student's death. When substance abuse, depression, or reckless behaviors are involved, parents may exhibit disbelief upon learning the news. Some parents know their children were struggling or engaging in dangerous acts but never thought it would lead to their death. Other parents simply have no idea these issues were facets of their child's life.

Circumstances surrounding the student's death may still be under investigation when the family arrives on campus. Refer their questions about the exact cause of death to the attending medical staff or law enforcement. One way to facilitate this is to arrange such a meeting for the family. If emergency personnel are not releasing sufficient information to the family or if the student's residence is the actual crime scene, acknowledge the family's frustration and see which specific questions you can get answered for them. In cases of homicide, the family faces multiple fears, including that their child will somehow be blamed for his or her death, or that the assailant will not be caught or convicted. Student affairs personnel should listen for which fears seem to most concern the family and verbalize them.

College students' suicides deserve special discussion as suicide is the second leading cause of death among this cohort. Suicidologists stress that the act of ending one's life is not about wanting to die but rather being unable to find a way to live. A mother whose daughter committed suicide said, "She desperately wanted to live; she died because she thought she had no alternative" (Andrews, 2000, p. 2). Later she expressed, "From the moment we learned of my daughter's death, I knew that the word 'suicide' had the power to erase her life while emblazoning her death in neon letters" (Andrews, 2000, p. 2).

It is difficult to accept that a suicide has occurred, even more so in a young adult with his or her entire future ahead. Some family survivors may not believe his or her loved one's death was by their own hand, insisting this must have been a terrible accident or even homicide (Scott et al., 1992). Therefore, even if the death was clearly a suicide, it is better to say, "This may have been a suicide" until medical professionals provide the cause of death.

Survivors may ask repeatedly if anyone on campus knew their brother or daughter was suicidal, perhaps to ascertain their own culpability. Parents might immediately blame academic stress or their child's social group for the suicide. "Suicide leaves behind the haunting pall of responsibility" (Scott et al., 1992, p. 233). Family members will probably blame themselves, to some degree. Harper (personal communication) remarked, "Parents are finding answers in their own way" and in their own time.

College students also die from lengthy illnesses. In this instance, the campus will stand witness to the act of dying, even if the student has returned home for the final stages of their illness. While no one wants to see a loved one suffer, some expressions of sympathy compound the griever's sorrow. Phrases such as "They're at peace now" and "It must be a relief" can create feelings of guilt and being misunderstood. The family is grateful their son or sister is no longer in pain, but they also wish things were different. Honor their sorrow by not proffering your theories on what they must be feeling.

Remembering a Student's Life

Part of the healing process is the coming together of community to express the collective sense of loss and sorrow. Students grieve profoundly and often organize memorials for their deceased friend, especially if they are not able to attend the funeral. It is appropriate, meaningful, and compassionate to display pictures of the student, hang wreaths, or wear ribbons. There is a clear indication that parents and siblings want to be a part of a wider circle of bereavement.

The planting of trees, the setting of memorial benches and other physical markers, contributions to significant charities, and the sharing of stories that celebrate aspects of the deceased's life can all add to the parents' and siblings' recognition of the impact their loved one had on the lives of others (Riches & Dawson, 2000, p. 159).

Student and campus leadership should make their best effort to attend the memorial. Leaders can include the student body president, university president, and residence and student life staff, as well as the student's professors. "The presence of senior school officials demonstrates to the family that the student was important and respected" (Iserson, 1999, p. 153). Not all families or all family members will be ready to participate in a memorial. If they do wish to attend, it is a nice gesture to have both a student and staff member who knew the student well escort them to the service. If a student's funeral is being held in his or her hometown, student affairs personnel should plan to send a university representative.

In the months after the student's death, peers often seek additional means to express their grief. Notes of condolence as well as a video montage highlighting positive memories have been helpful to both the friends left behind and the families that receive these gifts. Parents want to know the campus has not forgotten their child. One way to eliminate this fear is by sending a card on the student's birthday and/or one-year anniversary of their death. While this may strike some as morbid, families desperately hope someone will acknowledge how difficult but important these milestones are.

Proactive Measures: Training for the Worst

Student affairs staff can never fully prepare for their students' dying. Each student is unique and each situation uniquely tragic. However, thorough and recurrent training minimizes fear and encourages student affairs personnel to consider what they can say and do for the devastated family. "The ability of people to adapt during crises is often a measure of their capacity to organize and to integrate their experiences following crises" (Dunkel, Griffin, & Propert, 1998, p. 148). Chapter One provides numerous suggestions for Critical Incident Response Team (CIRT) training. The following questions for consideration can better prepare student affairs staff to meet with surviving family members.

1.   What are the municipal procedures when a student dies?
2.   Where are the area morgues?
3.   Can an autopsy be done without a family member's consent?
4.   How are death certificates issued?
5.   Can surviving family members access the deceased's residence any time they wish?

An additional valuable training resource is to speak directly with parents whose college-aged child has died. There might be an individual on campus who would be willing to share such an experience. If not, Compassionate Friends (a national support group for the parents and siblings of deceased persons), Mothers Against Drunk Driving (MADD), and Parents of Murdered Children (POMC) may be willing to provide a guest speaker. Finally, crisis responders must explore their feelings and experiences of witnessing death and grieving. "Imagination, studying people, advance planning, and learning from experienced mentors is the only way to successfully perform this necessary, but tragic, task" (Iserson, 1999, p. 34).

Conclusion

A student's death is, in Jan Schultz's (personal communication) words, "the worst thing that can happen." She would know. Jan was the Residence Life Director at the University of St. Thomas and one of Logan's favorite people. As professionals committed to improving the quality of students' lives, student affairs personnel are obligated to continue serving them in their deaths. When heartbroken families come to campus, their sorrow cannot be eliminated nor set aside, but we can still offer our best — accurate information, means by which to stay in contact, and expressions of condolences and our own sorrow.

References

Andrews, J. (2000, July). Suicide: How do we say it? *The Compassionate Friends Newsletter*, North Oklahoma City chapter, Oklahoma City, OK.

Dunkel, W., Griffin, & Propert, B. (1998). Development of coordinated mental health counseling resources in times of disaster. *NASPA Journal, 35*, 147-155.

Elder, R. (1999, January). Dealing with grief: A sibling viewpoint. *The Compassionate Friends Newsletter*, North Oklahoma City chapter, Oklahoma City, OK.

Finkbeiner, A. K. (1996). *After the death of a child: Living with loss through the years.* New York: The Free Press.

Gilliand, B. E., & James R. K. (1997). *Crisis intervention strategies.* Pacific Grove: Brooks/Cole.

Iserson, K. (1999). *Grave words: Notifying survivors about sudden, unexpected deaths.* Tucson, AZ: Galen Press.

Riches, G., & Dawson, P. (2000). *An intimate loneliness: Supporting bereaved parents and siblings.* Philadelphia: Open University.

Scott, J., Fukuyama, M., Dunkel, N., & Griffin, W. (1992). The trauma response team: Preparing staff to respond to student death. *NASPA Journal, 29*, 230-237.

5

Telephone Notification Protocol

Kenneth Iserson

Modified from Iserson, V. V. (1999). Grave words: Notifying survivors about sudden, unexpected deaths. *Tucson: Galen Press. Death notifications should be done by the attending physician, campus police, or the coroner. It is not recommended that death notifications be done by telephone; ask the survivors to come to the hospital immediately. However, if the need arises to make a notification, call preparation is essential.*

Protocols, such as the following, are useful when making death notification calls or when teaching others how to make them. When making these difficult calls, callers should speak in a calm voice, consciously trying not to use a high-pitched voice that will sound alarming to a listener. Allow brief periods of silence during the conversation so the recipient can digest the information. When possible, an experienced person should make the call. If new personnel are present who may need to make these calls in the future, they should listen in so that they can learn how it is done.

Kenneth Iserson M.D., M.B.A., is a Professor of Emergency Medicine and Director of the Arizona Bioethics Program at the University of Arizona College of Medicine, Tucson, AZ. Dr. Iserson has authored of more than one hundred fifty scientific articles and nine books including Grave Words: Notifying Survivors About Sudden, Unexpected Deaths *(1999). In his spare time, he is a member and medical director of the Southern Arizona Rescue Association (search & rescue).*

BEFORE MAKING THE CALL

a) Get identifying information

Patient name

Patient age

Male/Female

Skin color

Eye color

Distinguishing marks

Patient social security number or other ID numbers

b) Get event information

Type of event (accident, sudden illness, injury, etc.)

When did event occur?

Where did event occur?

How did the person arrive at the hospital?

When did the person arrive?

c) Get the survivors' contact information

Survivor's Name

Survivor Address

Phone number

Alternate phone numbers/pagers

Relationship to decedent

Time(s) contact attempted

Time contacted

Second Contact's Name

Address

Phone number

Alternate phone numbers/pagers

Relationship to decedent

Time(s) contact attempted

Time contacted

d) Prepare

Calm down.

Find a quiet area with a phone.

Get any long distance access numbers.

Review what you will say.

e) How will you say it?

Concentrate on the telephone conversation.

Speak distinctly and slowly so you can be understood.

Repeat the message, especially the directions if the recipient hesitates when asked if he/she has the location/directions.

When the recipients say something, do not interrupt them. Wait until they are finished to add to or clarify.

If you cannot reach the person, leave a message.

Clearly pronounce your name and spell it, the name of your institution, the name of person you are trying to contact, a return telephone number that will be answered by a person who knows how to quickly locate you, and the date and time you called.

Note: Only leave this message on a phone machine or with an answering service if you are sure that the individual you called is the person you are trying to contact.

MAKING THE CALL

a) What will you say?

Hello. This is (your name) from (name of health care facility or agency). Is this (name of person you are trying to contact)?

Are you the (relationship) of (name of decedent)?

(Name) has been in a serious accident. We would like you to come to the hospital. (This can be used for any type of injury.)

(Name) has had a (name of illness). We would like you to come to the hospital.

Can you arrange to get here? Do you know where it is?

b) Tell them your location

Ask the person to get a piece of paper and pencil to write down the information.
Location (including address, parking, specific area—such as the emergency department—and a contact phone number).

Directions to facility.
Who to contact on arrival.

Are they alone? If so, can they get someone to transport them?

c) Give your contact information

Give them your name or a person who they can call back, if necessary.

Give them a working telephone number and any other specific instructions about how to contact the individual (pager, badge number, extension, etc.).

If applicable, tell them the hours that the contact person is available.

Be sure they write down all information you give them.

Have them repeat back all information.

Note: detailed contact information is especially important for long-distance notifications.

d) Recommended responses

If they say, "The person you want is not here."

"Do you know how to contact them? When they will return?" (Be certain that they have your accurate contact information.)

If they respond, "I am their son, daughter, etc."

"How old are you?" If s/he is a child, give only the contact information. If s/he is an adult, give the same responses as if you had reached the individual.

If they ask, "How is s/he?"

S/he's in critical condition."

If they ask, "Can't you tell me any more?"

1) "The (physician, surgeon, trauma team) is here with him/her. It's probably best if we discuss other specifics when you arrive." or
2) "S/he just arrived at the hospital, and we will know a lot more by the time you get there."

If they say, "I can't come in right now."

"I think that you need to come in right now."

If they ask, "Is s/he dead?"

"S/he's in critical condition; we can discuss his/her condition when you get here.

If they ask a second time, "Is s/he dead? Tell me now."

"I'm sorry; yes, s/he died (on arrival, despite our attempts at resuscitation, etc.)."

If they ask, "Who did it?" (Or other details of the event).

1) Briefly give only the details that are listed above in "Event Information."
or
2) For any others say, "I don't have those details. We can find some of them out when you arrive."

e) If they ask, "How will I other tell emotionally close survivors?"

For Local Calls:
1) "Would you like me to call them and ask them to come to the hospital also so I can speak with them?" or
2) "Would you like me to call them and tell them what I have told you?"

For Long-distance Calls:
1) "Would you like me to call them and tell them what I have told you? or
2) "Would you like to discuss the best way to do it?"

6

The Academic Professional as Spiritual Caregiver: Guidance through Seasons of Sorrow

Barbara S. Boyd and Tom W. Boyd

While the psychological process of grief is crucial to personal well-being in response to significant loss, we face a deeper challenge in dealing with these losses. This challenge is spiritual rather than purely psychological. Exploring the spiritual side of loss and the role professionals can play in assisting families with difficult questions is important. Academic professionals can recognize the need for spiritual care-giving and become better able to assist students in crisis.

> Those who will not slip beneath
> The still surface on the well of grief
> Turning downward through its black water
> To a place we cannot breathe
> Will never know the source from which we drink,
> The secret water, cold and clear
> Nor find in the darkness glimmering
> The small round coins
> Thrown by those who wished for something else.
>
> *The Well of Grief*
> David Whyte (1990, p. 35)

Dr. Barbara S. Boyd is the Director of Outreach for Religious Studies at the University of Oklahoma and is also faculty in that program, teaching in the area of Christian and Biblical Studies. B. Boyd is an ordained Presbyterian minister, published poet, and public speaker. Dr. Tom W. Boyd is a David Ross Boyd Professor Emeritus in Philosophy at the University of Oklahoma, where he is currently teaching in the Religious Studies Program in theory and ethics. T. Boyd is an ordained Presbyterian minister, a writer, and public speaker.

In the well of grief the waters run deep. Any significant loss in our lives draws us there, but it takes courage to plunge into those waters and seek "the small round coins" that rest on the bottom. Grief requires courage because the significance of our losses is measured by the suffering those losses induce.

The claim of this chapter is that, while the psychological process of grief is crucial to personal well-being in response to significant loss, we face a deeper challenge in dealing with these losses. This challenge is spiritual rather than purely psychological. As used in this discussion, "spiritual" is taken to refer to the most fundamental concerns related to life-meaning. In the present context, the spiritual aspect of suffering loss will be called sorrow. Sorrow moves beyond "the well of grief" and toward the sea of surrender and compassion.

Here we direct attention to spiritual sorrow as the higher calling through and beyond grief over specific losses. After working with and observing people suffering from profound loss, we have noted that they follow a more or less predictable process ranging from deepest anguish to recovery toward the fullness of life. Our aim is to describe this process in such a way that academic professionals may recognize it and become better able to assist students in crisis.

Before turning specifically to them, two topics call for preliminary comment: first, the role of the professional in the academy as a spiritual caregiver; second, the understanding of students and their context in light of profound loss and suffering.

The Academic Professional

To introduce the idea of "spiritual caregiver," especially in relation to secular institutions of learning, may appear strange, if not alien. Yet, if institutional response to student needs is to be comprehensive, it must include this dimension of human life. Profound suffering cannot be walled out of the campus, and the deeper spiritual reaches of such suffering in relation to significant loss goes to the core of what it means to be human.

Accordingly, the academic professional does well to develop a capacity for responding spiritually to students. To do so, professionals in the context of higher education are invited to attend at least four considerations:

1.   Spiritual caregivers are engaged with their own journeys through sorrow. Simply put, only people who are themselves "well-grieved" can seriously make themselves available to others who are experiencing loss.

2.   Spiritual caregivers are prepared to serve as spiritual mentors to students in need. This is a delicate process, because professionals cannot simply assume the role of spiritual mentor. Students do the choosing.

3. Spiritual caregivers develop specific resources for assisting students. Over the last two decades of the twentieth century, a resurgence of spiritual practices has gained currency and popularity. They include, but are not limited to, the following: reflective reading, spiritual mentors, meditation of various sorts, journaling, group sharing, retreats, spiritual directors, and a variety of more specific practices related to given religious traditions. The professional's role is never to dictate any practice but under fitting conditions to suggest possibilities, and where interest is shown, to encourage students to follow through on them.

4. Spiritual caregivers learn their limits and know when and to whom students should be referred. Academic professionals, with rare exception, are not specialists in grief and sorrow. This does not absolve them of a measure of responsibility, but it underscores the fact that, as with any professional, they should know the limits of their expertise. Furthermore, they need to be sufficiently knowledgeable of helping resources in their community to refer students to other more capable spiritual caregivers.

Students as Recipients of Spiritual Caregiving

If academic professionals are committed to anything, they should surely be devoted to students and their welfare. Since students are as vulnerable to loss and suffering as anyone else, special consideration needs to be given to what it means for students to grieve and become sorrowful. Consider the following:

Students often bring experiences of significant loss to campus and begin their student careers with anguish. Contrary to common presumptions, youth does not immunize against lose and suffering. Furthermore, students often encounter similar experiences during their years in the academy. While it takes considerable professional skill to ferret this out, in many cases, a student's educational success may well hinge on how well peculiar struggles are known and addressed.

Quite obviously, students belong to particular generational groups and are in the process of their own maturation. It is important to understand how a fledgling adult may handle new and unfamiliar personal crises. For example, crises of loss among students may become especially acute because students tend not to expect such losses during these years. Thus, the more professionals know about the cycles of maturation and generational shifts, the more likely they are to be prepared for responding to crises of loss and suffering. If dealt with well, such crises may prove important in the maturation of many students.

Loss and suffering are intimate experiences, and they call for deeply personal engagement with students. Depending on the size and the general philosophy of relating to students, institutions' capacity to be personally available to students in crisis can be highly challenging. In general, students often complain of impersonal conditions at colleges and universities. This becomes accentuated at times of loss and suffering. Simply put, students who hurt and are in anguish are no different from any of us: They long for the most personal response possible.

Caregiving through the Stages of Sorrow

> Sometimes with the bones of the black sticks
> left when the fire has gone out someone
> has written something new in the ashes
> of your life. You are not leaving.
> You are arriving.
>
> David Whyte (1997, p. 38)

Grief is not experienced in a linear fashion. It is always understood as a dynamic process within the psyche occurring when people experience loss. Yet, for the purpose of reflection and study, it is helpful to create models in order to understand the way grief manifests itself. The pioneering work of Elizabeth Kubler-Ross (1969) on death and dying is the model most widely employed when discussing the grief process. Her approach has imprinted the way most contemporary helping professionals understand and interpret grief. It is upon her well-established research and contribution to the topic that in this chapter we offer our own complementary model.

As grief is to psychology, so sorrow is to spirituality. Grief work is incomplete when it relies solely upon a psychological process, especially when the person who is in grief has beliefs and convictions of a religious or spiritual nature. Caregiving in this context demands that all aspects of the loss experience be acknowledged in order to work effectively with the grieving person. To rely totally upon the grief model to do the work of helping another, without exploring the depths of spiritual sorrow, can inhibit the interior process necessary to bring about full healing.

For those persons who claim spiritual interests, the grief model and the sorrow models may work in tandem. While students are involved in the psychological grief process, they may likewise be involved in the stages of sorrow. These levels of grief and sorrow are not in conflict, but rather they express different aspects of the loss experience. If caregivers are able to help students identify both processes, the possibility exists for a healthier response to the inevitable variety of emotions striking the person suffering from a loss. Thus, it could be said that grief and sorrow are necessary partners in realizing the deeper agonies of life.

The Kubler-Ross Grief Model is organized around five stages: denial, anger, bargaining, depression, and acceptance. While no human psychological process is ever understood to be simply linear, the tendency still exists for a grieving person to move through these stages toward wholeness in a fairly predictable fashion, regardless of the length of time involved. At any one time, depending upon the coping skills and the circumstances surrounding the anguish, the victim of grief can leap forward into an unexperienced phase of grief or regress into a stage through which they have earlier passed. Or a person in grief can be in more than one stage at a time as they transition from one emotional state to another. While the grief process should never be construed as moving neatly from one stage to another, neither does grief tend to begin with acceptance nor move toward denial.

The Sorrow Model presented here is orchestrated around stages similar to the Grief Model, albeit with spiritual overtones. The Grief Model, as perceived in this chapter, is deeply personal—an intimate engagement with the suffering created through personal loss. Our Sorrow Model, however, takes on a larger venue—the engagement with loss as an existential category of life, embedded in what it means to be human and to live meaningfully. To reiterate, these two models are not antithetical to each other but address different dimensions of human experience. One is located in the ego personality, accompanied by attendant emotions, thoughts, and responses to loss. The other is located in the soul, where the individual is concerned with the complexity of suffering in relation to the full sweep of life-meaning.

The Sorrow Model uses these terms: deep doubt, despair, surrender, joy, and compassion. These terms make use of spiritual language in order to describe a distinctive process going on within a person who has suffered a loss. We will discuss the stages of sorrow, along with the task of caregivers in helping students move through the cycles of their sorrow. In claiming this as a viable model for attending students, it is our belief that caregivers have clear tasks that require an acute perception of the importance of spiritual work within themselves and with students. For caregivers to be able to make use of the Sorrow Model requires that they accept, attend to, and understand their own spiritual nature.

Stage One – Deep Doubt

> To lose until we lose our life is to live our life and our death,
> And nothing that passes on exists that doesn't give constant proof
> Of the continuous emptiness of all,
> The silence into which everything falls
> And, finally, we fall.
>
> Pablo Neruda (2002, p. 69)

Case 1: Jennifer and Alice have been friends since middle school. Now juniors in college they have been roommates for several years. To Jennifer's disbelief, Alice was killed by a car while crossing a heavy-traffic intersection after her last class. Jennifer, a deeply religious person, finds everything she believes, including confidence in her own ability to make decisions, in question. From a place of isolation and grief she asks for help in addressing her doubt.

Some say that doubt, rather than fear, is the beginning of wisdom. This may be true in a philosophical sense, but for someone who is experiencing deep loss, doubt becomes an albatross upon the soul. In a time of suffering, doubt becomes that which challenges the meaning and significance of life itself. Doubt cannot, in this setting, be relegated to some minor concern over daily decisions. Doubt in the spiritual arena has the capacity to throttle the assurance that life is valuable and meaningful. As the first stage of our Sorrow Model, doubt presents itself as the capacity to bring disorientation into the lives of those who are full of sadness. The center of the universe shifts, and a primordial sense of place may be severely disrupted. What has been formerly understood to be stable and reliable is now perceived as transient and untrustworthy. The worldview shifts from security in one's place to a sense of disequilibrium that can bring devastation to the student's capacity to function even in daily tasks.

We propose that it might be in this very stage where the seeds of future disorientation and dysfunction, or their resolution, are buried. If students are unable to face the existential doubt generated by life itself, the future could easily be scarred by the residue of this unattended burden. Occasions of significant loss only accentuate this condition. When elemental doubt about one's place in the scheme of life is eroded, critical spiritual work is required to resolve the issues this produces.

During this beginning phase of the sorrow process, what Jennifer unconsciously seeks is clarity and understanding of the larger order of things. The temptation, however, is to settle for easy short-cut answers to the demanding questions of the meaning of one's existence. The confusion brought on by doubting the purpose for life easily masks the need for intense scrutiny into more troublesome issues. The doubting student tends to scramble for anything handed to her in the form of platitudes as a less painful means of facing more complex questions. The spiritual challenge in this situation is to provide a environment for the beginning of wisdom, of a basic grappling with the doubt itself. While the seeds are beginning to form that may blossom in years to come, the student's immediate task is to locate a source within herself for taking on the perennial uncertainties of human existence (Mezirow, 1991; Tisdell, 1999).

Most students have only begun, if at all, to attend to such internally profound matters (Evans, Forney, & Guido-DiBrito, 1998). When a substantial loss occurs, the skills to sort through doubt are not yet fully developed. While this can be the occasion for nurturing such skills, work with a competent caregiver may be necessary. The skill needed by the caregiver at this point in the cycle of sorrow is listening.

Listening is a commitment to hospitality—to inviting the griever into a safe place where the story may be told and retold. For the caregiver, the ability to listen to the soul struggle with doubt requires a willingness to be patient as the student unveils this unfamiliar set of feelings and thoughts. Doubt is, by its very definition, a state of spiritual bewilderment. Jennifer is somewhat incoherent as she struggles to share her inner concerns with the caregiver. The atmosphere cannot be hurried, nor should caregivers become exasperated. Guiding this student through the minefield of doubt into some clarity of the larger issues of sorrow becomes the central task. This requires affirming the stage of doubt and the willingness to allow Jennifer to express it fully without trying to 'fix' it for her.

The logical temptation of the caregiver is to try to help the student find answers. Yet, we know that there are no answers to all problems, and to sorrow there are no programmed solutions. It is what it is—a wasteland of perplexity. In a loss event doubt seeps in to undermine the student just at a time in her life when she is beginning to feel some of her own potency and possibility. The caregiver has a delicate role to play at this point: to provide a calm presence, listening as the story unfolds. This is not the moment in the sorrow process for rescue and never for dismissal.

Stage Two – Despair

> No one told me it would lead to this.
> No one said there would be secrets I would not want to know.
> No one told me about seeing,
> Seeing brought me loss and a darkness I could not hold.
>
> David Whyte (1992, p. 51)

Case 2: Eric comes to class regularly but sits in the back and never responds to anything or anyone. When approached by his instructor, he responds with a profound cynicism, and he persistently demonstrates self-destructive inclinations by deliberately not doing well on examinations, by losing jobs, by questioning any and all attempts of other people to draw him into conversations related to the future. He says he has none. Upon closer questioning, a professor learns that Eric is the only survivor of a skiing trip taken by the Engineering Honors Club.

To be lost in despair is to experience the depths of spiritual abandonment. This stage is recognized by its sense of isolation. This is a place without future, without sufficient sense of hope to imagine a future. The stage of despair may be the most difficult for students who, during these formative years, stand on the threshold of their entire future as adults. The isolation felt during this stage can lead students to reject every overture to help, as well as the comfort of friends and family. In this place of sorrow Eric may consider harm to himself or others as a way to stop the pain to which he is being subjected by the loss event. Through the lens of despair this student cannot frame a future beyond his own suffering.

Since hope is a spiritual category, Eric's work in this stage is to locate a sense of promise in the midst of a crisis that has brought him to the abyss of despair. How to stay connected with family, friends, and life itself during this stage of sorrow often becomes the key issue. As Eric withdraws and isolates himself, his temptation is to wonder why anything matters at all. To establish hope in the midst of despair is especially problematic for young adults.

Despair brings with it a built-in alarm mechanism for the caregiver. If Eric becomes unable to articulate a sense of life's promise, the caregiver must take this signal seriously. The spiritual work to be done by the caregiver is reassurance. This is not to promise "everything will be all right." Such platitudes never work, because students know better from experience. This is the time to help students recognize and acknowledge that, while the universe may occasionally resemble boundless chaos, it also includes order and purpose. During the stage of despair Eric should be encouraged to discover sources in which he may recover hope. This is often an interior investigation not previously undertaken.

For students who have a clearly defined religious sensibility, language can be chosen that will affirm a deliberately inward turn. For students who are not religious practitioners, but have some basic understanding of spiritual life as in Eric's case, the caregiver can encourage engaging in life.

Reassurance offers students a borrowed affirmation by which they can navigate the rest of the journey through the encounter with sorrow. While Eric may not yet be aware that it is possible to negotiate this trial of spiritual suffering, the caregiver can firmly aid him in moving from the urge to find answers to a willingness to let the moment of despair be what it is—a time to discover psychological boundaries and to connect with spiritual strengths. Despair itself can actually engender hope if students are assured that they themselves possess inner resources for dealing with sorrow. To learn that they are not merely desolate islands in this sea of sadness can be great solace.

Stage Three – Surrender

> I am but a footprint on the earth
> A wing against the sky, a shadow in the water
> A voice beneath the fire
> I am one footstep going on.
>
> Nancy Wood (1979, p. 79)

Case 3: Fire in a student fraternity has left two students in especially acute distress at the death of a best friend. James and Will were both in the house when it caught fire and had tried to save their friend. They could not and he perished. The two young men are paralyzed with grief and guilt as they appear in the office of Student Services seeking help and consolation.

Surrender is not a positive category in the American psyche. It is, however, central to the understanding of the spiritual life. Thus, to claim surrender as the pivotal stage in the Sorrow Model is to challenge all the precepts of what it means to be a Westerner. Yet, if the person who is in sorrow is to move through the birth canal of the process of the model, surrender will be required. As a spiritual category, surrender has nothing to do with "giving up." It is closer to "taking the plunge." Further, it entails that deliberate stillness that comes with the leap into the void of release. It is a deep and abiding trust that as one leaps, something or someone is there to break the fall. Surrender requires release of ego attachment to survival in order to enter the spiritual dimension of abandoned affirmation into the drama of life.

For a person involved in sorrow, there is a strong propensity to hold on to what is familiar or sane, to what can be grasped in the face of the turmoil of loss. Attachment is what is known, and fear of what is unknown drives students as they approach this stage of sorrow. This clutching at the normative is especially apparent in young adults who usually have little experience with which to interpret suffering. A resolute fear entrenches them in a reluctance to execute the important task of releasing the sorrow, along with the event that caused it. The spiritual work of allowing themselves to free-fall into the abyss of the seeming randomness of the universe requires the phenomenal courage of letting go. Yet, this work must be done in order for students to move into an integrated relationship with sorrow.

For James and Will to enter into the surrender stage requires that there be something advantageous about such a leap. The work here is trust, which is an oddity, given the fact that loss is what broke their trust in the promise of life. Recovery requires a deeply spiritual capacity because the person must have trust in something or someone. The task of the caregiver is to invite the student to consider where trust is possible for her. Once trust has been established, students are more likely to surrender to the actuality and authenticity of sorrow in such a way that equilibrium can be re-established. In this case, they face the challenge to surrender their burdensome past and to trust once again in the ordinary routine of life as it unfolds. Life is embraced as a gift.

Caregivers are central at this point in the process, for they become trustees and representatives of trust for the sorrowful. Fear, the antithesis of trust, is at its peak during this time. The integrity of intentions toward students must be evident and focused. Students need to experience confidence in the process and to allow the caregiver to midwife them on this path. In this stage the caregiver invites but never insists.

The work that James and Will are doing at this point is life-critical. This is not simply psychological development toward the acceptance of loss; it is the work of realizing that all of life requires our constant movement into the unforeseeable future. For all persons, engaging the unknown aspects of life makes heavy demands on us. It is the spiritual dimension through which the courage is derived to make such a journey. The task of caregivers is to enable students to locate this capacity for release within themselves and to adventure into the mystery and uncertainty of life here and now.

Stage Four – Joy

> Inside everyone is a great shout of joy waiting to be born.
>
> David Whyte (1997, p. 30)

Case 4: Michelle enters the office of a faculty advisor. She has been there many times over the past two years, since her roommate's paralysis as the result of a car wreck. Prior to the accident, Michelle had been an honor student and the recipient of several academic scholarships. However, her grades have slipped while facing her roommate's emotional and physical needs. After working hard for two semesters, she is told by her advisor that her grades have recovered and that she is being considered for an award from her program. She is giddy with elation, but immediately wonders if her feelings are appropriate in light of her roommate's condition.

The gift of relinquishing the agony of sorrow lies in a growing sense of well-being. The spiritual word for this is joy. Not to be confused with happiness, joy is a profound sense of reconnection and alignment with the whole of life and what it can offer. It is not a fleeting emotion as happiness often is, but rather joy initiates within us a deepened sense of the gracious capacity to own our lives. As sorrow begins to loosen its stranglehold on students through the act of surrender, a most welcome inner change infiltrates the soul. The heaviness of loss begins to lift, and a lightness of spirit fills the student. Laughter and delight in the ordinary return. Sighs cease. Long blank stares turn into energetic participation. Joy decorates the face, frees the body, and inspires the soul.

For most students authentic joy has yet to be experienced. Most have known happiness, instant gratification, pleasure, fun. However, the depth and breadth of lived joy is generally a new order of experience for most young adults. Spiritually grounded rather than psychologically based, joy invites the soul to become an inner sanctuary, even when life is troubled. The richness of the joyful experience is that, once realized, it can become a part of the permanent landscape of the spirit. Sorrow is precisely the experience that most decisively makes the discovery of joy possible; the two are found in tandem.

The work of the caregiver in this stage of the Sorrow Model is quite simple: participate with the student in the revelation that life does continue. It is appropriate at this point for the caregiver to help Michelle recognize those moments in each day that go well, that are successfully executed and bring praise and gratitude. In this state of the spiritual journey through sorrow, the work of the caregiver becomes encouragement—to facilitate a celebration of all the elements of life, both those of sorrow and those of delight. In helping Michelle to discover this deeper rhythm in life, the caregiver is nurturing a sense of balance that, in turn, leads to her spiritual, psychological, and emotional health and well-being. To help this student revel in the ordinary moments of lived experience nurtures, in the end, a person turned dramatically toward the embrace of life as a whole. Sorrow is understood, not as defeat, but as a spiritual resource.

Stage Five – Compassion

> Innocence is what we allow to be gifted back to us
> once we've given ourselves away.
>
> David Whyte (1997, p. 32)

Case 5: Pedro, a 19-year old freshman was found dead in his room. Police said his blood alcohol level was .40, five times the legal level of intoxication for adults. David was drinking that night, too. He finds himself torn between what he knows he must say about the death and concern for his own responsibility. In his sorrow he remains compassionate as he looks across the courtroom into the face of the mother of Pedro.

The unique feature of this Model of Sorrow is that it does not stay fixated on the self. Rather, this model recognizes that the person turns from sorrow back into the world, where the sorrowful one becomes compassionate toward others who have also known loss. The authentic journey through spiritual sorrow moves students beyond their own agony into empathetic engagement with all suffering. As students realize inner joy, the urge to completion takes hold and leads them beyond themselves and into their world. Once those who have known sorrow successfully work through their own story, a subtle change takes place in their interior life. They become less and less immersed in their own ego. Something within the human spirit draws the wounded into compassion for the wounds of others. The best healer is a wounded healer.

In reaching for others, students complete the cycle of sorrow by taking attention away from themselves in this turn outward. Through compassion, students move into the farther reaches of actualized spiritual growth. The move to the compassionate response calls on the resources of selflessness and care. Students find themselves becoming the caregivers. Furthermore, compassion has a chance to become a way of life. Thus, through the experience of their own sorrow and awakening to joy, students may come to participate as world citizens.

As caregivers acknowledge this stage of growth in the Sorrow Model, they begin to release the student and bring the process to closure. This may, in turn, cause yet another grief to occur—the loss of the relationship between caregiver and student. Caregivers can use this occasion to encourage students to work through this loss with the skills and tools gained during the previous process. Relinquishing the connection reminds students that loss is embedded in every human encounter. The strength of the work will be tested as students turn to face and embrace their larger worlds. Caregivers can help students become aware that the rhythm of loss and recovery will continue throughout life. The work will never be completed, but it can be done more wisely each time it is experienced. At this point caregivers invite the students with whom they have traversed this adventure through sorrow into a ritual of remembrance and release.

In many cases, perhaps even in most, caregivers will not experience the student complete this process we have just sketched. After all, it can take years to find one's way into wholeness. Therefore, it becomes important that caregivers help students recognize that grief and sorrow processes do not have time limits attached to them. There is no 'race to the finish' embedded in this model. It will be helpful to students to encourage their continued attention to their progression along the path into well-being, a lifetime adventure.

Caregivers, in walking students through the vicissitudes of these stages of sorrow, face three important reminders: The caregiver does not have to be an expert therapist or priest in this Sorrow Model. All that is required is that caregivers attend and nurture their own sorrow so that as the students with whom they are engaged are doing their work, there is a communal frame of reference. The experience of sorrow should not leave the caregiver feeling helpless. Rather, because it is a common human experience, if well attended, we can mutually offer guidance, assurance, comfort, and compassion along the way. Caregivers are no different from students when it comes to sorrow.

A critical message for caregivers to discern is the scope of the task. We cannot fix the world, but we may be able to help students one at a time face their fears and sorrows. Since caregivers are called to be people of compassion and concern, the tendency is to become despondent when facing such a daunting task. But in order to do good work, the first realization is that we cannot repair an entire civilization. We cannot even repair one other person. We can only be the occasion for a few to meet a face of grace and kindness along the way.

In the end, the source of strength and courage for caregivers must come from beyond themselves. Caregivers, too, must have a spiritual center from which to draw the energy and creativity to work with students who are in sorrow. Relying merely upon our own skills and gifts will eventually run the well very dry. Working with students who have known loss requires of us that we do the very thing we are asking them to do—reach into the depths of the soul and trust the response.

Finally, by way of conclusion, this chapter addresses a topic too long ignored in the academy: the importance of the spiritual dimension when addressing students during times of crisis (Love & Talbot, 1999). It is our hope that the Sorrow Model might serve as a guide when assisting students through the experience of sorrow. There is nothing automatic or fixed about this process. Rather, the model offered here only sketches in the abstract something that is dynamic, quite personal, and always open toward the unfinished promise of the future.

Formal presentations such as this can only point to the convoluted web of human life, where the agony and ecstasy of our quite personal existence unfolds.

References

Evans, N., Forney, D. S., & Guido-DiBrito, F. (1998). *Student development in college: Theory, research, and practice*. San Francisco: Jossey-Bass.

Kubler-Ross, E. (1969). *On death and dying*. New York: Scribner.

Love, P. & Talbot, D. (1999). Defining spiritual development: A missing consideration for student affairs. *NASPA Journal, 37*, 361-375.

Mezirow, J. (1991). *Transformative dimensions of adult learning*. San Francisco: Jossey-Bass.

Neruda, P. (2002). *The yellow heart*. Port Townsend, WA: Copper Canyon Press.

Tisdell, E. J. (1999). The spiritual dimensions of adult development. In M. C. Clark & R. S. Caffarella (Eds.), *An update on adult development theory (New Directions in Continuing Education, no. 84)*. San Francisco: Jossey-Bass.

Whyte, D. (1990). *Where many rivers meet*. Langley, WA: Many Rivers Press.

Whyte, D. (1997) *The house of belonging*. Langley, WA: Many Rivers Press.

Whyte, D. (1992) *Fire in the earth*. Langley, WA: Many Rivers Press.

Wood, N. (1979). *War cry on a prayer feather*. Garden City, NY: Doubleday.

Understanding Funeral Arrangements

Tara M. Nielsen

Death services are a part of the process of assisting families with student tragedy. Whether or not university personnel assist in the preparation of funeral arrangements, it is important to understand some of the pressures the grieving family encounters. Funerals are enormous tasks to organize and execute, and university administration can benefit from knowledge of the proceedings and methods by which funeral arrangements are done.

It is the premise of this chapter that educators, especially those who work directly on the provision of services to students, should know and understand where their responsibilities lie, what type of support, information, and details they can offer in the event that death occurs on their campus. It is particularly important to be knowledgeable concerning death, its related customs and rituals, and the funeral process. This premise is based on the unfortunate fact that students do die on college campuses and that the devastating experience of death is complicated by the many arrangements that must be made. Consequently, the preparedness, response, and training of professionals in student services should include an area we would prefer to ignore, death.

Death is part of the natural life cycle; it is constantly present in our world and it plays a part in many of the decisions we make. Death wears many faces; it can present itself through a normal cycle of life, disease, suicide, homicide, accident, or even terrorism. Trauma or sudden circumstances often accompany death in college. Whether it is cancer, heart com-

Tara M. Nielsen has a degree in Funeral Science from the University of Central Oklahoma and a Master's of Human Relations from the University of Oklahoma. A licensed Funeral Director and Embalmer, she is well known for her work in organizing and creating death awareness and grief support seminars and for her assistance in the Oklahoma City bombing.

plications, an automobile accident, fire in a residence hall, a gunshot, stabbing, or the collapse of a building by terrorist acts, these circumstances can create unnatural conditions. Sometimes it is necessary to discuss the details of death with the family of the student before decisions are complete about the final disposition of the body. When families are unsure of what direction to take with funeral preparations, providing general information about these arrangements could alleviate some of the anxiety and confusion being experienced.

First, it is necessary to present several definitions of funeral, the diversity of its meaning, and the issues involved for families when making that first call to the funeral home. This will allow for a discussion of the gamut of services provided by funeral homes with the following goals: (a) to help the reader understand the complexity of decisions facing an already vulnerable family, and (b) to open a knowledge path into an area that professionals in student personnel services usually do not know. The services funeral homes provide place emphasis on a series of concrete decisions the family must make requiring swift precision and timing. An analysis of these decisions opens room for several areas where university administrators could play a critical role. Finally, the intersection of culture, religion, and death will be examined.

The Role of University Administrator

When any member of a campus community dies, it calls for an immediate and compassionate response from administrators. This response can often cause uncertainty, creating difficulties and complexities if a campus community lacks guidance and policies for such a traumatic situation. Poor coordination of response efforts can cause several problems. Unclear lines of authority and responsibility may result in duplicated efforts or even conflicting goals, problems in scheduling space for support groups and other debriefings, and inappropriate contacts with survivors by multiple interveners unaware of others' involvement. (Swenson & Ginsberg, 1995, p. 544)

he disposition of the body, while commonly left to the funeral director and embalming professionals, should be considered vital to the role of administrators providing support during the death of a student. Although administrators do not have any legal rights to the possession, transportation, preparation, or disposal of a dead body, the family of the deceased may ask for assistance in the funeral arrangement process. Therefore, college student personnel should be familiar with some of the basic aspects and ethics involved in preparing for a funeral.

The responsibility of the disposition of the dead usually falls to the next of kin of the deceased or with those identified in any written instructions left by the deceased. The mandate for pre-stated written disposition varies from state to state; therefore, it is important to verify these regulations in states where the death occurred. Who constitutes the next of kin? If the decedent is married, the legal spouse is the next of kin; single decedent's next of kin would be parents, if alive, or an adult child. If the parents are not living, and the deceased did not have children, an adult sibling would act as the legal next of kin.

Before notifying the next of kin of the deceased with the tragic news of a death or expressing sympathy, administrators should be prepared to provide them with names of funeral homes and funeral directors in their area along with their contact information. Having an established relationship with local funeral personnel may help eliminate details that tend to be overwhelming and can provide a sense of rapport with and responsibility to the family that may rely on you for support. To assist the family, campus personnel could prepare families for the type of information needed by most funeral homes when making the initial call for assistance.

Families who are planning traditional services that include burial may ask university administrators to recommend pallbearers to carry the casket. This number can vary from four to eight depending on the weight and size of the casket. Any number of honorary pallbearers may be selected and may include individuals or groups such as fraternities, sororities, clubs, organizations, work affiliates, or other memberships. The participation of special organizations needs to be discussed with the funeral staff in order to arrange for special circumstances and time allotment during services. Collegiate personnel can play a significant role in informing all the necessary organizations from the college community about specifics and assisting in coordinating funeral details with the family and the funeral home.

Funerals

A funeral is a service performed in conjunction with a burial or cremation of a dead body.

The funeral from Ancient Egypt to present day America helps confirm the reality and finality of death. It provides a climate for mourning and the expression of grief. Allows the sorrows of one to become the sorrows of many. Is one of the few times love is given and not expected in return. Is a vehicle for the community to pay its respects. Encourages the affirmation of religious faith. Is a declaration that a life has been lived as well as a sociological statement that a death has occurred (Mayes Funeral Directors, 1994, pages not numbered).

Many factors are considered in determining the type of funeral each family desires. Public or private, religious or secular, and where it will be held all play a role in what a funeral will be. Other concerns may be whether the body will be present, will the casket be open or closed, will be a viewing or visitation, and will the remains be buried or cremated.

Some cultures believe the funeral is a passing for the dead to another place, a journey, or a celebration of life. Funerals can be determined by who the individual is that has died, what time of day or month it is, where the body is at the place of death, how the individual died, or even how long the body must be grieved before it can be interred. As rituals for the burial of the dead, funerals serve as mourning, celebration, and reflection for the persons left behind.

Recognizing the culture and the customs of the student who died is fundamental when approaching a family with details concerning embalming, cremation, funeral arrangements, preparation of the body, and its transportation (Iserson, 2001). Never assume anything; always ask when referring to customs and
the funeral intentions of the family. Each family assisted will not want the same
type of funeral. As discussed previously, funeral practices are influenced not
only by religious and cultural traditions; a huge consideration is based on cost
(Federal Trade Commission, 2004). The grieving process for each culture usually coincides with the funeral and burial rituals. Dissecting each religion would
require an intense study in itself. Therefore, a brief overview has been included
to provide insight into some cultures and religions throughout the world (National Association of Funeral Directors, 2004).

Buddhist. The customs and rituals surrounding Buddhist funerals have
evolved over time depending on regions and families. No set order has been
prescribed for Buddhist funerals. Each sect has different traditions. However,
there are three main components that are universal to Buddhist services: (a)
chanting, (b) burning of incense, and (c) post funeral memorial services. Cremation is the most common form of disposition. However, Buddhists believe in
washing the remains and then placing them in a coffin. The remains of the deceased often stay in the family's home until the day of the cremation or disposition. This "cremation wake" can last from one to three days. During such time a
monk comes to the home each day to chant from the Abhidharma. The coffin
remains open, and an altar (a "butsudan"), is set up with fresh flowers, fruits, a
water bowl, incense, and candles. A picture of the deceased commonly is placed
on the coffin.

Post funeral memorial services are of great importance to the Buddhist
faith. Memorial services occur seven days following a death and then every sev-
enth day until the forty-ninth day. Services will be held in the temple or a family's home. Families will gather on the anniversary of the death. Three years
following the death marks the end of formal grieving period for the immediate
family.

Native American. The Native American culture consists of various tribes
and traditions. Funeral aspects are diverse in each tribe; however, most believe
that the deceased has departed on a journey. Most families do use a funeral
home for embalming, yet nations may differ in tradition, so always ask. Bodies
may lie in state at a funeral home, a community all-purpose center, or the family
home. The Kickapoos commonly transfer the remains to a home, which is made
from wood and cattail reeds. Most Native Americans continuously guard or stay
with the remains until burial. The Osage people believe that the soul leaves the
physical body to say its goodbyes. For the spirit to come back to the body for a
proper burial, a person is constantly on watch to be certain the body is not removed.

The burial is usually on the fourth day after death and generally has four
songs at the ceremony. This pertains to everything happening in fours within
Mother Nature: the four seasons, the four directions, and the four stages in the

life cycle. Remains may be buried with moccasins, food, and other items to help them during their long journey. An eagle feather is often placed in the hands of the deceased. The feather symbolizes the highest-flying creature towards God, and it is believed to purify the body.

Muslim. Muslim funeral rites differ greatly from Christians'. It is to be understood that each Islamic individual practices a diversified belief system and religious conviction. Therefore, practices can differ from family to family. Since they do not embalm their dead, the burial takes place within the next sundown period. There are typically four stages or preparations for the deceased: (a) washing, (b) shrouding, (c) funeral prayer, and (d) burial. The body is washed on an elevated surface. The washer, the same sex as the deceased, must be trustworthy and pious. He must not speak of what they have seen, only what is good. The body is washed from the right side to the left side three times, or an odd number until the washer feels the body is cleansed. The shrouding of the body takes place following the cleansing of the body. The shroud, white and scented with perfume and oils, must be nice, clean, and large enough to cover the remains. Commonly, the shroud is cut into seven pieces of cloth and wrapped around the body three times for men and five times for women.

Funeral prayers are often recited in the mosque. Family and friends recite Suras as blessings from the Koran for the deceased. There is no set time to offer such prayers; however, prayers may not be offered at sunrise, noon, or at dusk except when there is fear of the body decomposing. The funeral prayers are given while standing, because prayers offered while sitting or riding without an excuse are not valid. Most Muslims absolutely forbid the use of music at the funeral, and crying is not permitted. Burial may be performed at any time of the day or night. Graves are dug deep enough for a man's standing height. Muslims do not use a casket or coffin for burial; however, cemeteries may require families to use an outer burial container to surround the remains. The remains are lowered into the grave by hand either feet or head first. Once the body is in position, with the face of the deceased turned to the right, the head is then placed on a brick or stone, allowing for the left cheek to be open to the soil. The shroud is then loosened, and three handfuls of soil are thrown near the head of the deceased. A close friend gives final instructions to the deceased in preparation to meet with Allah.

Jewish. In the United States, Jewish families use a funeral home. Like Muslims, they do not embalm or cremate their dead; therefore, they typically bury within 24 hours. Families' and friends' lives virtually stop until a proper service has been completed. Autopsies are discouraged, as they are considered a desecration to the body. Traditionally, Jewish families do not lay the body in state for viewing. As a sign of respect, the remains are not to be left alone until after the burial.

Often funeral homes can obtain a specially designed "Jewish" casket made of wood. These caskets contain holes in the bottom so that the body can be exposed to the earth at burial. In preparation for burial, the body is thoroughly cleansed and wrapped in a simple, plain linen shroud. Jewish tradition believes that the dress of the body and the coffin should be simple so that a poor person would not receive fewer honors in death than a rich person.

Catholic. Funerals have three distinct parts: (a) the visitation (Wake or Rosary), (b) the church service (Mass of Christian Burial), and (c) the graveside service (Rite of Committal). The evening before the Mass, a practicing Catholic is allotted a Rosary or Wake service in which the casket is typically open. This service consists of Scripture, prayers, hymns, blessings, and sometimes, social festivities will be offered. Following the Mass of Christian Burial, services will proceed directly to the committal service most often at a Catholic cemetery. At the committal service the priest leads the family in words of comfort and commits the body back to the earth (Rite of Committal).

Protestant. There are tremendous variations among Protestants, and perhaps the only similarity is to have a funeral followed by a committal service. Usually a visitation period precedes the funeral, and the worship service includes the Bible readings, prayers, a sermon, and a eulogy, interspersed with music (Iserson, 2001).

Funeral Homes

Funeral homes provide a wide range of services. Basic professional services of funeral directors and staff may include consultation with family, clerical and administrative services, preparation and filing of legal documents and necessary permits, and consultation with clergy, cemetery, crematory, or common carriers. They provide assistance with insurance documents, planning the funeral or memorial service, and writing and placing obituary notices. Other services offered include embalming, washing, disinfecting of unembalmed remains, dressing, and casketing. Cosmetology, post autopsy care, post organ donation care, restoration, and refrigeration are also offered. The use of facilities and equipment for directing funeral or memorial services is another service that is available. Most funeral homes also have automotive and transportation services.

Calling the funeral home. The first call to a funeral home, crematory, or embalming service commences the process of accepting the fact that a death has occurred. This phone call remains the responsibility of the legal next of kin of the decedent. It is important that the family have proper information about local facilities that provide the services the next of kin desires. The first call to the funeral home can be overwhelming or confusing, and families will have to make many decisions in a time when duress welcomes any source of familiarity. Therefore, it is important that college administrators offer the family any information about funeral details. Being able to offer that assistance can often calm the family because they know they have someone who can offer some basic guidance.

The person contacted at the funeral home will usually ask for the following information: name of person calling, phone number, and relationship to the deceased; the full legal name, permanent home address, telephone number, date of birth, time of death or time found dead, and social security number of the deceased; address, and phone number of the location of the body; and if a physician or medical examiner (M.E.) will be handling legal documents of the death. It is important to know if the body has been released by medical personnel and is able to be turned over to a funeral establishment. The full name, address, and phone number of next of kin and the relationship to the deceased will need to be provided (see Figure 1).

The funeral home will also ask to set a time for the family to come in to the funeral home to make final arrangements. It is recommended for this meeting to take place as soon as possible and to take priority over other details the family is desperate to understand about such death.

Recovering the body. Once a funeral home has received the call from the family asking for their services, they will confirm the location and condition of the body, and if the body is ready to be released to the funeral establishment. If not, the funeral establishment will leave its contact information stating that it has permission from such family to recover the body once it is ready to be released.

The place of death is often not where the body is recovered by the funeral director. Recovering a body can take place from the medical examiner's or coroner's office, hospital, nursing facility, morgue, or the original place of death, but note this is not typical of a death on a college campus. Should the removal of the deceased occur from the place of death directly to the funeral home the deceased most often was in critical condition or under hospice care. This is a rarity among a college community, but the same rules apply: a physician must release the body in order for a funeral establishment to make a removal.

The recovery of the deceased may traumatize the family members, so it is advisable to inform them of the removal process. Generally, funeral directors will transfer the body to a collapsible cot and stabilize the deceased by strapping the body securely to it. Then a blanket is placed over the entire body. The funeral director will then exit the room and proceed to the vehicle to load the deceased. Be aware that if the family follows the deceased to the vehicle they may encounter another corpse in the process of delivery or removal.

Autopsy. Most often when dealing with a dead body from a college or university, the medical examiner will be in charge of the remains. Usually this means that the body will undergo an autopsy. The main reason to have an autopsy is to determine the cause of death. The results of the autopsy often take weeks and may result in pending information for a legal death certificate. This can create problems for families needing the full cause of death on death certificates to finalize personal details of the deceased. Once the body has been released to the funeral establishment, a director or embalmer will recover the body and personal effects that were on the body at the time of death. Sometimes blood, human fluids, feces, and elements inflicted at the time of death will be present on the body or on personal items. Another factor that could be present is odor or a strong unusual smell. Again, administrators should know that such conditions might exist in order to know how to approach the family with some of these horrific realities. Indeed, additional training and education may be

Figure 1

Information sheet: First call to funeral home

Call received by:

Time of call:

M.E. called: yes / no

M.E. case number:

Date:

Name of person calling:

Name of deceased:

Location of deceased:

Directions:

Deceased S.S. number

Age: Date of birth:

Deceased home phone number:

Next of kin:

Relationship:

Next of kin address:

Next of kin phone number:

Attending physician's name:

Attending physician's phone number and address:

Time of death:

Time found dead:

Release of the body by the attending physician or the medical examiner:

Permission for embalming: Y/N.   Given by:

Cremation:

Direct burial:

Donate to science:

Time of arrangement conference:

recommended to address such circumstances. The reader is encouraged to examine the book *Death to Dust* (Iserson, 2001), where the author discussed the details of what happens to dead bodies.

Embalming. The funeral personnel must ask for legal permission for a body to be embalmed. If the body is not embalmed it may be necessary for the body to be placed in a refrigeration unit until the family makes a decision about final disposition. It is important to realize that any remains not cremated may need to be embalmed to cross state lines or to be shipped abroad. This often raises concern and emotional stress for families abroad whose religious beliefs demand that the physical nature of the dead not be disturbed.

Cost of a Funeral

The least expensive type of funeral service is direct burial, direct cremation, or donation to science. Families can expect a full traditional service to cost anywhere from $6,000 to over $10,000 depending on the services needed and selected (Consumer Affairs, 2005).

It is not uncommon for families to be financially stretched. Sometimes paying for a funeral or memorial service would cause an extreme hardship. There are several options and resources available to families in need of assistance. These means, however, are not publicly recognized or offered. For example, the county of death often has funds to assist in the direct burial or direct cremation of individuals who need financial assistance. Funeral homes, vault manufactured cemeteries, flower shops, casket providers, and sometimes crematories will donate or discount services and merchandise. This financial assistance must be sought because most funeral service providers do not want to lose revenue.

In a collegiate community, administrators should offer assistance or funds for this type of circumstance. In some instances, the university may assume financial responsibility for the transportation of remains out of the state or country. However, not all universities have appropriate funds set aside to assist families. Nevertheless, the Funeral Consumers Alliance (1999) has recommended that when a death occurs during a course of study, scholarly activity, or a university-sponsored event, administrators should consider funding the transportation of remains regardless of financial need or responsibility.

Merchandise. Merchandise can be an area where families are often confused and conflicted, especially when they observe the cost of certain items. Encourage the family to inquire about other alternatives when discussing these matters. Also realize that the type of merchandise can differ among funeral homes, between regions of the world, and from culture to culture.

The merchandise that families often ponder when thinking of funeral arrangements is casket/coffin selection. Often and unfortunately, price is the dominating factor. The expense of caskets/coffins can be overwhelming, so it is up to the family to decide what is really important for them. The funeral director is required to present a Casket Price List when such options and prices are discussed (Federal Trade Commission, 2004). Caskets/coffins costs may vary depending on the type of material that is used to construct them, with an average cost between $2300 and $10,000. It is important to understand that regardless of cost and type of material the casket/coffin will not preserve a body forever. Even a metal casket with "sealer" gaskets designed to delay the onset of moisture into the casket and prevent rust will not preserve a body eternally.

Clothing. The funeral director usually asks the family to bring undergarments, stockings or socks, and outerwear (not necessarily a suit or dress) to the arrangement conference scheduled during the first call placed to the funeral home. Jewelry, eyeglasses, perfume, and hairdressers are other items that need to be addressed. If jewelry or eyeglasses are placed on the deceased for viewing, does the family want these items removed and returned before burial?

Transporting Human Remains

The collegiate population in today's society is extremely mobile; therefore, when a death occurs human remains often need to be transported across state lines. This is not a difficult procedure, but families must realize it takes time to process, to get all the necessary documents filed, and to obtain permits for transportation. Families who are unfamiliar with this process can often spend money that is not necessary. There are many options and resources available for families; collegiate administrators should be able, when approached, to suggest such services.

Transporting human remains across state lines. To begin, a decision of where funeral or memorial services will be needs to be made. Will the body be present at these services, will there be remains present, does the family want to view the body, where is the body, and what is the condition of the remains? If the family selects a traditional service, most states require that the remains be embalmed to cross state lines. Should a state not have such a requirement, most common carriers do. Will a traditional service be held in the locality where the death occurred? If so, a casket would need to be purchased; otherwise a casket could be selected after the remains are shipped. If the family prefers cremation, do they want to view the remains before the cremation? This would require the family to travel to the locality of death or that the remains be embalmed for shipping.

All observances that can be saved for the state of final disposition would considerably lessen the expense for the family. Families should not call a local funeral home, but allow the funeral directors from the state of final disposition to call on embalming or nationwide shipping services. Families should not specify using a particular shipping or embalming service because some funeral homes are corporately managed and are required to use a funeral home affiliate unless the family asks for other arrangements to be made. If the decision has been made to use a local funeral home, the family should inquire about the price of the package for "Forwarding Remains," which is required by the Federal Trading Commission (FTC). Usually this package includes the pick-up of the body, the basic service fee, embalming, and possibly a shipping container as well as transportation to the nearest airport. Occasionally, there is no need to have visitation and a full funeral service in the state of burial. If this is the case, families should ask the receiving mortuary for the price of "Receiving Remains," which is another one of the FTC required options. Most often this includes picking up the body at the airport, filing permits, and transportation to the cemetery.

Transportation via land or air. Sometimes it will be necessary to transport the body via an airplane. The air trays or shipping containers generally are available in two types. One carries just the body; the other covers and protects a casket. This is not always included as part of the funeral service package, so it may be helpful to know what is reasonable (Funeral Consumers Alliance, 1999). Most airlines offer a bereavement rate at a discount for people flying to a funeral. The funeral home handling the services will be asked to provide a letter stating the name, relationship, date of service, and place of service of the deceased in order to verify the need for the regular fare to be reduced.

It is legal for a family to transport the remains between state lines in most areas. A family could use a van or a large utility vehicle to transport the body. This option might be far less expensive than airfare, and such a journey could help in the grieving process. Immediate attention is given to out-of-state permits and requirements when a family requests that transportation of remains be made across state lines. In fact, most states have specific forms that need to be completed and faxed to the Office of the Chief Medical Examiner, coroner, or other officials for authorization. The medical examiner will then verify with physicians the cause of death and establish that there are no allegations or circumstances surrounding the death that may warrant further investigation of the remains. Once this is established the medical examiner will fax the funeral establishment the authorization for transportation, a process that usually takes one to two days. These forms must accompany the body throughout the transportation process.

International shipping of human remains. Customs, language barriers, and regulations are often a challenge when human remains need to be transported abroad. Proper documentation and meeting each country's requirements are essential in order to reach the intended destination. Often one detail can create an error in where the remains are delivered or will be accepted. It is advised to inquire about previous experience of international shipping before making a decision to use a funeral service. As could be expected, most airlines carriers will not ship without all proper documentation. When shipments require in-country flights, such as in Europe or the Far East, many smaller passenger planes cannot accommodate the size of typical American air trays or shipping containers. All airlines have restrictions on how remains are shipped, so attention to critical detail must be followed. Documentation and permits often needed to ship human remains abroad include:

- Certified copy of death certificates
- Translation of death certificate by an official translator on a funeral home stationery
- Embalming certificate stating solutions used, statement of death, statement of no contagious or communicable disease

- Translation of embalming certificate by an official translator on funeral home stationery
- Burial transit permits
- Translation of burial transit permits by an official translator on funeral home stationery
- Statement specifying type of container's remains is placed inside (some countries require a hermetically sealed casket)

Certified Copies of the Death Certificate (DC)

In most states there are three types of death certificates: (a) Certificate of Death, (b) Medical Examiner Certificate of Death, and (c) a Certificate of Fetal Death (Stillbirth). Details needed to complete the death certificate are usually recorded on the "First Call Information" sheet (Figure 1). Generally, the funeral home will complete the death certificate and send it to the physician who has the authority to sign it and note the cause of death. The doctor then notifies the funeral home that the DC is completed. The funeral home must then file the DC with the county, followed by the state, in which the deceased died. This process takes about two weeks.

If medical examiners or coroners are involved the death certificate will be filled out and signed by them first, and then the funeral home completes the other necessary information in order for the certificate to be filed. The Medical Examiner's office files all DCs for cremation, homicides, suicides, penal deaths, accident victims, unsupervised medical deaths, and others.

Most campus deaths will be filed through the medical examiner of the state where the death occurred. Depending on the state of death, some bodies cannot be transferred to another state or country until the death certificate is complete and filed. Unfortunately, this situation sometimes can delay the burial or service arrangements.

Conclusion

A multitude of information is required in preparation for the final disposition of the dead and funeral services. Whether or not college personnel assist in the preparation of funeral arrangements it is important to understand the pressures the family encounters. Planning a funeral is alone an enormous task. Not having resources or an understanding of what is needed, available, or legal creates unnecessary burdens and stress.

References

Consumer Affairs. (2005). *Preneed funeral arrangements.* Retrieved May 26, 2006. Available: http://www.state.nj.us/lps/ca/brief/preneed.pdf

Federal Trade Commission. (2004). *Complying with the funeral rule.* Washington, D. C.: Author.

Funeral Consumers Alliance. (1999). Retrieved May 26, 2006. Available: http://www.funerals.org.

Iserson, K. (2001). *Death to dust: What happens to dead bodies.* Tucson, AZ: Galen Press.

Mayes Funeral Directors. (1994). Brochure. Norman, OK: Mayes Funeral Services.

National Association of Funeral Directors. (2004). *Arranging a funeral.* Retrieved May 26, 2006. Available: http://www.ifishoulddie.co.uk/religious_traditions.htm

Swenson, D. X. & Ginsberg, M. H. (1996). A comprehensive model for campus death postvention. *Journal of College Student Development, 37,* 543-549.

Voices in Crisis

The personal experiences that follow provide vivid first-hand accounts of events during a crisis. From stories of identifying the deceased to interacting with the media, these vignettes enable readers to become more aware of the emotional distress and the immobilizing trauma of students and administrators alike.

The Early Morning of November 18, 1999

Robert Wiatt

Mr. Robert E. Wiatt became the Director of the University Police Department at Texas A&M in February 1983. He became the oldest still active law enforcement officer in Texas with 53 years of continuous service, until his retirement in July 2004. Mr. Wiatt's legendary experiences during his FBI tenure earned him the moniker "MR. FBI" when he exchanged himself for two hostages held by a killer; shot and killed a man kidnapping a Texas Highway Patrolman in a 300 mile, 125 car caravan, made into the movie Sugarland Express; *and helped to end the longest prison siege in country—11 ½ days—during which he was shot twice but killed one of the three convicts in Huntsville, Texas in 1974.*

Since October 1951, I have worn the badge of law enforcement continuously—almost 30 years as a Special Agent of the FBI, two years as Investigator-Intake Attorney for the Brazos County District Attorney's Office, and almost 20 years in my current position of Director of Security and University Police at Texas A&M University. During this time I have observed injury and death befall a number of citizens due to accidents or as victims of crime, and, on two occasions, I was required to administer the knell of death to two of the criminal type. Aside from notifying the next of kin on a number of these occasions (except for those of the two criminal types) there was very little opportunity in remaining to render support for the grieving ones or salubriousness in retaining their suffering in my mind for an inexorable length of time.

This built-in defense to diminish rampant emotionalism was shattered the early morning of 11/18/99, when my phone rang at 2:45 A.M. and one of my dispatchers excitedly announced that the Bonfire had just collapsed and many students were trapped under it. The Aggie Bonfire, a university tradition for years, is built by students around the clock for weeks, to be ignited the evening prior to the Thanksgiving Day football game with arch-rival University of Texas. This stack was 55 feet tall, comprised of 7,000 logs cut from surrounding forests, and weighed an approximate 2,000,000 pounds. About 70 students had been working at all of its levels when everything suddenly collapsed.

My arrival at the scene 30 minutes later was "mind blowing" with people running every which way, screaming and crying, while a cacophony of sirens added to the frenzy. I remained at this horrific site for almost 2 days as emergency personnel worked frantically to rescue 27 injured students and remove the bodies of 12 others who never had a chance. This was the largest loss of life at one time that I had witnessed in 51 years of wearing a badge.

Many of the arriving parents refused to remain at a Crisis Center established in one of the campus buildings and demanded to be allowed to go to the collapsed site to be near the efforts to rescue their children. It was here where I delivered the final news to 3 sets of parents whose children had been removed and carried to a temporary morgue established between 2 school buses shielded by a large tarpaulin screen.

My most singular traumatic instance occurred when a father, accompanied by his minister, requested to be taken to his son. I originally refused since the young man had been severely mangled by the deadly logs and his face, especially, was grossly disfigured.

The father and his minister pleaded even though I tried to explain that his son would not look like his son. I ultimately relented to their wishes. As we entered the makeshift morgue area, walking by the covered bodies of those awaiting transfer to local funeral homes, we stopped by one and I carefully pulled aside the cloth covering his son. The father blanched, briefly recoiled, then sobbingly knelt to touch the mangled face, then supported between myself and the minister, shuffled away.

It was a number of hours later when the father and his minister returned to the scene where rescue efforts were still occurring frantically. Seeking me out, the father grasped my hand and tearfully said a simple "thank you," turned, and departed while his minister said that closure had been brought to the father to be able to see his son to say, "I love you" for the last time.

Mourning and the Media

Daniel Nugent

Daniel Nugent was a 19-year old resident assistant on the third floor of North Boland Hall, the site of the January 19, 2000 dormitory fire at Seton Hall University. Mr. Nugent graduated with a BA in Communication from Seton Hall University in 2003. He has remained at Seton Hall and currently is the Associate Director of the Alumni Relations.

In the aftermath of the Seton Hall fire on January 19, 2000, I was faced with many challenges and emotions that I never thought I would have to deal with in college. I was a 19-year-old student who up until that point had concerns like every other student: classes, grades, and girls. I never imagined that I would be faced with a trauma so powerful that it would thrust my classmates and me into the international media spotlight.

When people ask me what I remember most about that day I think of dozens of answers. I remember it all, as vividly as the moment it happened. The tragedy, emotion, and countless acts of kindness that I saw will never be forgotten. There is one theme that is present throughout all of my memories: the presence of the media. As a public relations student I had only just begun to learn about media relations, what could be expected from press interaction, and how to deal with cameras and reporters.

The hours after the fire were awful for all of us. For myself and the rest of Seton Hall's resident assistants, the hours passed slowly. The pain of not knowing the whereabouts of "my" residents made hours seem like days. It was in these first early morning hours that the press became a huge part of the equation. Most of us learned about the fire's deadly effects from CNN reports on televisions in our cafeteria, our temporary shelter, counseling area, work space, and information center. The university's administrators also held regular briefings with students.

Not long after the actual event, television stations worldwide showed live pictures of our campus, and radio stations interviewed students and parents over the phone. Camera flashes went off all around us. Everything we did, every word we said, was being broadcast to the world as it happened. My initial feeling was that of anger. I couldn't understand how the media could be so insensitive, so cruel as to invade us at our most vulnerable time. Then I realized they weren't being cruel; they were doing their jobs.

One thing that I will always be thankful for is the quick action taken by the university's Public Relations Department. Seton Hall's spokesperson immediately met with students to instruct them of Seton Hall's policies regarding media on campus, where to find "media free zones," and things to remember when talking to the press. The main message sent to students was to be honest, say what you feel, and don't feel obligated to answer or refuse to answer any questions.

As pressure on students began to mount to take part in interviews, to go live on television and tell the world how they felt, the general student population began to feel the way I initially did: resentful. I realized that the media would only be pressured more from networks and agencies to find answers when students weren't talking to them. Someone has to step up and talk to the mass media. After talking with my friends, family, and fellow resident assistants I decided that I would make an attempt to talk to the media myself, in the hopes that it would make it easier for other students.

I sought out the advice of Seton Hall's head spokesperson, the director of University Public Relations. I told her that I wanted to address the media as a whole, give them answers to some of the questions that they had been asking and tell them that we understood their jobs and responsibilities but that we also needed time to deal with what was for many of us our first real brush with death and tragedy.

The PR Director went over all of my options, things I might want to say, and the possible outcomes of such an action. The format was decided; I would read a statement in my own words to an open press conference of all reporters covering the story. I was too shaken and upset to take questions.

Immediately Seton Hall's Public Relations Department offered me assistance and guidance. I met with Kathleen Rennie, my Public Relations professor, and we began to organize my thoughts. After a few hours I was ready. The media was alerted, and I was escorted to a door. On the other side of that door reporters sat awaiting my arrival. I got a final vote of confidence from my parents, from Kathy Rennie, and from other members of Seton Hall's administrative community. I was ready.

As I walked through the door into the pressroom, everything moved in slow motion. I paused for a moment as the University spokesperson spelled my name for the assembled press. Looking at the cameras, the microphones, and tape recorders that packed the small space I began to feel nervous. My parents walked me to the podium and stood by as I began to read my statement. I was shaking; every time I lifted my head I was blinded by the lights and camera flashes. I read through my statement quickly and then asked the press to allow my fellow students and me time to cope with and accept all that had happened. I finished my remarks, and the pressroom fell quiet, the reporters knowing that I would not be answering questions.

I left the room, escorted by State Police officers who had agreed to escort my family and me to our car and off campus in order to avoid further contact with the press. Through it all, Seton Hall's Public Relations Department stood by me, helped me, and guided me, and for that I will always be grateful.

Mourning any loss is difficult. Mourning a tragedy at a college campus can be more difficult as so many lives are touched and affected. When tragedies happen on college campuses they make the headlines for days, and in Seton Hall's case, for years. Although I feel no student can really be prepared for the trauma that can arise from seeing the most painful images replayed daily on the evening news, I do believe that colleges and universities can take steps to make sure that support is immediately in place for students when the unthinkable occurs.

Seton Hall University resident assistants and other student employees now go through regular media training. Response from students thus far has been good. Those of us who were students at the time of the fire tell our story, and new students learn life's most important lessons.

It is now close to three years after the fire that killed three of our residents, one of whom had become a close friend in the short time that I had to know him. The investigation into the cause of the fire is still ongoing, and the phone still rings. The reporters still call and ask how we're all doing, what progress we're making, and if we're finally learning to cope.

When I walked into that press conference, I was nervous and I felt nauseous. Since that time has passed I have had media training, I've talked with countless other reporters and news agencies, and I now feel comfortable doing so. I know how to answer questions so that my true message is carried through; I know that no matter what I say Seton Hall University will stand behind me 100%. It is this knowledge that allows me to feel confident knowing that although I may have to "mourn in the media" I can still be a private person and have the strength and support of a university that cares about me.

Part III

Responding
to the Situation

9

Residence Life: Responding To Loss of Life

Wayne D. Griffin

Effects of loss on the student community can be multi-faceted and long-term. Because campus residence fosters close student relationships, administrators can benefit the university with an intervention model for Residence Life programs that includes death notification, psycho/educational services, and rituals of remembrance. By responding to concerns that include working with family and survivors, realizing the impact of large scale crisis, an awareness of potential traumatization of staff, and tips for working with the media, administrators can be more effective in times of crisis.

Students are born into, nurtured, and challenged within the context of relationships. They become a part of social networks comprised of family, friends, and colleagues who play meaningful roles in their development. This important process is continued as part of their higher education experience. Living on campus provides many opportunities to develop these important relationships. Residence Life communities are fertile grounds in which to develop friendships, encounter and explore diversity, and experiment with new values and lifestyles.

College students also experience the suffering that comes from the loss of persons in their network of support, be it a loved one, friend, or member of an affiliation group. LaGrand (1982) reported that 28.4% of the college and university students responding to his survey had experienced the death of a loved one or a sudden death. Seventy-three percent of the students in the study reported having experienced some form of significant loss including death, the end of a love relationship, friendship, or separation from a loved one.

Wayne D. Griffin is a Clinical Associate Professor and Associate Director in the Counseling Center at the University of Florida. He writes extensively in the area of trauma response team, mental health issues in time of disaster, and crisis management in the higher education setting. He also designed and teaches a graduate level course in trauma theory and crisis intervention for the Department of Counselor Education at the University of Florida.

An important developmental lesson interwoven in the student's experience of loss is the value of the support to be found within their social groups. These relationships become the sources for comfort and intimacy, challenge and learning, and inspiration and hope. The ability to cope with such loss is important to the affected student's continued matriculation and long term ability to manage and integrate similar experiences over the course of his or her life. For many students, living on campus becomes their first home away from home. Results from the *Chronicle of Higher Education's* (2006) annual survey of first year students indicated 81.4% planned to reside in on-campus facilities, 79.3% in residence life halls. For these students, the residence hall becomes a place where daily life skills are honed, the search for autonomy is balanced with the needs of the community, and interpersonal competencies are developed through new relationships. Students learn the skills necessary to refine expectations, negotiate privacy through cooperation, and manage conflicts that arise from differing lifestyles. The diversity in their new neighborhood and presence of differing opinions challenge students' worldviews and values. This interplay can increase self-awareness and support the value found in collaborating with persons of differing socio-economic, cultural, and racial attributes. These opportunities often forge emotional connections and a sense of loyalty towards each other. Their new home becomes a source of support for the challenges inherent in their educational pilgrimage.

This chapter focuses on how loss affects students living in residence halls and how institutional interventions can facilitate individual and community bereavement. The discussion is divided into sections that address topics associated with planning and implementing these helpful programs including: (a) the experience of loss associated with the college-aged cohort, (b) the effects of loss on the student community, (c) an intervention model for Residence Life programs including death notification, psycho/educational services, and rituals of remembrance, and (d) the response to special concerns including working with family and survivors, impact of large-scale crisis, vicarious traumatization of staff, and dealing with the media.

Impact of Loss on College Students

The 18 to 24 year old cohort is viewed as a high risk-taking group. Its membership is often associated with lifestyle change including exploration of affiliation groups, experimentation in the use of alcohol and other substances, and increased sexual activity. Higher risk taking behaviors are associated with an increased chance of significant injuries and death. Three out of four deaths in young people aged 15 to 24 are the result of unintentional injuries, homicide, or suicide, in that order (CDC, 2002; NIMH, 2002). Given the risk profile of their chronological cohort, age of parents, and advanced life span of grandparents, it is not unusual for students to experience the death of someone during their time in college.

This developmental period in students is also associated with an attitude of invulnerability, a sense of permanence that encourages risk taking while obscuring personal vulnerability. Students may not wish to think about or have death enter into their realm of reality as it interrupts a sense of an open horizon (Rick-garn, 1996). When death does occur within a student's peer group, it is experienced as a loss of connection and a threat to one's sense of permanence. Similarly, the reaction to loss is also affected by a student's prior experiences. In the aftermath of a death, a period of existential insecurity may trigger the memory of and associated reactions to earlier losses or trauma. Thus, a loss of the family pet may produce a strong reaction in light of a prior divorce of parents, death of a childhood friend, or recent death of a peer (Rando, 1993).

A substantial body of literature describes the effects of loss on individuals. Normal reactions of bereavement include a period of adaptation, some degree of impairment in ability to concentrate, changes in mood with periods of deepened sadness and reflection, and possible disruption of daily life functions including sleep, appetite, energy, and interest in being with others (Rando, 1993; Redmond, 1996). Complicated bereavement may result in even greater loss of time and productivity in work, impair or delay academic progress, increase isolation from needed support, and alter the person's meaning system and worldview.

Traditional age college students (18 - 25 years of age) are typically engaged in developmental tasks that promote their increased sense of autonomy, use of social support systems, clarification in sense of purpose, and construction of a meaningful worldview (Chickering, 1981). The death of a family member, friend, or close peer can impact a student's ability to focus on academic and personal development. In a study of bereaved college students, Balk and Vesta (1998) identified the presence of intrusive and avoidant thoughts, trouble with concentration, and disruption in the use of support systems. Unaddressed, these symptoms may become a distraction or impairment to the student's well-being and ability to successfully accomplish her academic goals.

A sense of belonging is a fundamental dimension of the human experience (Chickering, 1981; Erickson, 1963). Participation in a residence hall and affiliation with persons who reside in the setting becomes a part of the student's campus identity and experience. A death in the residence life community may disrupt the perceptions of students in the following ways:

When members of the residential community die, their presence and influence in the group is suddenly absent. Patterns of interaction are altered, often in ways not determined for some time following the loss. There is change in the physical and social ecology, when, where, and what kind of interactions were initiated with the deceased. Rituals of communication around meals and other daily life activities are disrupted. The roles of the deceased are vacated, thus requiring changes in personal status as roommate, suitemate, officer, companion, and study mate.

When a member of the residential community experiences a loss (e.g., death of a parent, sibling, or close friend), fellow residents must determine how this affects their ongoing relationships. How and when to interact or what to say to the grieving student become salient issues. A lack of personal experience, change in the behavior of their grieving peer, or fear of making a mistake and further hurting the grieving person may leave students confused on what to say or how to help.

Individuals grieve in different ways that vary in timing, form, and substance. Some students will feel quite connected to the deceased or the peer experiencing the loss and express their grief openly. Students who feel less connection, or are more private in their expression, may respond in more subdued tones. They may appear to withdraw or stay on the perimeter of the group process. These differences in perception and experience can result in some students unfavorably comparing their reactions to other members of the group. Consequently, they may feel less a part of the campus. They become secondary victims of the loss and are in need of support to keep them attached to the community.

Students with a prior history of loss or trauma may find their reactions either blunted or exacerbated by the current experience. These students may not know how to relate, choose to withdraw, or unexpectedly react with strong emotions to the situation. The experience triggers personal memories and may leave them feeling disoriented, uncertain of their experience, and unclear on how to relate to others. Counseling may help this population of students integrate their prior loss with the current experience and sustain their place in the community.

The loss may result in the identity and cohesion of the student group being compromised. When the death is the result of suicide or a high risk taking behavior (e.g., DUI, unintentional drug overdose, reckless driving) members of the community may feel some responsibility, wonder what they or others could have done to prevent the incident, and experience feelings of anger and frustration towards themselves, others, and the deceased.

When death occurs from violence or communicable disease, the safety and security of the residential community becomes a significant concern. It is normal for students to want information to relieve a fear of the unknown and perception of being out of control. In the midst of a criminal investigation or public health fact-finding, the lack of readily available information becomes a source of anxiety and confusion.

Lastly, the experience of the loss may precipitate questions about the value of community. Death is often unexpected and brings into focus both the benefits of living with and caring for others and the related potential for personal suffering. Providing a venue for discussing and normalizing these dynamics can help students choose to continue their engagement in the community.

Planning the Institutional Response

It is important for the residence life program to provide support to on-campus residents during the crisis of loss. Planned interventions communicate the institution's commitment to the students' well being and quality of life, restore confidence in the safety and security of the living environment, and promote use of campus and community resources (Everly, 2002). The short term goal of interventions is to assist students through the transitional issues related to the loss, such as coping with the initial grief response, effectively communicating with others, and adjusting to changes in environment and the social network.

In the long term, the interventions help students transform their experience into developmentally meaningful lessons that affect their world view, value of life in the community, and integration of intellect and spirituality.

Effective interventions in the residence hall environment require attention to several concerns. First, it is necessary to identify the scope of persons impacted by the loss. Knowledge of the various constituents affected by the death shape the focus of the planned response. Second, it is important to understand how the nature of the death can influence the bereavement process and students' efforts to derive meaning and develop hope. Awareness of these dynamics helps define the concerns of those affected and identify resources appropriate for intervention. Third, issues of safety and security need to be addressed in order to provide an environment in which the community can grieve. Tragedy can increase the fear of threat and sense of personal vulnerability and impair the process of adaptation. In summary, interventions respond to the needs of specific groups, promote inclusiveness and the values of community, focus on the developmental needs of those mourning, and provide a bridge to the future to promote hopefulness.

The Scope of the Community Impacted by the Loss

It is important to identify who has been affected by the loss. Determine whether the incident affects roommates only, members of the floor or building, or the larger campus community. Residence life staff, faculty advisors, organizational officers, and residents may be in a good position to provide information on the range of persons impacted by the event. It is helpful to responders and empowering to the students to involve the residents in helping to identify the affected groups. Through electronic mail and instant messaging (IM), students interact across a number of affiliation groups on and off campus. This pattern of communication results in larger numbers of persons being aware of the loss.

If the scale of impact is broad, a campus wide response team may be helpful in developing a comprehensive intervention (Griffin, 1998; Griffin & Lewis, 1995; Scott et. al., 1992). The type and number of interventions depends upon the identification and location of the groups of persons affected by the loss. For example, in a multi-building residence life area or in a case where the student served in a leadership capacity the likelihood is good that a number of students will have known the deceased or interacted with the students directly affected by the loss.

The Nature of the Loss

Knowing how a loss occurred is important to understanding its impact on survivors. Factors that complicate the bereavement process include: (a) the trauma of a loss through violence, (b) unexpected timing, (c) the young age of the deceased, (d) a perception the death could have been prevented, (e) an uncertainty of cause, and (f) the survivor's history of prior loss (Rando, 1993; Redmond, 1996).

A death caused by suicide and/or excessive risk taking is often accompanied by surviving peers using cultural and religious systems to develop some meaningful way to understand what happened. Residents may also question their responsibility to have prevented the loss. Those closest to the deceased may wonder if they missed specific signs or behavioral cues that forewarned the tragedy. Others may question the reasons those closest to the deceased permitted certain things to happen that may appear to have contributed to the loss, such as excessive drinking, experimenting with drugs, or driving while overly tired. Students holding religious views that condemn the behavior thought to result in the death may experience conflict with their community. These students' theological or spiritual meaning system may be viewed by their peers as calloused towards the deceased and detached from their community's experience of grief. Effective leadership needs to be sensitive to and address these issues in order to help students sustain communication and a sense of cohesive community.

Issues of Safety and Security

When death occurs through violence or as a consequence of unexpected illness, the campus will need to address an increased perception of personal vulnerability. This is especially the case when the event occurs within a residence life setting. In the aftermath of tragedy, it is important for survivors to feel their safety is secure before they can proceed to process the affects of loss (Young, 2001).

Some deaths are associated with a perception of ongoing threat. For example, the death of a student from bacterial meningitis or other communicable disease can increase concern that the illness is a threat to the current living environment. Reisberg (1999) found that 83 cases of meningococcal disease, which includes meningitis, were reported at academic institutions in the previous school year. Six of those cases were fatal. The annual incidence among 15 to 25 year-olds has doubled to more than 600 cases since 1991, leading some to speculate that the rate may increase for the near future. The infections and deaths have fueled a debate on the merits of campuses requiring immunization for the disease (Reisberg, 1999). This, along with current discussions on the potential threat of diseases such as smallpox or anthrax being used as a weapon of mass destruction, and the development of emergency vaccination plans are important reminders of how significant these issues are for our campus community.

In cases where a communicable disease is suspected as a cause of death or the loss has been associated with violence, it becomes very important to provide accurate information on the nature of the death and ongoing potential risks to students. The fear that it could happen anywhere, even on the campus or in the residence hall, leaves students feeling vulnerable. Residents will want assurance that actions are being taken to protect them from further harm and apprehend the offender. Law enforcement, medical personnel, and persons functioning in positions of authority are useful as resources. They can provide helpful information and promote student confidence in the institution and their living environment.

Focus and Timing of Interventions

Effective interventions are designed to meet the specific needs of the groups affected by the loss. The intervention is shaped around the knowledge of who has been impacted, the nature of the event, and any potential safety and security issues. It is helpful to keep the following objectives in mind when designing the interventions: Each intervention is designed to be as inclusive as possible of those persons within the targeted group (e.g., residence hall roommates, floor members, unit residents, and staff). Knowing the students most intimately involved with the deceased helps determine the persons most appropriate for individual and/or group interventions. Attention to multicultural, gender, and other distinctive attributes of the group is important. Familiarity with the attitudes and cultural values associated with the death represented is central to establishing trust and communicating effectively. The experience and communication of grief varies within North American cultures. Emotional expressions, spiritual meaning systems, and rituals related to death are distinctive to class, ethnicity, religion, and family traditions (Fukuyama, & Sevig, 1999). Consultation with cultural and linguistic specialists may help to clarify critical information and is the most effective means of communication. It is helpful to identify campus or community resources that specialize in these areas of knowledge.

Interventions are scheduled as soon as it is possible to obtain accurate information and assure attendance by the affected population. With college students, this may necessitate a late evening response and attention to the various extracurricular activities in which the residents participate. Consideration of religious holidays, exam schedules, and campus and athletic events can be very relevant to attendance. Announcements for the intervention include the subject of the meeting, encourage attendance, and promote support of community cohesion.

The goals of the initial intervention are to provide timely and accurate information on the loss, address the immediate impact of the event, and prepare the residents for what lies ahead. Providing timely and accurate information on the death empowers the students to begin dealing with the loss. It also helps to avoid reactions that may emerge from rumors. Misinformation can increase perceptions of vulnerability and cause students to engage in unproductive speculation.

It is helpful for residents to normalize their bereavement process. This can occur through the opportunity to share their own and listen to others' reactions to the loss. Recognizing the personal and group experience of loss promotes a sense of connection with their peers. Likewise, providing information on how people generally respond over time can empower the students to understand and place their subjective experiences within a context. This is an important time to provide information concerning campus and community helping resources to assure the residents that the institution is concerned for their ongoing well being.

Types of Interventions

Following the assessment phase of planning, interventions are developed to address the specific needs associated with the incident. These programs are organized to allow for the emergence of information related to the incident. The type and number of programs depends on the nature of the death, identified concerns of targeted populations, and availability of resources. There are three basic types of interventions.

1. The Information Sharing Response, a program designed primarily to convey information related to the nature of and concerns about the death. The goal of information sharing is to provide the knowledge necessary for students to have a basic understanding of what happened, clarify any concerns related to their safety and security, and prepare for the next set of developments.

2. Psycho/Educational Outreaches, an intervention that focuses on the normalization of the personal and community bereavement process. The goal of this program is to increase awareness of the personal experience of grief and the group's reactions to the change that loss brings.

3. A Ritual of Remembrance, an activity that addresses the community's need to pay tribute to and remember the deceased. The goal of a Ritual of Remembrance is to facilitate the community reaction to the loss and promote group cohesion and a bridge to the future.

Information sharing responses. Information sharing responses include individual and group death notification, and incident updates. A death notification conveys information about the loss to the affected persons. Campuses vary on which agencies assume this responsibility. Law enforcement, student affairs, counseling, victim advocates, campus ministers, and sometimes residence life staff members are often assigned this function. Advance assignment of personnel responsible for death notification allows for training and coordination between campus and community agencies. Staff assigned this responsibility need to possess the skills, training, and personality to work effectively with both the reactions of the person(s) being notified and their response to the distress experienced in the process.

The National Organization for Victims Assistance (NOVA) (Young, 2001) provides a comprehensive curriculum for carrying out this important function. Additional resources can be obtained from the National Center for Post Traumatic Stress Disorder (2003). The following is an outline of considerations to be incorporated in death notification for both individuals and groups in the campus setting:

A. Individual death notification

1. Determine if the information is correct. Avoid making a false notification by obtaining the specifics necessary to confirm the identity of the deceased. Full name, permanent place of residence, Social Security or institutional identity number, date of birth, place of birth, and other information may confirm the identity. Corroborative information related to the student's educational status can include the year in school, campus address, academic major, and graduate committee chair. Be aware that in some cultures, surnames are broadly shared in the population. Acquire as much information as possible about the full name of the deceased. Collaborate with community or campus law enforcement to as-

sist in confirming the identity. While this process takes some time, it is important to act on the best information available. The goal is to avoid a mistaken identity or mistakenly informing a survivor.

2. Whenever possible, notification is to be done by two persons, with one person assigned the role of lead communicator. The other individual is available to provide support, obtain additional resources, or communicate on behalf of the person being notified. Utilizing the lead communicator role decreases the potential for the survivor to become confused by more than one message or different communication styles.

3. Have conversations in an environment that is perceived to be safe for the persons being notified. Attention to privacy, lighting, restrooms, and exits is helpful. Within a residence life facility, this may be the student's room or a staff member's office. It is helpful to have a means available for the student to communicate with family or other supportive persons. Sometimes students will want a roommate or friend to accompany them. Following the notification, offer to help the student communicate with family, friends, faculty, and clergy. The shock and strong emotions associated with the news may temporarily impair a student's ability to communicate clearly.

4. It is important the information be given in a timely manner to prevent others less trained or concerned from communicating the news. Care should be taken in the use of electronic and cell phone technology. Discussions related to the verification and notification should take precautions with technologies that are not secure from unauthorized interception including cell phones, electronic mail, and fax machines that may be located in public settings.

5. Personal notification is preferable to communicating such important news over the phone. Members of family or family friends may call to obtain a student's contact information in order to inform the student. They may want college or residence life staff members to know about the death in order watch out for their student. Before giving out a student's personal contact information, follow institutional and legal guidelines to confirm the identity of the person requesting the information. If there are questions about the contact, enlist the help of law enforcement or administrative services to assure the contact and provision of information is appropriate. It is helpful to offer the family the campus services to assist with the death notification. The benefits of institutional involvement include the presence of trained personnel to follow up on the student's reactions, assistance to help plan for the next steps, and resources to address questions related to academic progress and responsibilities. If family or others wish to convey the information, arrange for the notification to occur when trained campus personnel are present or readily available. This can be done in the student's room or staff office where privacy and safety are assured.

6. Notification is done in clear language that avoids misunderstanding or false impressions. Avoid the use of dosing techniques that build up to

the announcement. Statements like, "You know how your father has been ill and not doing well" or "There are times when we all get some bad news and it's important to be strong" often increase the student's anxiety and lead to unnecessary speculation. Additionally, clearly state the terrible news that has to be shared. Their loved one has been involved in an activity that has resulted in their death, such as a vehicle crash, accident at work, act of violence, or their loved one has died from a medical complication. Avoid the use of colloquial sayings to convey the message (e.g., passed away, succumbed, left us, gone on to a better place, or isn't here any more). Trained personnel are prepared for the reactions and questions that follow hearing or reading such painful news, including the confusion and emotional numbness that requires having to repeat the message. It is often necessary to restate the message to help assure the person has gotten the basic information. Prepare in advance for the student who may have difficulty understanding the message because of a hearing impairment or cultural difference. Identify personnel with expertise in sign language and different cultural dialects to interpret during the notification. Ideally, these persons will have undergone training in the notification process, be accountable to confidentiality and privacy standards, and aware of the diverse cultural makeup of the student body. A centralized list of language specialists with key contact information can be made available through administration, student affairs, or law enforcement.

7. Prepare to assist the respondent in knowing what to do next. Keep in mind issues of safety. In the sense of urgency to be with family, a student may want to leave and make a five hour drive home in the middle of the night. Develop plans to communicate with next of kin and other supportive persons to arrange for the next steps that help the student feel connected and assured of safety.

8. Remind the student of the support of the residential community. Ask whom they wish to know this information and what details they want shared with roommates or other members of the community.

9. Help the grieving student understand his or her reactions. Offer and provide the support of campus counseling resources, and tell the student there will be someone available to talk and help make arrangements.

B. Group death notification

1. The goal of group death notification is to effectively and compassionately provide information to groups affected by the loss. As with the notification of an individual, communication requires attention to the accuracy of information and use of trained personnel. While there is some sense of urgency to communicate the message, the timing and location of a group notification aims for participation of the greatest number of participants.

2. Sensitivity to the racial and cultural diversity present in the community becomes essential. Select language and suggest actions that support the

personal and community values and customs essential for making meaning of difficult experiences.

3. Where acts of violence have occurred, residents may experience increased concern for their safety and security. Some students may become suspicious of others within the group because of stereotypes or biased attitudes. These concerns can provide an educational opportunity to increase self-awareness and community development.

4. Students may not know how to relate to persons who have experienced loss. Helping students understand the experience, preparing to encounter those grieving, and learning to express their sympathy are important aspects of the group intervention.

C. Incident Updates

1. Beyond the initial death notification, students benefit from having information that clarifies the circumstances around a death, dispels rumors which arise in the campus and larger community, and helps them gain a sense of perspective on upcoming events, such as the visit of family members, presence of investigative personnel, or concern of campus administrators.

2. Scheduled updates are especially helpful when death has occurred in a manner that threatens the safety and security of the residents (e.g., threat of a communicable disease, fear of further violence, or risk of additional damage from a natural or human made disaster). Providing students with accurate information about the loss and any potential threat to their safety empowers their decision-making and assists the process of bereavement. It also provides them information that can be shared with family who may be interested in their well being and considering whether to allow them to remain in residence or continue their academic studies at the institution.

3. In an incident update, it is often helpful to incorporate specialized resource persons who can address the associated safety or health issues. The credibility of these sources is a critical factor during a crisis.

4. Information regarding ongoing investigations, matters of public health, and the integrity of the campus organization is best provided by authorities like law enforcement, medical and public health experts, and campus administrators.

Psycho/educational programs. Education and occasion for personal and group reflection can help students understand the impact and experience of loss. Psycho/educational programs focus on the psychological, physical, and spiritual dimensions of student experience. They include issues related to personal and community grief and address topics like coping with loss, community development, surviving the effects of trauma, stress and anxiety management, interpersonal communication, and the value of counseling/consultation. Educational interventions demonstrate an institutional presence and ethic of care and encourage trust and use of campus resources. Leadership resources for these programs can include counselors, campus ministers, student affairs staff, faculty members, and community agencies like Hospice.

These outreach programs provide counselors an opportunity to determine the degree of personal and group distress. Individual students who are experiencing significant difficulty can be provided specialized attention and referral for ongoing care. Interaction between the counselors and residents also promotes trust and encourages use of the campus helping resources. Follow up sessions can be provided to address emerging issues and assess the group's adaptation to the loss over time.

Rituals of remembrance. A residence life community can be helped to meaningfully remember and integrate the crisis associated with loss through the use of rituals of remembrance. The term ritual of remembrance is culturally characterized by words such as funeral, memorial service, commemoration, eulogy, tribute, or recognition. Rituals of remembrance are often embodied in some form of service for members of the grieving community. Activities associated with these services are products of cultural tradition and linked to the nature and scope of the incident. The general purpose of a ritual is to provide occasion for personal and social expression of mourning, confirmation, and utilization of social support and emphasis on ongoing life. Rituals of remembrance also contribute towards integrating loss into a faith and spiritual paradigm that underpins the meaning of life and value of relationships.

Students involved in residence life organizations often develop a strong sense of loyalty to one another. A ritual of remembrance provides an outlet for expressing their personal grief and creates a way the deceased can remain a part of the group's memory. Some student organizations have specific liturgies and programs that are used at these times. Often students have limited experience with loss or exposure to memorial events. Even fewer have participated in planning and implementing such a program. Thus, it is important the institution recognize the significance of this type of intervention and provide leadership to empower and facilitate students in developing a meaningful experience.

The following discussion elaborates on some of the issues relevant to the planning and implementation of a ritual of remembrance. Some concerns may be more salient given the nature of the campus community and mission and type of the institution.

The memorial is focused on the needs of the particular student group impacted by the loss. Group attributes such as racial/ethnic and gender diversity, cultural customs and religious/spiritual beliefs are important considerations for the program to be as inclusive as possible. A mixture of students from various faith traditions, such as Islam, Judaism, Buddhism, Sufism, Christianity or non-traditional religions, will likely pose special challenges to timing, language, and content. Colleges often have working relationships with local religious officials familiar with the school's goals for respect and are able to help intersect and translate varying customs during this time.

The decision to invite or involve others in the ritual needs to be a thoughtful process. Members of the family, friends, and interested campus or community members may wish to participate. While this inclusion may be helpful, it is important to keep in mind the goal is to meet the needs of the targeted student group.

Leadership for the ritual can come from several sources. There may be campus ministers or community religious leaders who are sensitive to the development needs of students and the culture of the campus. The selected leaders should be made aware in advance of the need of inclusiveness in language, readings, and other activities. Identify qualified leadership resources in advance. This permits time for training and promotes an increased level of trust and coordination during crisis.

As far as possible, the timing and location of a service of remembrance needs to consider involvement of the greatest number of affected students and staff. This requires a working knowledge of the formal and informal academic and activity calendars. Announcements of the ritual need to focus on those groups for whom the event is planned with emphasis on the dignity of the event.

Be aware of campus guidelines that might affect a ritual's design. Where and when activities are allowed to happen, who authorizes the various types of activities, and who provides for safety and security are important to successful program planning. A large scale event open to the larger campus or community will require different logistical support than a service that requires a smaller setting for a limited audience.

College students often desire a visual or verbal reminder of the deceased. Exercise caution when incorporating video images or recorded remarks by the deceased into the ritual. Audience reactions to the content of images and voice recognition may become complicated because of the nature of the death, unknown aspects in relationships, and sensitivity of family and survivors. If video or audio content is utilized, it is helpful to provide some advance notice for persons who may otherwise not be prepared for or desire such an experience.

A ritual of remembrance in the residence life setting may be conducted within a commons area or other setting on or off campus. Rituals often consist of an outlined program that may include introductory remarks, readings of inspiration from literature or sacred texts, remarks by selected speakers, and perhaps a contribution of music. There may also be a period in the service where students and others are invited to share memories of the deceased or aspects of their experience that provide hope.

Examples of other rituals include candlelight vigils, circles of dialogue, or a time of quiet. Sometimes students wish to create something more permanent, as symbolized in the dedication of a tree planting, wall or building plaque, statuette, landscape garden, posthumous publication of art or literature, signature books for the family, poetry, music, songs, and establishments of grant or scholarship awards.

There are many ways people can come together to remember the contribution of a friend or colleague. In planning and implementation, the focus is always on how the ritual can be developmentally meaningful to the bereaved, provide a context for the affirmation of community, and promote a sense of perspective and hopefulness.

Special Issues

The experience of loss is sometimes associated with additional factors that require foresight, planning, and response by the campus. Special issues include: (a) preparation needed for parents and members of the family when they come back to campus to pack and remove their loved one's personal effects, (b) need for a comprehensive plan to respond to crises in which multiple deaths and injuries may occur, such as fires in residence life areas, on-campus shootings, and auto crashes, (c) institutional initiatives to attenuate the effects of stress on campus personnel who work with family and survivors during critical incidents, and (d) campus plans to collaborate with the mass media to provide information that is accurate and respectful of the bereaved and reflects the institutional ethic of care.

Working with family and survivors. Family members or designates often return to campus to pack and remove their loved one's personal belongings. This is a very difficult task and often an occasion for remembering the loved one and expressing the depth of sadness and confusion experienced from the loss. For the survivors, coming to campus is akin to being in the last place their loved one lived, played, and carried on the process of achieving personal and family dreams. It is the heartbreaking task of putting in boxes what should be actively used by their loved one. The following suggestions can help prepare staff to assist family and survivors:

Plan the date and, to the degree possible, the arrival time. Provide this information to the students impacted by the loss and help them understand how they can interact and what they might say to the family. Sometimes students wish to convey their sympathy and present family members with signature books, wall posters with remarks, or group photos. Often they do not know how to relate their thoughts and feelings to the family. Give them an opportunity to prepare for the interaction and provide some suggested language, for example, "I am so sorry about [name of student.] I am glad to have shared some time with him or her." Help normalize the reactions they might see from members of the family who may be crying, agitated, aloof, or inquisitive. Remind them that there will be staff available to help the family members. It is also important to provide permission to students who do not feel comfortable being around the family. Remind them that it is okay if they choose not to be present; others can convey their sympathy.

Packing up the belongings of the deceased can be traumatic for the family members. Offer to do it for them or assist in the process. Some families would rather avoid the experience of packing but would like to see the room as their loved one left it. Plan for this visit; select staff members for packing the room and prepare them in advance for the experience. Remember family or survivors may, as part of their visit, wish to speak to someone familiar with their loved one. Offer to have boxes available for the family and preview the amount to be removed so they can plan for adequate transportation. Though the family may have recently been involved in moving their student, at this time they are not likely to recall the specifics of how much was involved.

Select members of campus staff to be present when family members or their representatives come to pack. It is preferable that a counselor trained to work with survivors of loss or other trauma be present to respond to the reactions of those grieving. The counselor who escorts the family will need to visit the room in advance to obtain knowledge of the environment. The counselor will use this memory snapshot to help prepare those packing for what they will see. Have guidelines in place on what to do if items that may be distressful to the family are present in the room (e.g., photographs, literature, videos, beverage containers, etc). The decision to remove something from the room or from plain view is to be taken thoughtfully. It is to be consistent with the defined legal and privacy rights and in consideration of the emotional impact on survivors.

Be sensitive to the needs of a roommate or suitemates in this process. Ascertain if they wish to be present, what of their property they wish removed that might be confused as a belonging of the deceased, and whether they wish to interact with the family. Introduce these persons to how the family or survivors might respond and their need to hear about their loved one. Role-playing a typical interaction can sometimes help prepare and build their confidence. If they choose not to be present, discourage feelings of guilt and shame on their part.

If possible, have a counselor present to escort the family while another university official may need to be present as well to provide access to the room. Provide a time and location for the counselor to prepare the family for the experience. This preparation includes determining their desire for any possible student interaction and helping them understand the impact of being in their loved one's last living environment. Exposure to the living area can trigger strong reactions. What the family and friends see, smell, touch, and feel in the room constitutes a strong reminder of the deceased and serves to kindle the grief process. The visit is a powerful reminder of their loved one. It is helpful for the counselor to provide a visual memory snapshot of what will be seen when entering the room and go through a suggested process for the experience. This might include: (a) staff and counselor accompanying them to the room, (b) the counselor taking them into the room and staying for a few moments while the family adjusts, (c) the family being provided a period of privacy, and (d) assistance being offered for packing or moving the effects to their vehicles. It is helpful for a staff member and counselor to be present or readily accessible during the process of packing.

According to the wishes of the family, plan when contact with other students or roommates might occur. Be prepared for the family or friends to ask questions about the deceased. Sometimes residents and staff are viewed by the survivors as the last persons to know their loved one. They have a need to gain some sense of enduring impression of their student. In the event the death is the result of a suicide, the counselor may need to respond to questions motivated by the survivors' need to know what happened. The survivors may be coping with feelings of shame, guilt, anger, and questions about whether anything could have been done to prevent the tragedy. Trained counselors will be able to recognize and respond accordingly to these understandable but complicated concerns.

Saying goodbye is a difficult process for the family and survivors. Packing up a loved one's personal belongings is the concrete reminder of their absence. Thoughtful planning can assist in making the task and environment safer for remembering their loved one and their expression of grief.

Campus crisis with multiple deaths. A crisis in which multiple losses occur can tax residence life and campus resources. A coordinated campus crisis response program is an effective way to provide interventions that can address the needs of various groups affected by the tragedy. Multidisciplinary teams that meet on a regular basis form around a network of counseling, administrative, health, and academic resources (Griffin, 1998; Griffin & Lewis, 1995; Scott et al., 1991). These teams often train and hold simulation exercises to prepare and refine interventions that address the impact of traumatic loss. Membership from the residence life program on the team helps to assure the impact of trauma on group living environments is included in planning and training for interventions.

Residence life programs can also benefit from cooperative relationships with campus and community counseling services including crisis centers, emergency rooms, and hospice centers. Liaisons from these resources can provide training for residence life staff and direct support during critical incidents. Where campus counseling services do not exist, conversation with community based agencies or private practitioners can augment the lack of existing on-campus expertise.

Preventing compassion fatigue. Campus personnel involved in responding to incidents of loss are exposed to a wide range of reactions by those impacted by death. The reaction of the crisis intervention staff is predicated on their knowledge and training for such work, degree of ongoing exposure to stress, and integration of their personal history of loss or trauma (Figley, 1995).

Among the needs to be addressed by administrators is the emotional fatigue that accumulates in members of campus personnel directly involved in planned interventions. Staff responding to a series of crises can be affected by vicarious traumatization or compassion fatigue, a process by which responders can develop symptoms similar to those persons they serve (Figley, 1995). The crisis responder working with death notification or in support of those affected by loss may experience the need for bereavement support. It is important to develop guidelines that help protect respondents from too frequent involvement in a schedule of interventions and provide ongoing training to increase knowledge on the symptoms and effects of compassion fatigue.

An effective means of caring for personnel is to require post response interventions that allow for de-escalation, normalization of reactions, and integration of healthy coping skills (Young, 2001). Trained counseling personnel from the campus or community can be identified to provide this important service. It is important to remember the effects of trauma are cumulative on victims and responders alike. Efforts to minimize the negative aspects of post intervention reactions are a means of keeping staff healthy and effective.

Working with the media. News media are often interested in critical incidents and their affects on the campus community. Working relationships with representatives of the media can help assure published information is accurate and consistent with the campus ethic of care. Survivors of loss need their privacy and mourning respected. Untimely questions or inaccurate stories about the death may result in survivors feeling re-victimized and their personal suffering made public (Young, 2001). The following steps can be taken to facilitate the media getting the information needed while respecting those directly affected.

If the campus or residence life program has a public affairs or information officer, he or she can provide guidelines for the media. These guidelines should include defining expectations for the privacy of the bereaved, identifying a central resource for campus information, such as a public affairs officer or institutional representative, and promoting a discussion of campus concern for the dignity of the bereaved. Guidelines should also include the rights of on-campus residents to refuse comment or deny entrance to their private living environment. It is helpful to remind the media of the rights of students and the privacy considerations related to their living environments.

During campus interventions, it is appropriate to ask if representatives of the media are present. The presence of media representatives may put a chilling effect on the willingness of students to participate and thus be counterproductive to the institution's efforts to provide care. The media can be directed to speak with institutional personnel and made aware of the goals and guidelines associated with the event. While confidentiality cannot be assured at all public gatherings, the media representatives can be asked to respect the privacy of others and clarify any information through the designated campus contact.

In some circumstances, interventions like psycho/educational programs conducted by licensed counselors or events held in what are considered private residence facilities may be protected under existing privacy and confidentiality standards. In these instances, where representatives of the media and other unrelated parties are present, they may be referred to a staff member present for clarification regarding their attendance and directed to campus information resources. Statutes and standards related to confidentiality and privacy can be clarified through campus or community legal counsel.

The question of whether the mass media is to be present at a ritual of remembrance merits discussion and planning. If permitted, several issues need to be addressed. Concerns to be clarified include the types and location of audio/videotaping equipment allowed, restrictions on flash photography, presence and location of certain types of technology that generate noise, access to interviews, and placement of media personnel within the event. Properly involved, the media can play a constructive role in supporting the campus ethic of care and demonstrate respect for those who are mourning. The significance of mass media's influence on the experience of survivors and campus community warrants cooperation and planning.

Summary

As noted at the beginning of the chapter, students are born into, nurtured, and challenged within the context of relationships. They become a part of networks of family, friends, and colleagues who play a meaningful role in their development. Students continue to develop these important relationships during their experience in the higher education setting. Residence life programs are fertile grounds for them to continue to develop friendships, encounter and explore diversity, and experiment with new values and lifestyles within a community setting.

During their college years, students may experience the suffering that arises from the death of a loved one, friend, or member of an affiliation group. An important lesson to be learned from such a loss is the value of a continuing community. This chapter proposes ways residence life programs and staff can respond to and promote student well being when the on-campus living community experiences the death of one of its members. A variety of services can be provided including death notification, psycho/educational outreach programs, community information sessions, and help in remembering the deceased through rituals of remembrance. Careful work by the residence life program can enhance the experience of the family as they pack up their loved one's belongings and begin to bring closure to their student's college experience. Campus collaboration with mass media can assure that accurate information is conveyed to the public and the institution's ethic of care is communicated and supported. Thoughtful planning and consideration of the varied aspects of student life can help assure that the important work of responding to loss can support the living environment, mobilize campus resources, enrich the personal and community experience of bereavement, and build a bridge to the future.

References

Balk, D. E., & Vesta, L. C. (1998). Psychological development during four years of bereavement: A longitudinal case study. *Death Studies, 22*, 23-41.

Centers for Disease Control and Prevention (CDC). (2002). *Final 2000 Mortality Statistics: National statistics for health statistics.* Hyattsville, MD: Centers for Disease Control and Prevention. Retrieved on December 07, 2002 from: http://www.cdc.gov/nchs/releases/02facts/final2000.htm.

Chickering, A. W. & Reisser, L. (1993). *Education and identity.* (2nd ed.). San Francisco, CA: Jossey-Bass.

Erickson, E. (1963). *Childhood and society.* New York, NY: W.W. Norton and Company, Inc.

Everly, G. S. (2002). Early psychological intervention and college personnel services. *ACPA Commission VII Counseling and Psychological Services Newsletter*, Fall 2002. Retrieved July 12, 2003 from http://www.acpa.nche.edu/comms/commo7/c7 news.htm

Figley, C. (1995). *Compassion fatigue.* Bristol, PA: Brunner/ Mazel.

Fukuyama, M., & Sevig, T. (1999). *Integrating spirituality into multicultural counseling.* Thousand Oaks, CA: Sage Publishing.

Griffin, W. (1998). Crisis management in the higher education setting: A multidisciplinary approach. *Talking Stick: ACUHO-I,* 16, #2, 6-7, October 1998.

Griffin, W. & Lewis, L. (1995) The Trauma Response Team: An institutional response to crisis, *ACPA Commission VII Counseling and Psychological Services Newsletter, 22*, #2, 3-4, October 1995.

LaGrand, L. E. (1982). How college and university students cope with loss. In R. A. Pacholski, & C.A. Corr (Eds.), *Priorities in death education and counseling* (85-97). Arlington, VA: Forum for Death Education and Counseling.

National Center for Post Traumatic Stress Disorders (2003). *Casualty and death notification.* Retrieved June 27, 2003 from http://www.ncptsd.org/facts/ disasters/fs _death_notification.html

National Institute of Mental Health (2002). *Suicide facts: 1999 mortality data.* Retrieved December 7, 2002 from http://www.cdc.gov/ncipc/wisqars/fatal/help/datasources.htm#6.3

Rando, T. (1993). *Treatment of complicated mourning.* Champaign, IL: Research Press.

Reisberg, L. (1991, July 9). Meningitis deaths renew debate about vaccinating students. *The Chronicle of Higher Education*, p. A41.

Redmond, L. M. (1996) Sudden violent death. In K. J. Doka (Ed.), *Living with grief after sudden loss.* Washington, D.C.: Hospice Foundation of America.

Rickgarn, R. L. (1996). The need for postvention on college campuses: A rationale and case study findings. In C. A. Corr, & D. Balk (Eds.), *Handbook of adolescent death and bereavement* (273-292). New York, NY: Springer.

Scott, J. E., Fukuyama, M. A., Dunkel, N. W. & Griffin, W. D. (1992). The trauma response team: Preparing staff to respond to student death. *NASPA Journal, 29*(3), 230-236.

Siegel, M. & Barefoot, B. (2002). National survey of first year co-curricular programs. *National Association of Student Personnel Administrators;* Retrieved on November 15, 2002 from: http://www.naspa.org/netresults / article.cfm?ID=608& category=Feature.

Young, M. A. (2001). *The community crisis response team manual* (3rd ed.). Washington, D.C.: National Organization for Victim Assistance.

10

When a Student Athlete Dies:
Dealing with Death in College Athletics

Kelly A. Norton and Shaun R. Harper

The death of a student athlete can have a profound effect on an institution, in-cluding its students, staff, administrators, and alumni, as well as community members and athletics supporters. Campus administrators and counselors of-ten coordinate the coping process within an athletics context with the student athlete's family and attending to the grieving process among athletes and ath-letics staff.

For more than a century, athletics has coexisted with institutions of higher education. Among the thousands of college athletic programs across the country are the highly publicized institutions of the National Collegiate Athletic Asso-ciation (NCAA), as well as smaller and less well-known colleges, independent and religious-affiliated institutions, and two-year schools. Although the athletic programs at these institutions are as varied as the schools themselves, the stu-dent athletes within them share many commonalities. With a fervent work ethic, these athletes have surpassed competitors to gain a place among the college ranks. They have been trained to succeed at the highest level of amateur compe-tition, molding their bodies into instruments of skill, poise, and determination. They have formed strong bonds of interdependence and loyalty within their sports, with each athlete fulfilling a vital role on the team.

Due to their regimented training, athletes are often considered among the healthiest and most physically fit students on campus and are sometimes thought

Kelly A. Norton is the Director of Academic Services Center at High Point University in North Carolina, a private liberal arts university with approximately 3000 undergraduate and graduate students. She is seeking a doctorate in Higher Education Administration from the University of Florida. She writes on issues of diversity, athletes, and disabilities. Shaun R. Harper, Ph.D., is a Research Associate at the Center for the Study of Higher Education and Assistant Professor of Higher Education, at Penn State and writes about race and gender in higher education.

by themselves and others to be indestructible. Students and fans assume partial ownership in the team's successes and failures, regardless of the sport, patting themselves on the back for outstanding play and scolding themselves for sub-par performances.

However, athletes are not as unbreakable as they appear as they, too, are vulnerable to the same life-threatening risks and dangers encountered by other college students. In fact, some may argue that their rigorous workout routines and play conditions, sometimes in extreme temperatures, put student athletes at higher risk of injury or even death. The death of a student athlete can have a profound effect on an institution, including its students, staff, administrators, and alumni, as well as community members and athletics supporters across the country and around the world. The cultural environment that rewards strength, grace, and composure in the athletic area offers little comfort to those grieving for a lost teammate. The expectation to "be strong" and "suck it up" interferes with the natural grieving process, which causes additional anxiety for the athletes. Tragic situations may be further complicated by media coverage, forcing surviving teammates to grieve in a public forum. The fans that cheer on their favorite players mourn alongside the team and staff as if they themselves are part of the athletic family.

For these reasons, a death within athletics extends beyond those people who were close to or personally acquainted with the student. Counselors, student affairs administrators, and athletics staff must contend not only with the roommates, classmates, and teammates, but they also must offer support to the general student body and fans who knew the student as #24 on the basketball team, the middle hitter on the volleyball team, or the school mascot. They must consider the numerous athletic staff members who were in daily contact with the student. Administrators who promoted the spirit of the institution through the determination and hard work of the student must also be consoled.

Recent student athlete deaths have prompted discussions of bereavement within athletics. This chapter serves as a resource for campus administrators and counselors coordinating the coping process within an athletics context. Three areas specific to athletics will be addressed: (a) understanding the nature of the death, (b) coping within the student athlete's family, (c) grieving among athletics staff. Examples of practices will be drawn from recent events at colleges and universities across the country. Because each incident requires an individualized approach, this chapter does not offer a recipe for all institutions to follow. Instead, it serves as a guide for administrators in creating or modifying existing protocols for dealing with the death of a student athlete.

The Nature of the Death

In the wake of a student athlete death, survivors in the university community are left bewildered by the loss. They attempt to gain control of a seemingly uncontrollable situation by asking themselves unanswerable questions. How could that athlete have contracted such a devastating medical condition? Why was the player involved in that fight? Could someone have prevented that situation? Why was that person driving the team van? As much as we attempt to gain and maintain control on our campuses, student deaths are often unpredictable and uncontrollable, even those situations we see so clearly in hindsight. Although the loss cannot be changed, the circumstances surrounding the death may play a vital role in how friends and teammates grieve, how the athlete is memorialized, and what preventative steps are taken to avoid future tragedies.

A heart condition caused the 1990 death of All-American Hank Gathers from Loyola Marymount University, who collapsed on the basketball court (Huber, 2000). In 1997, drastic weight loss attempts claimed the lives of three wrestlers—Billy Saylor of Campbell University, Joe LaRosa of the University of Wisconsin-LaCrosse, and Jeff Reese of the University of Michigan (Field & Plona, 1997, 1998; NCAA News Release, 1998). These were the first reported wrestling deaths since the NCAA adopted the sport in 1928. Reese was trying to lose 22 pounds over four days in order to drop to a lower weight class. In 2001 Florida State University linebacker Devaughn Darling succumbed to cardiac arrhythmia (Seminoles LB Darling dead, 2001). Heat-related factors caused the deaths of freshman fullback Eraste Autin from the University of Florida (Darlington, 2001). Northwestern University safety Rashidi Wheeler died from asthma complications (Hayes, 2001). Autin and Wheeler died just nine days apart. The following year, Kevin Dare, a Pennsylvania State University pole vaulter, fell during a vault attempt that resulted in a fatal head injury and subsequent death (Penn State Athletics Press Release, 2002).

These athletes died while participating in their sports, either in formal competition representing their institution or while practicing or conditioning on their campuses. They were surrounded by coaches, trainers, teammates, friends, and fans. Yet, their lives could not be saved, a solemn testimony to the unpredictability and impartiality of death.

Other student athletes have died in situations unrelated to athletic training or competition. Natsha Wakida Sachiko, a cheerleader and mascot for the University of California, Santa Cruz, died in an automobile accident on Christmas Day in 1998 (Greenwood, 1998). Because school was adjourned for the winter break, many friends and university supporters did not learn of the tragedy until the beginning of the next term. An automobile accident also claimed the life of University of Tulsa freshman tennis player Juan Bertoldi, who was killed in Argentina on his way home from a tennis tournament (Hefner, 2000). Bertoldi's parents also died in the crash. Additionally, eight University of Wyoming cross country and track team members were killed by a drunk driver on an interstate highway just 17 miles south of their campus in 2001. The drunk driver, who survived the accident, was also a student athlete at the university.

Unfortunately, student athletes are not immune to the dangers life presents. Morgan McDuffee, senior captain of the Bates College lacrosse team, was stabbed and killed during a street fight in 2002 (LaFlamme, 2002). At the time this chapter was written, the details of the incident are unclear, and the assailant remains unidentified. Six months later, University of Minnesota sophomore football defenseman Brandon Hall was fatally shot in downtown Minneapolis

(University of Minnesota, 2002). Hall had played in his first college game the night of his death; he recorded one solo tackle.

When searching for answers, survivors often blame the criminal actions that caused the athlete's death. However, in some situations, an athlete's behavior and decisions directly or indirectly led to death. Substance abuse, automobile accidents involving alcohol, and suicide are among these circumstances. The Boston Celtics drafted University of Maryland basketball standout Len Bias in 1986. Three days after the draft selection, Bias died of a cocaine overdose. The news rocked the college, the nation, and the athletics community. More than 11,000 mourners turned out for the memorial service at Cole Field House on the University of Maryland campus.

Coping within the Student Athlete's Family

Perhaps the most challenging part of coping with the death of a student is responding to familial reactions and concerns, especially those of parents. When students leave for college, their parents entrust them to campus administrators, faculty, and athletics personnel. Although student claims of responsibility and maturity are sometimes overstated and premature, parents are assured their children will be provided safety, security, and protection from danger by the university. Administrators, faculty, and staff assume the roles of mentor, knowledge-sharer, chaperone, morality coach, rule-enforcer, and many other positions inside and outside of the classroom, including the athletic field or court. Nowhere is the notion of *in loco parentis* more evident than the college campus, and nowhere on the campus is it more apparent than in athletics.

During recruiting, athletics staffs meet with prospective athletes and their families and attempt to gain their trust. A seasoned recruiting coach knows the job of winning over students often begins with winning over their parents. The parents want to know if their child will be okay. Will she have what she needs to do well in college and in her sports? Will someone be there to help him if needed? Will someone make a personal investment in student athletes' successes, both on the court and in the classroom? The responsibility of *in loco parentis* falls on athletics staff at all ranks. But in the eyes of the parents, the crux of supervision is often placed on the coaching staff. These are the adult women and men who promised to be actively involved in the athlete's well being and development—academically, athletically, and personally. When signing the letter of intent to compete at an institution, the athlete places trust in the coaching staff, the athletic program, and the university at large. The parents also trust that their child will be cared for and they will be notified if trouble arises. When a student athlete dies, the grieving parents may be left to wonder how the university, and more specifically the coaching staff, could have allowed such a tragedy to occur.

Although they are grieving, the athletics community can offer comfort to the family. In the wake of tragedy, those who were close to the athlete can relate personal anecdotes and memories of times they shared with the athlete. Just as the parents placed their trust in the coaching staff, the coaching staff can provide a source of support to the family. The parents may be dealing with feelings of guilt for not being with the child, yet coaches can assure them that nothing could have been done to prevent the incident, if that is true, or apprise them of the measures being taken to help prevent similar incidences in the future. Knowing their daughter or son made an impact on so many people can be a source of comfort to grieving parents.

Grieving among Athletics Staffs

In the wake of a student death, athletics staff members often focus their attention and efforts on grieving students. Coaches must show concern for surviving teammates; advisors are also concerned about players on other teams, close friends, and significant others; residence life staff keep watch over roommates and other residents; and faculty tend to the athlete's classmates.

In the midst of such sadness, little attention is given to mourning among the athletics staff. Within the athletics community, the staff is often as deeply hurt by the loss as the students. Many athletics programs are small enough for administrators and support staff to know each athlete personally. A loss in such a close-knit environment can have a devastating effect on those who worked closely with the deceased student athlete. Yet they feel a self-imposed pressure to be strong for the students. Such staff may involve coaches, trainers, academic advisors, and sports media personnel. Volunteer coaches, equipment managers, graduate assistants, secretaries, and other peripheral staff also are part of the athletics family and should be offered support as well. Athletes are in contact with people in these positions on a daily basis, perhaps more often than with full-time professional staff. Survivors will seek help from the people they trust and respect, regardless of job title or status. Therefore, administrators should make available the latest information to the entire athletic community so they are able to accurately assist grieving students.

Institutional Response for Memorial and Remembrance

Athletics communities are known for their celebratory symbols of recognition. Trophies, plaques, and cups are awarded for superior performances. Photographs and jerseys of star athletes adorn the walls of gymnasiums and field houses across the country. The names and statistics of former players are painted on softball and baseball outfield walls. Players' numbers are retired, running shoes are displayed, and athletic facilities and city streets bear the names of great athletes and coaches. Winning teams and standout players are featured in several popular press publications, books, and television programs. From high school programs to intercollegiate athletics to professional sports, great athletes and their legacies live on long after their last touchdowns are scored, cheers are led, or laps are swum.

Symbols of remembrance enable teammates, fans, families, and athletics staff to celebrate the lives of fallen athletes. Hank Gathers' Loyola Marymount jersey was retired. A plaque commemorating Eraste Autin hangs inside the field where he last practiced. Autin had been at the University of Florida less than six weeks at the time of his death. More than 50 athletes traveled to his funeral service. He continues to be recognized in the media guide and on his teammates' game jerseys. The Hatsha Wakida Leadership Award is awarded to a UC-Santa Cruz athlete who embodies "the spirit and commitment of athletics." The University of Wyoming created a memorial garden in honor of the eight cross country and track team members who were killed in 2001. The garden is located near the field house where the team warmed up and cooled down before and after practice. Eight boulders, each representing one of the runners, form a ring around a larger boulder bearing a bronze plaque designed by a cross-country teammate. The plaque is imprinted with the runners' names and the words "Come Run With Me." The boulders were taken from the highway where the tragic automobile crash occurred. These are just some examples of institutional response to student athlete deaths.

The remainder of this chapter is devoted to providing programmatic recommendations and possible institutional responses. Strategies for facilitating coping and healing among teammates, parents, fans, and athletics staff are offered below. Emphasis is placed on the strategic timeliness of institutional responses to death in college athletics. While many of the approaches may be appropriately enacted or replicated at a variety of institutions, a "one size fits all" approach is discouraged. Ultimately, responses should be crafted with the unique needs and culture of the institution in mind. Appropriate memorial efforts at a smaller Division III college may be ineffective at a large Division I university. Therefore, the recommendations provided herein should be carefully considered and used as a catalyst to assist athletics departments in developing institutionally appropriate, symbolic, and programmatic responses to student athlete deaths.

First Steps: Immediate Call to Action

In all walks of life, death is often unanticipated, yet ultimately inevitable. Teammates and various others in the campus community are typically shocked to hear of a student athlete's death. Even more devastating is actually witnessing a player collapse and ultimately die on a field or court or in an athletic training facility. Furthermore, teammates and coaches are stunned to receive the news that a player was fatally injured on the way home from practice or immediately following a game. "We just saw her" is the usual response offered by many. Given the unpredictable nature of death, institutions are often forced to offer immediate responses upon hearing about the loss of a student athlete. Many students, especially those who played on the same team with the student who died, depend on campuses to provide quick responses, which range from counseling to campus-wide memorial activities. Moreover, various members of the campus community, as well as external media constituents, often demand information and formal institutional reactions.

Counseling strategies. Upon learning of a student athlete's death, campus administrators and athletics personnel should immediately call upon the professional staff of the university's counseling center. Counselors should be apprised of the tragedy and urged to make themselves available for consultation, as teammates will undoubtedly be devastated by the news. Few grieving athletes may seek the services of the counseling center, especially male students whose masculine identities typically lead them to circumvent counseling services and cope with emotional losses on their own (Gilbert & Gilbert, 1998; Gilligan, 1993). Bringing counselors to the athletics facilities may be necessary and advantageous. It is far easier and more realistic to have two to three counselors gathered in a venue where basketball players are grieving the loss of a teammate, as opposed to expecting those same team members to go to the counseling center for help.

Also, counselors may achieve greater success by allowing the team members to depend on one another for support during grieving sessions, particularly on the first day. Given the preexisting bonds that tend to link college student athletes, they may derive greater comfort from teammates, especially those who are coping relatively well with the loss. Hence, it may be more beneficial for the counselors to simply have a presence, pose guiding questions to the team, and assist grieving students when input is sought. Coaches and athletics staff members may also benefit from participation in these sessions. The comfort inspired by student athletes and counselors could have a similar impact on grieving staff.

Realizing that athletes will not be the only students affected by the loss, it may be necessary to have counselors available in the residence halls and other campus facilities. Since NCAA regulations prohibit the existence of student athlete exclusive on-campus lodging facilities, chances are that students who live in the same suite, on the same floor, or even in the same residence hall building will be negatively impacted or potentially devastated by the loss. Again, many students may not seek support from the counseling center; therefore, having counselors available in the on-campus facility where the student athlete resided would be beneficial. Obviously, a shortage of counseling center staff will make this problematic. Therefore, having counselors simultaneously represented at the athletics facilities and in the residence halls may not be feasible. In this case, preference should first be given to assisting grieving teammates, then other students with whom the fallen student athlete may have been acquainted. In the case of extreme shortages, coaches and other athletics personnel, as well as faculty and residence hall staff (hall directors, RAs, etc.) should strongly encourage grieving students to visit the campus counseling center.

Organizing services. In an era of political correctness, many higher education institutions intentionally avoid religious programming for fear of failing to accommodate the spectrum of religious diversity that exists on campus (Love & Talbot, 1999). However, a campus prayer service may be exactly what students, athletics staff members, and fans need to cope with the death of a student athlete, especially on the day of the tragic loss. The opportunity to pray individually or collectively in one venue—be it a gymnasium, chapel, residence hall lounge, or campus auditorium—could offer some sense of spiritual comfort and calmness. In an effort to be inclusive and respectful of the religious differences that may exist among the mourners, it would be most appropriate to simply offer a venue where people can gather and reflect on the loss as they see fit, instead of having the campus minister or local clergy lead the prayer services. Teammates and coaches will likely take advantage of the opportunity to lead a prayer, as will other students, faculty, and staff who come from different religious faiths. Many who need help coping with the initial shock of a student's death would appreciate having a venue where they may gather for reflection on the day of or day after the tragedy.

Offering collegial support. As noted earlier, athletics staff—including coaches, equipment managers, secretaries, media personnel, and various others—are also greatly affected by the loss of a player. Athletics personnel who serve in comparable roles at sister institutions (including rival schools) should serve as external sources of support. For instance, the soccer coach at one school in the conference may contact another to offer her condolences upon hearing the news. In that conversation, the coach may ask her colleague if she would like to talk about it or how she feels.

Athletics staff members are often forced to camouflage their true feelings and suppress their emotions in order to respond to the pain of the students. In fact, they are barely afforded the opportunity to grieve at all, as news reporters are demanding interviews and statements; presidents and administrators are requesting meetings to brainstorm appropriate responses; and the parents of the deceased student are looking for answers. In the midst of this chaos is unexplored pain. Therefore, a private telephone conversation initiated by a colleague who also works closely with student athletes in the same sport could provide the coach the opportunity to do the grieving he could not do publicly. Despite the historic rivalries that may exist between many schools and personnel at those schools, this type of outreach from one athletic professional to another, particularly on the days immediately following the tragedy, is likely to result in much-needed support, companionship, and opportunity for bereavement.

In Memoriam: Paying Tribute to a Lost Team Member

A series of programmatic initiatives should occur after the initial shock has been dealt with on campus. Given that student athletes are important to several constituency groups (e.g., teammates, athletics staff, local fans, national spectators), it is critically important to appropriately honor their lives, contributions, and achievements. While some efforts can be implemented immediately, others may require a slightly longer passage of time. In most cases, well-coordinated tributes that take weeks or even months to orchestrate are far more meaningful than loosely planned events that occur immediately after the student's death. For instance, the memorial garden at the University of Wyoming was dedicated exactly one year after the eight student athletes died. In the interim, the University employed other memorial efforts. Timing is critical; therefore, the undertaking of multiple initiatives is usually necessary.

Campus memorial services. A formal program that is open to students, faculty, staff, and community members should be offered within one to three weeks following the death of a student athlete. The service should include a variety of speakers who may include, but are not limited to, the president, the athletics director, members of the coaching staff, teammates, and other students who were well acquainted with the deceased student. Poetry, prayer, silence, and music may also be part of the program. The memorial service could be held in an on-campus auditorium or athletic facility.

Given that most program participants will be speaking from their hearts and vividly reflecting upon the student athlete's life, this type of service should require a comparatively low degree of preparation. Most attention should be devoted to publicizing the event and ensuring that all interested persons, including those external to the university, are invited and encouraged to attend. Athletics personnel should work with the university ceremonies office to make certain that protocol is being followed (at least to some degree) and consistency is upheld. That is, the memorial service for a softball player in 2003 should be somewhat similar to the campus-wide program held in honor of the football player who died in 1999. Consistency is important so that parents and members of the campus community do not feel that some student athletes' lives and contributions were more or less important than others. Obviously, more extensive memorial services would be necessary and appropriate in the case of multiple deaths, like a commuter plane crash carrying the entire golf team.

Symbolic remembrances. Since the tragic February 2001 car crash that led to the death of football player Brandon Cole Pittman, the University of Texas has engaged in a number of symbolic recognition efforts. Cole's locker has been encased with glass; the Longhorns retired his jersey; teammates wore a "CP" decal on their helmets the following season; his picture and a memorial message appeared on the scoreboard throughout the football season; and his number was painted on a hill in the end zone of the field. Similar symbolic initiatives have been used at several other institutions. It has become commonplace for teams to affix black armbands or stripes to their uniforms as a display of grief for a lost teammate.

In addition to displaying retired jerseys and uniforms, many athletics departments also exhibit students' pom-poms, running shoes, and other personal sports-related gear as a symbol of tribute. Some programs have even retired players' numbers, meaning there will be a perpetual gap on the team's roster in honor of the deceased student. On the one hand, this is a significant and powerful recognition effort, while on the other, some teams place themselves at risk of running out numbers. What happens when multiple student athlete deaths befall a team over a short period? Eventually, too few numbers could remain. Also, retiring actual numbers instead of jerseys is somewhat risky as athletics personnel and various others may not deem a player's contributions worthy of permanent number retirement. As mentioned earlier, consistency is important when memorializing student athletes. Parents may be particularly displeased if their daughter's jersey was retired when the actual number of the woman who died the previous year was permanently removed. Retiring a player's jersey or uniform offers a safe and appropriate alternative.

Many of the symbolic remembrances offered in this section could occur within weeks or months following the student athlete's death. They are usually most effective at this time because players' hearts are still sore, as their deceased teammate's presence is still missed in practices and games; athletics personnel still feel particularly compelled to do as much as possible on behalf of the program; and fans are deeply interested in showing their respect for the fallen players and their families.

In Auxilium Parentis: In Support of Grieving Parents and Family Members

When tragic events lead to the death of a daughter or son, college and university administrators, faculty, and staff must shift their attention from acting in place of the parent to acting in support of the surviving family members. As mentioned earlier, parents expect athletics staff members (namely coaches) to ensure their children's safety, protect them from harm, and most importantly, help sustain their lives. When student athletes die, staff members feel a tremendous responsibility to the families. Sometimes, grieving parents even hold athletics staffs accountable for the death of their daughters or sons, especially if the death occurred during athletic training or a sporting event. College and university administrators, as well as staff members in athletics departments, can engage in a number of outreach efforts to parents and family members.

First and foremost, universities should emphasize to parents exactly how important their deceased children were to their teammates, the athletics program, the larger campus, and the surrounding community. Telephone calls or in-person visits (pending distance) from the president of the university, athletics director, and coach are logical first steps. Arranging transportation for teammates and other interested students to attend the athlete's funeral or hometown memorial service would also confirm for family members that the person was important to and loved by affiliates of the institution. If invited, a member of the coaching staff or a teammate may even offer a few reflections during the funeral service.

Campus memorial services were discussed and advocated elsewhere in this chapter. Given the suggested timing of the service, it may or may not be feasible to have parents and family members participate in the program. Obviously, they should be invited to attend and offer remarks on behalf of the family. However, it should not be an expectation that the family will be strong enough to address an audience of the deceased student's peers, fans, and supporters. In many cases, the parents are simply incapable of doing this but are able to send another representative from the family (e.g., a sibling, aunt, or cousin). The coordinators of the memorial service should invite, but not push family members to speak. Regardless of their decision to participate, the campus memorial service should be videotaped, and the tape should be given to the family members.

Video recordings of teammates, athletics staff, faculty and administrators, and other supporters may be another treasured gift to family members. Hearing each of these people spend two to three minutes reflecting upon the ways in which the deceased student touched their lives would undoubtedly aid parents in the healing process. Perhaps athletics staff members who cared deeply for the student (e.g., secretaries, graduate assistants, equipment managers) but were given minimal opportunities to contribute in the planning and execution of other memorial activities, could coordinate this task. Clips of the deceased student in practices or athletic play would provide an added touch to the memorial video-tape. Given the public and commercial nature of college athletics, it should not be too difficult to locate video segments that include the student. If video pro-duction capabilities are limited or nonexistent, putting together a scrapbook of newspaper clippings, photographs, and handwritten letters from various univer-sity affiliates could be just as effective. Videotapes and scrapbooks are gifts that family members will treasure forever.

A framed memorial resolution from the faculty senate or local or state gov-ernment is another gift that family members can proudly display in their homes. The resolution should be read and presented in a public forum. The campus memorial service may or may not be the most appropriate place to do this be-cause of timing. Pre-game or halftime at a sporting event during the following season or the end-of-the-year athletics banquet may be more desirable venues for this presentation. Because he died in the off-season, a presentation was made to Cole Pittman's family at the first University of Texas home football game of the 2001-2002 season.

Given the minimal costs that would be incurred by athletics departments, offering complimentary lifetime season tickets to the parents of a student athlete who died would be a polite gesture. Furthermore, dedicating two reserved sta-dium seats for family members that are affixed with plates that say "In memory of [student's name]" would be a nice way to honor the family and the athlete. Even if the families do not use the lifetime season tickets or reserved seats, they should be offered annually.

In some instances, family members do not have adequate life insurance to help cover funeral and burial expenses. Therefore, they are forced to rely upon personal savings, donations, or even loans to help offset costs. In this case, the athletics departments and larger institution should solicit donations to assist the family. Although some larger athletics programs are financially capable of mak-ing a sizeable contribution to the student's family, raising the money would be a more meaningful gesture, as once again, family members will see exactly how important their daughters and sons were to the institution. In concert with the university development office, athletics departments should launch an immedi-ate campaign to raise the money to assist needy families. Because it is for the burial expenses of a student athlete, many different groups—including booster clubs, alumni, and local businesses—are likely to contribute. In some cases, student athletes who die leave behind surviving children. Undertaking a devel-opment campaign to create a college scholarship fund for the children of fallen athletes would make a bold and powerful statement. Some day the child will say, "My mother [or father] was so important to this institution that they raised the money to pay for my college education."

Although the campus memorial service may occur too soon for parents and family members to comfortably address an audience, they should be invited to speak at other forums (e.g., athletics banquets, booster club meetings, during halftime at a sporting event). In many instances, family members will request an opportunity to publicly express their gratitude and celebrate the lives of their daughters and sons. They should be invited to participate in sports-related activities long after the short-term memorial efforts have ended. In fact, inviting parents to say a few words years after the tragedy would assure them that their children's contributions to the athletics program were meaningful and worthy of long-term recognition. Eventually, staff and administrative turnover may cause some families to be forgotten or overlooked; it is, therefore, important that records be kept to advise new staff members of the protocol and traditions regarding outreach efforts to families of fallen student athletes.

Lastly, many perpetual symbols could let the family members know how important the deceased student was and will always be to the institution. In addition to displaying retired jerseys and encasing lockers with glass, the athletics department could also employ a number of permanent strategies to pay tribute to fallen students. For years to come, parents and other family members could visit the campus to view and relive the legacies their loved ones left behind. All the initiatives described herein, while they cannot completely erase the pain associated with death, would help family members better cope with their losses, both in the short term and long term.

Gone, But Not Forgotten: Perpetual Symbols

There are several ways to permanently celebrate the lives of fallen athletes and recognize their contributions to the institution. Memorial gardens, portraits displayed in athletic facilities, permanent memorial pages on institutional websites, dedicated rooms in athletics buildings and seats at stadiums, and named annual scholarships and performance awards are just some of the ways that institutions might permanently honor the lives of student athletes who died while in college. Given that many student athletes receive some type of scholarship award to cover their tuition and fees, a tremendous opportunity exists to name some of those scholarship awards after deceased players. Perhaps those named scholarships can be awarded to a student athlete who comes from the same state or hometown as the person for whom the award is named. Besides being a symbol of recognition, naming certain portions of athletics facilities (e.g., locker rooms and meeting rooms) after fallen student athletes will prompt future generations to inquire about the person the room is named for. Therein lays the opportunity to teach countless student athletes about the life and contributions of a former player.

Also, it is important at annual athletics banquets to recognize all the student athletes who died during their college years. At minimum, their names should be read and the audience should engage in a moment of silence in their honor. This is important far beyond the months or years immediately following the student athlete's death. Paying tribute to them annually, though in a seemingly small and effortless way, keeps their legacies alive and imparts a spirit of honor to younger generations. Again, new coaches and athletics staff members should be given the names of those who died and apprised of the tradition.

In Honor of the Fallen: Ongoing Lifesaving Efforts

Perhaps the best way to honor the lives of fallen student athletes is to engage in efforts to prevent the same tragedies from claiming the lives of others. If a drunk driver killed a student athlete, her teammates may reduce future tragedies by speaking to high school students about the dangers of drunk driving or becoming spokeswomen for special community or national programs to discourage driving while under the influence of alcohol and drugs. Similarly, if a student athlete died of alcohol poisoning, his teammates could advocate responsible drinking and lead alcohol education programs for other college students, locally and nationally.

Lifesaving fundraising initiatives are additional ways to honor those athletes who died during their college years. Admittedly, this chapter has disproportionately focused on death from unnatural causes, especially automobile accidents. There are, however, illnesses and diseases that claim the lives of college student athletes; breast cancer, leukemia, and HIV/AIDS are just some of them. When these diseases lead to death in college athletics, teammates, staff members, and other university affiliates can engage in campaigns to fund research, treatment programs, and educational initiatives that may save the lives of others.

Players and affiliates are apt to be most passionate about affecting change in the months immediately following the student athlete's death. Thus, their willingness to champion educational and research endeavors through the commitment of personal time and solicitation of financial donations is likely high. Even if they were previously unaffected by or unconcerned with the cause, they will become passionate about it in honor of their teammate, fellow student, or favorite player.

Conclusion

Death is inevitable and often unpredictable. In times of loss, survivors must, and do, endure. Parents lose a child, and they grieve. A piece of the team is missing, but teammates continue to put forth the effort expected of them. Students lose a close friend. Faculty must contend with the empty desk in the classroom. Fans can no longer cheer on their favorite player. And all are left to question, "Why?" Yet an institution will survive the death of a student athlete.

University officials and athletics department staff aid in the grieving process of all who are touched by the student's death. From initial response to long-term memoriam, survivors look to the institution to lead them through the shock of loss and the pain of grief to the solemnity of remembrance. Decisions made will have a profound effect on the relationship of the institution with the family, the recovery of teammates and athletics staff, and the student's place in the institution's history.

Recommendations for and examples of action and inaction have been presented; however, each institution must take into account the circumstances of the student's death and the culture and history of the institution. Decisions should be consistent yet personalized, organized yet heartfelt and sincere. In light of recommendations provided, perhaps the most important is to meet the grieving needs of survivors within the bounds of the family's wishes.

Another student athlete will die. Another family will lose a son or daughter. Another college campus will be left to pick up the pieces. The cycle of life and death is inevitable. By denying the possibility that a death will occur on their campus, university officials are in turn allowing themselves to be ill-prepared for the event when it occurs. Ignorance will only hinder their ability to cope with the situation. Instead, they should examine the culture of their institution and the needs of their students, consider the contingencies, and formulate preemptive guidelines for dealing with the death of a student athlete. By examining such scenarios, administrators are equipping themselves with the knowledge and experience of others and making the most of a somber situation.

References

Darlington, J. (2002, August 26). One year later: UF freshman Eraste Autin's mark still left on Gators a year after his death [Electronic version]. *The Independent Florida Alligator*. Retrieved October 15, 2002, from http://www.alligator.org/edit/sports/issues/02-summer/current/d08autin26. html

Field, J., & Plona, K. (1997, December 11). Michigan wrestler dies while exercising [Electronic version]. *The Michigan Daily*, Retrieved June 11, 2002, from http://www.pub.umich.edu/daily/1997/dec/12-11-97(special)/ news/ news1.html

Field, J., & Plona, K. (1998, January 7). Wrestler's death evokes grief, spurs training reforms [Electronic version]. *The Michigan Daily*. Retrieved June 12, 2002, from http:// www.pub.umich.edu/daily/1998/jan/01-07-98/news/news4. html

Gilbert, R., & Gilbert, P. (1998). *Masculinity goes to school*. New York: Routledge.

Gilligan, C. (1993). *In a different voice: Psychological theory and women's development*. Cambridge, MA: Harvard University.

Greenwood, M. R. C. (1998, December 31). *Administrative messages: Death of Natasha Wakida*. Retrieved October 15, 2002, from http://www.ucsc.edu/ oncampus/currents/98-99/01-04/wakida.htm.

Hayes, M. (2001, August 21). Supplements becoming a major concern [Electronic version]. *The Sporting News*. Retrieved May 27, 2002, from http://www.sportingnews.com /voices/matt_hayes/20010821.html

Hefner, V. (2000, August 22). TU loses tennis player in automobile accident [Electronic version]. *The Collegian Online*. Retrieved October 15, 2002, from http://www.utulsa.edu/collegian/article.asp?article=194

Huber, J. (2002, March 15). Remembering Hank: Memories of fallen star remain 10 years later [Electronic version]. *CNN Sports Illustrated.* Retrieved June 12, 2002, from http://sportsillustrated.cnn.com/inside_game/jim) huber/news/2000/03/15/hubersportinglifeinsider_gathers/

LaFlamme, M. (2002, March 4). Bates senior, 22, stabbed to death. *Lewiston, Maine Sun. Journal Online* [Electronic version]. Retrieved on October 15, 2002, from http://www.sunjournal. com/story.asp?slg=030402bates

Love, P., & Talbot, D. (1999). Defining spiritual development: A missing consideration for student affairs. *NASPA Journal, 37,* 361-375.

NCAA News Release. (1998, January 13). *Wrestling rules changes address dehydration.* Retrieved June 3, 2002, from http://www.ncaa.org/releases/ makepage.cgi/rules/1998011301ru.htm

Penn State Athletics Press Release. (2002, February 23). *Nittany Lion Student-athlete Kevin Dare dies at Big Ten Men's Track & Field Championships.* Retrieved November 17, 2002, from http://wwww.gopsusports.com/pressreleases/pressrelease.cfm?anncid=2336

Seminoles LB Darling dead. (2001, February 27). *CNN Sports Illustrated.* Retrieved March 27, 2002, from http://sportsillustrated.cnn.com/football/ college/news/2001/02/26/fsu_death_ap/

University of Minnesota. (2002, September 11). In Memoriam, Brandon Hall. *The Source.* Retrieved October 156, 2002, from http://www.1.umn.edu/urelate/thesource/BrandonHall/

11

International Students:
An Administrative Response

Connie Shoemaker

Universities should be aware of and attendant to international students and cultural differences when responding to an international student's death. Challenges to responding successfully to the death of international students include formulating an administrative plan for dealing with a crisis situation, training counselors in culturally-appropriate techniques, obtaining thorough information about the student's background and the situation of her death, gaining knowledge of the student's culture related to death and grieving, and providing language translation.

In spite of the impact of the September 11 tragedy, international students continue to view educational institutions in the United States as their first choice, and our campuses continue to welcome them because their presence in our classrooms brings a stronger understanding of global issues, a broader perspective of world cultures, and hope for peace and development around the globe.

A total number of 572,509 international students were studying on university and college campuses in the United States during the academic year 2003/2004 (Institute of International Education, 2004). The majority of these students are long-term visitors who are in the U.S. to earn undergraduate or graduate degrees. A smaller number are here for shorter term English as a Second Language or specific types of training programs.

Connie Shoemaker is the founder and director emeritus of Spring International Language Center in Colorado. She has extensive teaching experience in colleges and universities in the USA as well as abroad and is a prolific author and trainer on issues of international education and ESL.

Open Doors 2004 also reports that international student enrollment has decreased by a total of nearly 2.4%, pointing to the first absolute decline in foreign enrollment since 1971/72 (Institute of International Education, 2004). However, growth is particularly strong at community colleges, where enrollments of all international students total up to one-fifth. Whether in a university, a four-year college, or a community college, situations of loss and grief are inevitable in the international population studying here in the United States. The trauma of a student dying on a university or college campus is always a disturbing and highly emotional event, but when an international student dies, the trauma is intensified. Not only does it affect the campus and surrounding community, but it also affects the international student's family and cultural community. In addition, the way in which university officials respond to the death becomes more complicated by differences in culture. Some of the most common challenges to responding successfully include formulating an administrative plan for dealing with a crisis situation, training counselors in culturally appropriate techniques, obtaining thorough information about the student's background and the situation of her death, gaining knowledge of the student's culture related to death and grieving, and providing assistance with needed translation.

This example from Xavier University illustrates the complexity and the challenges of responding to a death situation.

Case 1: A Korean Student

This October our campus experienced its first death of an international student, a 30-year-old Korean ESL student who died of a heart attack. Of course, we followed the overall university policy regarding the death of a student, but the fact that this was an international student made the situation different. We had no specific written policies, so we worked out the details day by day. Sadly, the student was a newlywed. When he went into cardiac arrest at home, his wife called 911. It was impossible to revive him, so body identification was not necessary and his wife spoke with the doctors, coroner, etc. An autopsy was performed to determine the cause of death.

As the director of the Intensive English Program, I was informed of the death the next day by a group of Korean students. Luckily, they had appointed a representative of the Korean community to act as a channel of communication between the family and the school. We cancelled classes that day because our students were so upset. We have a small program of 60-70 students, so almost everyone knew the deceased. The campus Director of International Student Services worked with the family and tried to expedite the parents' visas to the U.S. When it turned out that the parents did not even have passports and could not come to the U.S. to make arrangements, we focused on getting the body home as soon as possible.

The major situations we dealt with were contacting the insurance company used by the University to find out procedures for repatriation of the body, obtaining the required death certificate, holding a private mass off campus the day after the death, embalming, and arranging a funeral home visitation, which was held expressly, I believe, for the other ESL students and staff. This was a wrenching experience and the Koreans told us, "We don't usually do this [open casket] and see the face."

We also called the airlines to arrange body transport, excused one or two Korean students from class each day to stay with the body per Korean custom that the soul stays with the body for seven days and the body must not be left alone during that time, wrote letters of condolence to the family, refunded tuition, and planned a memorial service on campus. The Korean Catholic community stepped in and did so much, which wouldn't happen in most cases. The fact that the student was married also left many decisions to his wife.

I hope we never experience this again, but it pointed out the need to be prepared for an international death if it does happen in the future. (Conzett, personal communication, 2003)

As one can see, cultural differences are a major complication in dealing with the death of an international student. Contacts with the deceased's family may involve use of his first language; hence, the need for a translator. The student or scholar may be sponsored by an embassy or foreign company. Both the sponsor and the US Department of Homeland Security (formerly Immigration and Naturalization Services) must be notified. Ways of dealing with death, possible transport of the body, and/or burial also must be culturally appropriate.
"The immediate psychic disorientation that accompanies a crisis and not just for those stricken by it can render any of us virtually unable to think straight and 'do the right thing' instinctively" (Burak & Hoffa, 2001, p.xxii). (Readers are encouraged to read Part 2, Crises involving international students in US campuses, in the book *Crisis Management in a Cross-Cultural Setting*, by the authors just mentioned). This makes it even more crucial to engage in advanced planning, which leads to the development of response procedures before a crisis occurs. The response protocol should be implemented by a team of campus administrators who have discussed and practiced the procedures.

Organizing an Administrative Team
The Foreign Student Advisor (FSA) or, in the case of an intensive ESL program on campus, the director, is often the central person on the team who serves as the institutional link between the university's various entities and the family of the deceased. The FSA can be the guide in dealing with cultural issues, such as repatriation, or sending the body of the deceased to the home country. Members of the team may vary depending upon the institutional organization. The team may include representatives from the Office of International Students and Scholars, the Vice-Chancellor for Student Affairs, the student/scholar's major department, residence life if the student lives in campus housing, campus police, university relations, the health center, counseling and psychological services,

public relations, a consultant who is familiar with the student's culture, a campus attorney if legal issues are involved, and a representative of campus ministry.

Initial Steps in Responding to the Death of an International Student

The following nine steps should be part of the first response to be initiated by the FSA or another designated member of the team:

1. Consult the file of the student for essential background information, such as telephone numbers of family members and local contacts.
2. Contact the office of the senior student affairs officer or the Dean of Students to keep that office informed of the situation.
3. Assemble the administrative team and identify the person in charge. Assign tasks to members of the team.
4. Start a list of contacts and telephone numbers.
5. Identify the body. This may become the task of a close friend of the deceased, a professor, or college official who knows the student.
6. Establish the cause of death. Determine the circumstances of death. The best source of information is the Medical Examiner's office (MEO), which is usually a county governmental agency having jurisdiction over the location where the death occurred. In order to receive a death certificate, some states require that the MEO present a letter certifying that there are no contagious diseases present in the body. Generally, this letter will accompany the body to the funeral home. As many as five copies of the death certificate should be ordered, a copy each for the insurance company, the student's file, two copies to accompany the remains during repatriation, and one copy for the family.
7. Inform the family. Consider the language and cultural issues involved before making the telephone call. Choose the best person to inform the family. If there is a local or emergency contact, it is best to contact the person first to seek advice about the best way to inform the family. It is critical to ask students from the same country not to call their own families with the news until you are sure the deceased's family has been notified. No family wants to learn their child has died in a foreign country and no one has bothered to contact them officially. The person designated to make this call must be sensitive to the religious beliefs and cultural traditions of the family. Listen to the family's needs in order to make proper decisions about funeral or memorial service arrangements and burial or repatriation. For example, the family's religion may require special cloths for washing the deceased's body. In certain faiths, the body may need to be buried before sundown, and in others, it would need to be cremated after ceremonial washing. In the initial example, an open casket viewing may not have been the choice of the Korean community.
8. Some families may request an autopsy depending on the circumstances of the death, and many states require that an official autopsy be performed by the MEO in cases where the deceased dies under suspicious

circumstances or when the deceased dies alone. Other families may re-
sist the procedure. The cultural difficulty in this case is that autopsies
are often perceived by people from non-Western cultures as barbaric
and disrespectful to the deceased and his family.

9. Notify the consulate of the student's country of origin and any sponsor-
    ing agency. The consulate should be very helpful and supportive in
    dealing with the total response to the crisis.

In the case of the Korean student, the wife and members of the Korean
church community assisted with many of the initial response tasks including
those on the day of the student's death, the private mass, and arrangement of the
airline transport. The Director of International Student Services on the Xavier
campus obtained the death certificate, worked with family in Korea, and tried to
expedite the relatives' visas to the U.S. The Director of the ESL program arranged for students to be excused from classes to stay with the body, got a re-
fund of tuition through the Bursar's office, expedited students' visits to the funeral home, and planned a memorial service on campus. The memorial service
was videotaped and copies were sent to the wife and parents in Korea.

Making Arrangements for the Deceased's Body

Making arrangements for the body of the deceased is one of the most difficult and complicated tasks. If the family chooses to have an autopsy, the county
coroner will fulfill this request. It is also necessary to obtain multiple death certificates. The family must decide whether to repatriate the body, to cremate it in
the U.S. and return the ashes to the home country, or to have a burial in the
United States. Some families will want to view the body within 24 hours; others
will not want the body embalmed for religious reasons. These decisions often
stem from cultural considerations. Repatriation is frequently a family choice.
These three steps are necessary:

1. Contact a reputable funeral home that understands the international re-
    quirements of transporting a body via air, including the requisite em-
    balming. Check to see that the funeral home knows the rules and regu-
    lations that govern shipping bodies across borders because these vary
    from country to country.

2. Arrange transportation with an airline if this task is not assumed by the
    funeral home. In some cases, the airline of the country involved will
    make space readily available and will cover the cost of the transporta-
    tion. The contact with the consulate may help to facilitate this step.

3. Assist the family with travel arrangements. Find out who the family
    representatives are, when they will arrive, and on what airline. An offi-
    cial delegation, accompanied by an interpreter, if necessary, should
    meet family members at the airport and transport them to their hotel.
    When using an interpreter, speak directly to the family, maintaining eye
    contact with them. If complicated medical issues need to be discussed,
    refer these matters to the attending hospital, which often employs inter-
    preters proficient in medical terminology. At this meeting, the delega-

tion can offer their condolences, review the current plans, and determine the immediate wishes of the family. If the family does not choose to travel to the U.S., a representative of the administrative team may establish contact with the family and/or embassy for disposition of the deceased's body.

Case 2: A Taiwanese Student

Our only experience of the tragedy of a student death came when a Taiwanese student was hit by a car while he was changing a tire on the highway. At the time, we did not have a coherent policy to deal with such an experience, but since then we have developed some guidelines.

The American Language Program (ALP) was notified by the receiving hospital, and my staff immediately contacted the insurance company and called me so that we could arrange to have a university representative call the family right away. I was the Academic Coordinator of the language program at the time, and our Dean of Extended Education was the acting director. He contacted university officials, and a Chinese-speaking professor was designated to call the family immediately. At the same time, I notified all of our faculty and students. My staff was wonderful, spending all weekend in the office, contacting the local police, insurance company, hospital, and dealing with all possible details for the family.

Our dean called the Taiwan Economic and Cultural office attaché here in Los Angeles, who also called the family and helped them make arrangements. The family arrived and with the help of the attaché made arrangements for the body and the memorial service held at a local mortuary for friends and family.

At the campus memorial service, university representatives spoke, and the Taiwan attaché addressed the group in both Chinese and English. The most moving moment was when one of the teachers and a student who had been friends with the deceased read memories of the student written by his friends and teacher. A teacher collected all of the memories into a booklet, which was presented to the family.

After the campus service, university counselors held bereavement counseling sessions for students, with matriculated students present as translators to assist students through the grieving process. Because four students had witnessed the accident, we spent additional time counseling them. Later, the family and the attaché were invited to meet with university officials, staff, and students who had known their son. The university, our former students, professors in the English department, and the Counseling Center all came together with us to help the family make arrangements and to counsel the grieving students in their own languages.

In the aftermath of this tragedy, we have developed guidelines for dealing with a student death, and because of the circumstances of the accident, we have added freeway safety precautions to our orientation materials. (Richmond, personal communication, 2003)

Planning a Memorial Service

The memorial service is important not only for the campus and the community but also for the family of the deceased student. In the previous case study, the campus memorial service drew together administrators, teachers, students, family, and the representative of the Taiwan Consulate. It demonstrated to the family that their son was respected, well liked, and an integral part of the campus community.

Arrangements for the memorial service should include the following:

1. If possible, involve the family in the choice of a place for the service: a campus location, local church, or mortuary chapel. Be aware of any cultural or religious considerations.
2. Excuse students from class for the memorial service.
3. Assist students and family with transportation to the site of the service.
4. Provide a translator for portions of the service.
5. Prepare a formal program and order of service. Observe culturally appropriate religious rituals. Determine whether or not flowers are appropriate. Involve the deceased's friends and teachers in the service. In some situations, music may be provided by a student or teacher. Speakers may be campus officials, teachers, and/or student friends.
6. Provide the family with a memory book or videotape of the service.

Other Support Services

The aftermath of an international student's death involves not only counseling but details related to the student's possessions, costs of dealing with the tragedy, a possible memorial, and maintaining contact with the family after they leave the United States.

1. Make counseling available for the family before they leave the United States, and continue to have it available for friends and others involved in the grieving process. In the case study, counseling was offered immediately after the memorial service. It was available in the languages of the students, staff, and family.
2. Dispose of the student's personal belongings. With the direction of the family, personal belongings may be packed, shipped home, or otherwise disposed of by the university. Critical and very personal belongings such as passports, death certificates, jewelry, and photographs need to be returned as soon as possible. International mail is not the most secure way to do this. A fellow student can return these items personally, even if it means the university covers travel expenses. Another option is to air express the items via an international courier service. Some insurance policies have an accidental death benefit that may cover moving company expenses to pack and ship all belongings. After

this is done, discuss with the family what they would like to see happen with the student's other belongings, car, and so on. Make it clear the campus is more than willing to securely store these items for a period of time.

3. Make certain that life and medical insurance benefits have been properly requested. Assign a team member to monitor bills and payments. These may include bills from the ambulance company, the hospital, and the funeral home. Rather than sending the bills directly to the family, it is important for a campus official to forward them to appropriate insurance companies. Coverage by the student's medical insurance and, in some cases, coverage by auto insurance, may require some sorting out and pressure for payment.

4. Request that the family be reimbursed for tuition and fees for the semester.

5. Inform the Immigration and Naturalization Service of the death.

6. Maintain contact with the family. A team member may continue to assist the family in interfacing with the insurance company and in dealing with other issues that may arise.

7. Consider the establishment of a memorial to the student.

In the event of a student death, the goal of the university is to inform, assist, and offer its sympathies in a fashion that is most respectful to the family's beliefs, situation, and culture. The importance of listening to the family and the students affected by the tragedy is well illustrated in the case study that follows.

Case 3: An Ecuadorian Student

Twelve students from Ecuador were on their final ski trip in the Colorado mountains as part of a special winter program that included intensive English study and weekend skiing. At the end of the day, all but one of the students, Fabian, returned to the van for the trip home to Denver. When the accompanying teacher contacted the Loveland ski patrol, she was informed that they were bringing down a skier who was killed when he struck a tree. The skier was Fabian.

Shock and extreme emotion engulfed the group as the details of the death were dealt with by the teacher and officials of the language center who hurried to the ski area. The body of the young man remained at the coroner's in the county where the accident occurred, and the students returned late that night to the campus in Denver where their host families and I met them. After discussion of the accident, students were allowed to stay together, if they chose, that night at two of the host families' homes. Counseling began that night and continued throughout the remaining weeks of the program.

A cousin of the deceased contacted the sponsor in Ecuador who, in turn, contacted the parents who were out of town. The parents chose not to come to the United States, but were represented by the student's aunt and uncle who flew in from Miami.

The meaningfulness of the days that followed were the result of 'taking a cue from the students.' The eleven students requested that they be taken back to the mountains to view the body and to visit the place where Fabian died although some of the host families were shocked by what they thought was an unusual request. The drive through the mountains was quiet and somber. The president of the intensive English program and I accompanied them to the coroner's office where those who wished could see the body. Some of the students wanted to go on the trip but chose not to view Fabian's body. Others asked that the president and I go with them in small groups to view the body. This was difficult for us, but important to the students. Fabian's best friend placed a letter he had written in Fabian's pocket. Then the Loveland ski patrol took everyone by ski mobile to the place where he had died. The students placed flowers at the base of the tree and a small plaque that read "God Has Called Him Home" on the tree. On the way back to Denver, the group seemed to have a better sense of the reality of Fabian's death. They were relaxed, talking, laughing a bit, and remembering good times with their friend.

A memorial service in Spanish was held in the Immaculate Conception cathedral in Denver. It was videotaped and given to the family. Fabian's aunt and uncle met his host family and packed his belongings. The body was repatriated within 10 days. We sent flowers for the funeral service to be held in Ecuador. One very important element of the process was maintaining contact with Fabian's family during the ensuing months. On the first anniversary of his death, his father and younger brother came to Denver. His mother was not at a point in the grieving process in which she could accompany them. She still had not opened the suitcases that had been sent home and couldn't bring herself to look at the video. The father and brother met Fabian's host family who had communicated with them during the year and had sent them a gift, and they visited some of the places Fabian had enjoyed while he was in Colorado. Then they were assisted by the Loveland Ski Patrol to visit the site of his accident.

We pray that this will never happen again, but we have prepared a crisis notebook to assist us in the event of another tragedy. (Hind, personal communication, 2003)

This case study exemplifies the stress and emotion involved in the death of a member of the international community. It also demonstrates that the tragedy can be a learning experience and an opportunity to show true care and concern for the family and friends affected by the tragedy.

Each of the case studies or illustrations in this chapter demonstrates a unique response to the first death of an international student on its campus, and in each situation, the university or college involved dealt with the crisis without advance planning. After the initial crisis all of the institutions recognized the advantages of formulating a crisis management plan that focused on cross-cultural sensitivity. A crisis management plan designed to respond in a culturally sensitive fashion can make all the difference in an institution's appropriate, comprehensive, and timely response to the death of an international student. However, the crisis management plan is not in itself enough. It will only be as effective as the team members' awareness of their responsibilities and the challenges posed by the death of an international student.

References

Burak, P. & Hoffa, W. (Eds.). (2001). *Crisis management in a cross-cultural setting*. Washington, DC: NAFSA.

Institute of International Education. (2004). *First absolute decline in foreign enrollments since 1971/72*. Retrieved December 18, 2004 from http://opendoors.iienetwork.org

Davis, T. M. & Chin H. K. (Eds.) (2004). *Open Doors 2004: Report on international educational exchange*. Retrieved May 1, 2005. Available at opendoors.iienetwork.org.

12

By One's Own Hand:
Suicide on the College Campus

Nancy Crist Welch

There are several ways the university community can respond sensitively and responsibly when a student completes a suicide. Noting trouble signs is an important step in assisting families with grief and shock issues. Student affairs personnel must address the aftermath of a suicide by responding to students, families, and friends. With sensitivity and caring, a tragic occurrence can be addressed and handled in a way that can promote healing for all.

The fall of 1999 was full of hope and excitement. Newly employed as a psychologist at the Student Counseling Service at my alma mater, Texas A&M University, I eagerly awaited opportunities to help students in need by providing individual therapy, couples and group work, consultation and outreach, and crisis intervention. Little did I realize the extent of crisis intervention skills I would learn, not by way of continuing education units, but through on the job training. In one short, tragic semester, Texas A&M suffered a series of debilitating losses, challenging the campus and local community as never before. In the span of three months, the university lost 21 students to violent death—on several occasions losing more than one student—a sky-diving accident, automobile accidents, the collapse of the traditional Bonfire stack, which killed 12 students, and two completed suicides.

Of the student deaths one may expect to encounter in a university setting, suicide is often the most difficult to understand and process. It is difficult to accept that a suicide has occurred, even more so in a young adult with his or her entire future ahead. There is nothing else quite like the feeling one has when

Nancy Crist Welch, Ph.D., is a licensed psychologist with the Student Counseling Service at Texas A&M University and is also an adjunct professor in the Department of Educational Psychology. She often works with students who are dealing with grief and loss issues and also works with trauma and PTSD issues in both individual and group therapy contexts.

college administrators, student affairs staff, faculty, counseling center psychologists, and students hear of a suicide that has taken place in their midst. Such an event gives rise to questions that have no easy answers: (a) What happened? (b) How did it happen? (c) Are you sure it was not an accident? (d) Did anyone know that s/he was suicidal? (e) Could this have been prevented? (f) Who will tell the parents and friends? (g) And the most troubling question of all—Why? The "why" question appears early and may never be fully answered—for the loved ones, faculty and staff, and student body at large.

Texas A&M, with over 45,000 students, is a large university campus. Because the college community is a microcosm of our larger communities, it could be reasonably expected that suicides will occur. Yet when one does, the entire campus is shocked and saddened. Certainly, our campus counseling center sees students with some degree of suicidal ideation on a regular basis—it is part of the college counseling experience at most universities. Thankfully, through psychotherapy (sometimes including medication or other psychiatric services as well) these suicidal crises usually pass. However, for some anguished students the option of suicide is the one ultimately chosen.

This chapter will focus on ways the university community can respond sensitively and responsibly when a student commits suicide:

1. What are the stress and risk factors for college students who are considering suicide?
2. What can campuses expect, and what can they do after a student kills him/herself?
3. How can we help the grieving family and friends when their loved one commits suicide?
4. Is suicidal contagion or "copycat suicides" a possibility?
5. What can we teach students who survive a peer's suicide?

Stressors of College Students

The statistics on college student suicide are sobering. Suicide is the second leading cause of death among college students (after automobile accidents), and the third leading cause of death among 15-24 year olds nationally (Centers for Disease Control [CDC], 1997). More women than men attempt suicide, while more men than women complete it (usually due to the violent measures more often chosen by men, such as firearms or hanging). An understanding of the particular stressors that college students face will help us meet their needs more proactively.

Developmentally, young adults in college are undergoing concurrent life transitions. Often they have moved away from home for the first time. Related to this move is the absence of daily family support, hometown friends, and other established ways of dealing with stress when it occurs. Adults sometimes downplay "homesickness" as a necessary but benign phase for newly entering college students, but there are those students for whom this is a wrenching transition. As one would expect of this age group, romantic relationships are important as well, and a break-up can be a tremendous stressor, especially if it is the first "serious" relationships. Some college students may be facing grief for the first time with the death of a family member or friend. Another stressor is the expectation of academic achievement. For many students, getting the high marks they received in high school is more difficult in college, especially one with high expectations or rigorous academic demands. Over half of Texas A&M's entering freshman students are in the top 10 percent of their high school class ("Texas A&M," 2002). The transition from being a member of a select group in high school to a milieu in which excellent grades are the norm may be difficult for some. Sometimes students' study skills are not sufficient and need refining. For others, being away from home for the first time leads to the mismanagement of time as students learn to balance academics with a social life (and sometimes employment). The college years are often a time of experimenting with higher risk-taking behaviors, such as sexual activity or the use of alcohol or recreational drugs (Rickgarn, 1994; Rivinus, 1990). While finding and establishing a sense of self-identity is key for all college students, gay/lesbian/bisexual/transgendered (GLBT) students face an additional transition. International students also encounter a unique situation–managing the rigors of a demanding college life while taking courses in a secondary language as well as the cultural stressors of living in a different country. Any of these transitions can contribute to a college student's feelings of isolation and loneliness. But does the presence of stressors unique to college students relate directly to the incidence of suicide?

Most researchers agree that there is no single reason a person chooses suicide, but rather it is associated with an interaction among several stressors (National Institute of Mental Health [NIMH], 2000; Rickgarn, 1994; Whitaker & Slimak, 1990), thus pointing to the cumulative effect of multiple struggles that may erode into suicidal ideation.

Risk Factors for Suicide

The American Foundation for Suicide Prevention (AFSP, 2002) estimates that 95 percent of college students who commit suicide suffer from some form of mental illness, usually depression. It is important to note that while most depressed people are not suicidal, most suicidal people are depressed (AFSP, 2002; NIMH, 2000). Increasing this risk is the presence of substance abuse, anxiety, impulsivity, rage, hopelessness, and desperation.

Risk factors identified by AFSP and NIMH include:
1. Clinical depression or other mental illnesses. It is estimated that more than 60 percent of all people who complete suicide suffer from a mood disorder, usually major depression. If alcohol abuse is present, this figure rises to 75 percent.
2. Substance abuse. Alcohol is a factor in almost 30 percent of completed suicides.
3. Familial factors. A history of suicide in one's family increases the risk for suicide, as does the presence of mental illness, substance abuse, and violence in the family home.
4. Adverse life events. Among the college population, these may include identity confusion or feelings of isolation. Situational crises such as death or divorce cause emotional distress as well.

5. Cultural or religious factors. Some cultural or religious beliefs may hold that suicide is an acceptable solution for inescapable pain or dishonor.
6. Previous suicide attempts. This factor is considered by many researchers to be the single most salient risk factor for eventual completion of suicide (Jamison, 1999). Between 20 and 50 percent of people who kill themselves have previously attempted suicide. Having access to firearms, exhibiting impulsive or aggressive tendencies, and exposure to the suicidal behavior of others (by family members or peers, or through inappropriate media coverage or fiction stories) are also considered risk factors (AFSP, 2002; NIMH 2000).

Common threads throughout these factors are the intense feelings of hopelessness and helplessness a suicidal student often feels, resulting in the belief that the only way to escape the emotional pain is to take his or her life. Suicidal students usually maintain negative feelings about themselves and their self-worth. At a time in which students are newly engaged in adult pursuits, such as career exploration or hoping to find a lifelong partner, they may feel they are not measuring up to their own and/or society's expectations. For example, if students' primary identification has been with academic success and they subsequently find they are not doing well academically, their sense of self can be knocked off kilter and their self-esteem lowered. Again, it is important to remember that most people do not complete suicide even while enduring intense psychological pain; however, researchers find that in suicide cases, this is a key component.

Social Stigma of Suicide

Helping the survivors of suicide—the grieving family, friends, and college community left behind—can be complicated by the stigma associated with suicide. Parents, having just entered the nightmare of outliving their child, now must additionally confront the manner of death itself. This deals a second devastating blow. Not only have the parents experienced the sudden, violent death of a child, but they may also feel guilt, shame, and/or embarrassment over the nature and circumstances of the death (Bolton, 2001; Fine, 1997; Prend, 1997). Sometimes the site of death is treated as a crime scene, adding further trauma to the family. The stigma surrounding suicide can complicate the grieving process for survivors, who may be wrestling with desperate, intense questions, such as, "Why was my son so miserable?" or "What could I have done to prevent this?" Parents want to protect their children, and it is nearly unimaginable for them that they were unable to prevent such self-inflicted violence.

Suicide has a long history of being forbidden and taboo; even the phrase, "committed suicide" connotes criminality. Indeed, suicide was considered a crime in some parts of the United States as late as the early 1990s and is still considered as such in some countries (Goldsmith, Pellmar, Kleinman, & Bunney, 2002; Jamison, 1999). (Wishing to distance the act from moral judgment, researchers now often replace the word "commit" with "complete.") From early centuries, suicide has been proscribed by Judaism, Christianity, and Islam as a sin, and for hundreds of years theologians and philosophers have debated whether or not suicide is a transgression against divine benevolence. The intricacies of this debate are beyond the scope of this chapter. What is evident, however, is that with the advent of increased awareness of mental illness, along with many religious institutions' mission of providing care and compassion to survivors, most major religions today do not discriminate against suicide victims and do offer traditional funeral rights ("Suicide," 2002).

What is noted among suicide survivors is the common feeling that others relate to them differently than if the death had been accidental or expected (AFSP, 2002; Bolton, 2001; Fine, 1997). Some survivors report that friends once considered close refuse to acknowledge the tragedy. At a time when grieving parents and other family members most need support from others, they do not receive the needed comfort and solace that may help make their journey more bearable. Because of this, the grieving family is often hesitant to talk about the way their child died for fear of being judged or of causing discomfort to others. Student affairs personnel should not compromise the family's grieving by casting their own moral and religious perceptions about suicide.

Working with the Grieving Family

When working with the grieving family, one should be prepared for a wide array of reactions. Some parents are eerily calm, almost robotic, as shock serves to protect them during this incomprehensible time. Others are extremely emotional, expressing anger and tears. Some may feel true physical pain. Others may simply deny that the death has occurred, or has occurred by suicide. Iserson (1999) emphasized that officials may speak of a student's death as a suicide only if it is "...very clear from the evidence and the police are treating it that way" (p. 35), noting that they must await the medical examiner's/coroner's ruling. Thus, it is important not to identify the death as a suicide until there is an official ruling as such. Dave Parrott, Dean of Student Life at Texas A&M, stated that the most important aspect of notifying others of someone's suicide (or any death) is to be "truthful but sensitive" (personal communication, December 4, 2002). Some parents want to know as many details as can be provided about their child's death, while others come to the campus, take care of affairs, and leave quickly. Each family's way of grieving and handling the news of their child's death must be respected.

Commonly, college personnel are concerned about saying and doing exactly the right thing when working with the bereaved family. Circumstances surrounding the student's death may still be under investigation when the family arrives on campus. Refer their questions about the exact cause of death to the attending medical staff or law enforcement. One way to facilitate this is to arrange such a meeting for the family. If emergency personnel are not releasing sufficient information to the family, then acknowledge the family's frustration. Listen for which fears seem to most concern the family and verbalize them. Do not dismiss them as irrational or "thinking too far ahead," and express your confidence in local law enforcement. It is also important to realize the value of simply being with them during this time, answering questions as accurately as possible, and most of all, listening. Being present during those first terrible moments, whether knowledgeable about all the facts or not, authentically relays to them that the college is also shocked and grieving. No "perfect" conversation needs to take place, no profound words need to be spoken; just the "power of presence" is helpful (Christian, 1997). The value of another accepting human being with a calming presence does more than one realizes. Student affairs staff may feel helpless after a student has completed suicide, but the truth is we can offer the family and friends valued assistance in the form of speaking and listening with sensitivity, truthfulness, and accuracy.

Kristin Harper, Senior Associate Director of Student Life at Texas A&M, stated that university personnel are not generally the ones that give death notification; that is more apt to be delivered by police officers, emergency medical personnel, or hospital staff (personal communication, December 19, 2002). However, following Texas A & M's Critical Incident Response Team (CIRT) procedures, a member of the CIRT team often goes to the hospital or funeral home to meet with the parents and offer condolences and support (2002). Harper stated, "The truth is, I don't know their son or daughter," but they can count on her to be professional, compassionate, and knowledgeable as she helps them navigate the university bureaucracy in tending to their child's affairs. If the hospital or funeral home has not provided a chaplain (and one is desired), the CIRT representative will offer to contact one of the university's campus ministers.

We live in a culture that fears death and avoids talking about it. Often we resort to euphemistic sayings that we feel somehow "soften" the blow. Most survivors are not comforted by these vague attempts to comfort, so it is recommended to avoid sayings such as "We lost him," or "She's passed over." The Compassionate Friends, Inc. (TCF) (1998), an international support group for families who have experienced a child's death, also cautions against references to "God's will" or other attempts to find something positive in the student's death ("At least you have other children;" "She didn't suffer"). The reality is that no words exist to make their child's death all right. Again, it is important to be aware of personal beliefs about suicide, moral or religious, and to avoid making statements that are insensitive and unhelpful. Assumptions should not be made about the family's religious views.

When working with bereaved parents, refer to the parents' deceased son or daughter by name. One of the greatest fears a parent has when a child dies is that he or she will be forgotten. Some people believe that bringing up the dead child's name will upset the parent or will cause the parent to begin thinking of their child. The truth is that their son or daughter is never far from their thoughts. Having someone remember their child by name can be immensely comforting. Harper noted that bereaved parents often express concern and worry about their child's friends on campus (personal communication, December 19, 2002). University staff can be instrumental in helping parents by facilitating communication and arranging personal meetings, phone calls, or delivering notes or messages. Sometimes parents do not know their child's friends well, and meeting them or having a way to contact them later will aid in their grieving process.

Harper related that years after she helped guide one family through the maze of university procedures following the suicide of their son, they have continued to keep in contact and commented on the special connection they feel with her (personal communication, December 19, 2002). She believes that some parents may sense that she understands much of what they are experiencing because she, too, has gone through losing a loved one to sudden unexpected death. While she does not mention to them the death of her younger sister when she was in high school, she mused that sometimes parents may sense this common ground between them (personal communication, January 20, 2003). The relationship she has with this family is treasured because their communication with her is heartfelt and genuine, and the family knows she has not forgotten them or their son.

Grieving parents are often not able to retain or remember verbal information in the initial meeting with a university representative; thus it is important to tell them that student affairs staff will put the information in writing. Because Texas A&M is a large university, student affairs staff can oversee many details for the parents without them needing to go to individual offices themselves. Communication with the student's professors and departments, such as financial aid and residence life, is often done by phone by a member of the Department of Student Life. Harper is also careful to forward the student's yearbook, provide the family with the cherished Aggie ring (had it been ordered), or arrange for the posthumous awarding of their child's college degree (if it had been earned). These are all examples of how student affairs staff can continue extending condolences and respect.

Critical Incident Response Team Procedures

Texas A&M, like most universities, has a Critical Incident Response Team (CIRT) which has been in place for several years, with its manual currently in its 11th edition. This team has been invaluable to the university as it responds to student crises and student death, including suicide. CIRT members include 22 representatives from the Division of Student Affairs as well as other campus and community representatives and meets at least once a year (2002). There is a smaller team comprised of eight on-call CIRT members, which is available seven days a week, 24 hours a day. This team meets weekly.

According to CIRT procedures, when a student completes suicide, a series of six steps is initiated. The University Police Department (UPD) is usually the first department on campus notified about the incident. UPD then contacts the CIRT Person On-Call via pager. During Step Two, the CIRT Person On-Call (CIRT PO-C) gathers necessary information on the incident and contacts the appropriate staff. Additionally, the CIRT PO-C proceeds immediately to the site of the incident or to the hospital. There, the CIRT PO-C may request assistance from other CIRT members. The CIRT PO-C works in conjunction with University Relations to coordinate press releases (if any). During Step Three, contact with the student's family, roommates, romantic partner, or other affected students is verified. CIRT also ensures that any additional services for the affected students are provided. Step Four entails arranging the campus visit for the family and providing them with an escort as they work to meet family needs. The family meets with the appropriate university administrators, police officers, and campus minister (if desired), and other officials as requested or needed in Step Five. The last step is for the CIRT to meet and debrief as well as to plan appropriate follow-up procedures. They also evaluate the procedures that were followed and make suggestions for revisions, if warranted (2002).

Friends Who Remain

While the family is involved in the process of taking care of university business and their child's belongings, the friends, roommates, siblings, and sometimes the romantic partner of the deceased are reacting to the suicide in their own way. Again, a wide variety of reactions can be expected and considered "normal," but shock and disbelief are initially the most commonly seen. When a student ended his life by jumping from the roof of a campus parking garage, his resident advisor commented, "I did not see any signs at all of him being depressed. I saw him yesterday and asked him how he was doing, and he smiled and said he was fine." A fellow dorm resident said, "We're all trying to figure out what's going on. There is a lot of silence" (Stirpe, 1999).

In another case, a grieving student who had been a high school and college friend of a senior who died by shooting himself said she had seen him that very night and related, "He was so happy that night, he talked about how he wanted to go to law school. When we were dropping him off at home he was talking about how we were going to an Astros game Friday night." Ironically, his acceptance to law school arrived by letter after his death. Of this same student, a friend remarked, "He had talked about suicide before, but I never said anything about it." She expressed regret that she did not inform others of his depression and was quoted in the student newspaper as encouraging students to tell someone if any of their friends ever said anything about ending their lives (Snooks, 1999). In both of these instances, friends are left with questions to which student affairs staff and counselors simply do not have the answers. There is, however, an opportunity to express the confusion and sadness we all feel, as well as to help them realize they are not responsible for not being able to foresee their friend's fatal decision.

Assisting friends who remain enrolled at A&M and who are still in profound grief is essential. As part of CIRT procedures, these students are identified early in the process, and actions are taken to provide them various offers of assistance. Sometimes notes are written to professors if these students will be missing class for a few days; other times students receive assistance with reducing their course load. Roommates are not always comfortable remaining in the dorm or apartment, especially if the suicide took place there, and a CIRT member will assist them with relocation.

The campus counseling center can be of immense help to bereaved friends of a suicide victim. At the Student Counseling Services (SCS), I have been involved in two different kinds of groups for these students. One group can be considered a debriefing group—friends come together and share their reactions—because real grieving has not yet begun. The second group takes place later, when more grief work is done. The Grief and Loss group offered at the Counseling Center provides a place of support as members journey on their paths of making sense of the death of their loved one or friend. The different stages of grief are processed, and members have opportunities to share with others who are experiencing many of the same kinds of emotions and reactions. Whether or not affected students avail themselves of these groups, it is important to offer them. Student Life administrators, residence hall advisors, and other student affairs staff, as well as faculty, are given information about the services of the SCS and are asked to encourage their students to use them.

The SCS HelpLine, a telephone crisis line staffed by trained volunteers, is also available to students in the aftermath of a friend's suicide. This service is open during all times the Counseling Center itself is closed, and it utilizes a back-up team of SCS psychologists to assist the HelpLine staff and to intervene in crises as necessary. Statistics show that the suicide rate on campus has declined since the implementation of the HelpLine in 1995 (S. Vavra, personal communication, November 21, 2002).

Remembering the Student

Some suicidologists feel that public remembrances of a person who completes suicide can result in what is known as "suicide contagion" or "copycat suicides" (see Gould, Wallenstein, & Davidson, 1989, for a comprehensive review of this subject). This phenomenon is most strikingly noted in cases of teen suicide, but has also occurred on college campuses (e.g., six students completed suicide at Michigan State University within three months of each other in 1997; New York University is investigating three apparent suicide deaths within 45 days of each other in 2003; and, Massachusetts Institute of Technology's suicide rate has also been under public scrutiny). NIMH (2000) described suicide contagion as

> ...the exposure to suicide or suicidal behaviors within one's family, one's peer group, or through media reports of suicide and it can result in an increase in suicide and suicidal behaviors. Direct and indirect exposure to suicidal behavior has been shown to precede an increase in suicidal behavior in persons at risk for suicide, especially in adolescents and young adults. (p. 19)

The CDC, aware that media coverage can influence the incidence of suicide clusters, presented recommendations from a national workshop on suicide contagion and the responsible reporting of suicide (1994). While suicide is certainly newsworthy, the recommendations state that sensitive and mindful media reporting can help reduce the risk for suicide contagion by following certain guidelines. These include refraining from presenting simplistic explanations for suicide (suicide is usually the result of many complex factors rather than one final precipitating event) or engaging in "repetitive, ongoing or excessive" suicide reporting. Another caution is avoiding sensationalizing the suicide, or divulging unnecessary morbid details of the death. Media coverage should also avoid providing detailed descriptions of how the suicide was completed in order to lessen the incidence of duplication. Also recommended is refraining from presenting the suicide as a way to accomplish certain goals (e.g., retaliating against parental discipline or dealing with a romantic break-up). Only focusing on the suicide completer's positive traits or otherwise glorifying or romanticizing suicide can also inadvertently increase the potential for suicide contagion (1994).

The report by the CDC concluded by stating, "...Reporting of suicide can have several direct benefits. Specifically, community efforts to address this problem can be strengthened by news coverage that describes the help and support available in a community, explains how to identify persons at high risk for suicide, or presents information about risk factors for suicide" (p. 17). In the Texas A&M newspaper, *The Battalion*, information about the SCS counseling services and the HelpLine phone number are always included when reporting news about suicides on campus.

Several high schools across the nation, following the CDC recommendations, have forbidden school-wide memorials or other public displays of grief, such as flying their flag at half mast, believing that these activities may glorify the student and/or his or her actions, and some universities may pattern this practice. Texas A&M does not prohibit memorials or other public displays of grief or eulogies for students' suicides. Dave Parrott, Dean of Student Life, stated that while suicide contagion can affect college-aged students, it is less likely and that "...age, life skills, and life experiences are dramatically different for adolescents than for young adults" (personal communication, December 4, 2002). Memorial services are often a comfort to students because they provide a forum in which they come together and remember the deceased student with others.

One of Texas A&M's oldest and finest traditions is that of Silver Taps. Rooted in the university's history as a military institution, this ceremony, begun in 1898, is a solemn remembrance service that honors currently enrolled students who have died during the past month. Held the first Tuesday of each month, it is eloquent in its simplicity and silence. The flag of the university is lowered to half-mast during the day, and notices are posted at several locations around campus. Lights across campus are dimmed at 10:20 p.m., and darkness and quiet surround the thousands of students who come to pay their respects. A twenty-one gun salute for each student is given, and a bugler plays Taps in the upper floor of the oldest building on campus, the Academic Building. As the ceremony draws to a close, the students disperse into the darkened campus. Afterwards, the bullet casings are collected and chromed for the families of the deceased students. This memorial ceremony is attended by the vast majority of grieving families, who are escorted by a Department of Student Life representative. Harper (2002) noted that this ceremony is "...not a time to mourn our deceased students, but a time to honor them" (personal communication, December 19, 2002). She related that families of suicide victims have commented on the meaningfulness of this remembrance and noted that several colleges and universities have inquired about this ceremony as they consider thoughtful ways of remembering students who have died.

There are other ways that parents of deceased students memorialize their children at Texas A&M. For the parents of one student who died by suicide, the establishment of a scholarship in the College of Business was helpful in their grieving process. Others galvanize their grief into action and decide to become more knowledgeable about suicide and its prevention, choosing to share their stories and information with others in an effort to stem the tide of student suicides.

From the time parents first hear of their child's suicide to several years later, university personnel can be of invaluable support and compassion. As Christian (1997) stated, "Standing with those who have experienced the pain of suicide is a special opportunity to serve." Student affairs personnel must not lose sight of their unique position to assist in the aftermath of a suicide with students, families, and friends. With sensitivity and caring, a tragic occurrence can be addressed and handled in a way that can promote healing for all.

References

American Foundation for Suicide Prevention. (2002). Retrieved November 20, 2002 from http://www.afsp.org/

Bolton, I. (2001). *My son...my son: A guide to healing after death, loss, or suicide*. Roswell, GA: Bolton Books.

Centers for Disease Control. (1994). Programs for the prevention of suicide among adolescents and young adults; and Suicide contagion and the reporting of suicide: Recommendations from a national workshop. *Morbidity and Mortality Weekly Report, 43* (RR-6), 1-18.

Centers for Disease Control. (1997). Youth risk behavior surveillance: National college health risk survey – United States, 1995. *Morbidity and Mortality Weekly Report, 46* (SS-6), 1-54.

CIRT: Critical Incident Response Team. (2002). *Official team manual* (11th ed.). Texas A&M University, Division of Student Affairs. Author.

Christian, R. (1997). After a suicide: What is the best way to serve those left behind? *Christianity Today International/Leadership Journal, 18*, p. 84. Retrieved January 7, 2003 from http://www.christianitytoday.com/le/714/714084.html

Fine, C. (1997). *No time to say goodbye: Surviving the suicide of a loved one*. New York: Broadway Books.

Gallagher, R. P., Sysko, H. B., & Zhang, B. (2001). *National survey of counseling center directors*. Alexandria, VA: International Association of Counseling Services.

Goldsmith S. K., Pellmar, T. C., Kleinman, A. M., & Bunney, W. E. (Eds.). (2002). *Reducing suicide: A national imperative*. [Electronic version]. Washington, D.C.: Institute of Medicine, National Academies Press.

Gould, M. S., Wallenstein, S., & Davidson, L. (1989). Suicide clusters; A critical review. *Suicide and Life-Threatening Behavior, 19*, 17-29.

Jamison, K. R. (1999). *Night falls fast.* New York: Vintage Books.

Iserson, K. V. (1999). *Grave words: Notifying survivors about sudden, unexpected deaths.* Tucson, AZ: Galen Press.

National Institute of Mental Health. (2000). Frequently asked questions about suicide. Retrieved December 28, 2002 from http://www.nimh.nih.gov/research/suicidefaq.cfm

National Mental Health Association and The Jed Foundation. (2002). *Safeguarding your students against suicide – expanding the safety net.* Proceedings from an expert panel on vulnerability, depressive symptoms, and suicidal behavior on college campuses. Alexandria, VA: Authors.

Prend, A. D. (1997). *Transcending loss: Understanding the lifelong impact of grief and how to make it meaningful.* New York: Berkeley Publishing.

Rickgarn, R. L. V. (1994). *Perspectives on college student suicide.* Amityville, New York: Baywood Publishing.

Rivinus, T. M. (1990). The deadly embrace: The suicidal impulse and substance use and abuse in the college student. In L. C. Whitaker & R. E. Slimak (Eds.), *College student suicide* (pp. 45-77). Binghampton, NY: The Hayworth Press.

Silverman, M. M., Meyer, P. M., Sloane, F., Raffel, M., & Pratt, D. M. (1997). The Big Ten student suicide study: A ten-year study on suicides on Midwestern university campuses. *Suicide and Life-Threatening Behavior, 27,* 285-303.

Snooks, E. R. (1999, September 14). Friends mourn passing of Texas A&M student. *The Battalion,* p. 1.

Stirpe, A. (1999, March 31). Student falls to his death. *The Battalion,* p. 1.

Suicide. (2002). Microsoft Encarta Online Encyclopedia. Retrieved December 29, 2002 from http://encarta.msn.com

Suicide FAQ. (n.d.). American Foundation for Suicide Prevention. Retrieved November 30, 2002 from http://www.afsp.org/index-1.htm

Suicide – Frequently Asked Questions. (1996). Retrieved December 29, 2002 from http://www.faqs.org/faqs/suicide/info/

Texas A&M facts & stats. (2002). Retrieved December 27, 2002 from http://www.tamu.edu/univrel/sheets/a02.html

The Compassionate Friends. (1998). *How can I help? When a child dies* [Brochure]. Oak Brook, IL: Author.

The Jed Foundation. (2000). Suicide and America's youth. Retrieved December 30, 2002 from www.jedfoundation.org/suicide.html

Whitaker, L. C. & Slimak, R. E. (Eds.). (1990). *College student suicide.* Binghampton, New York: The Hayworth Press.

Part IV

In Remembrance

13

Spontaneous Shrines:
The Expression of Communal Grief at
Texas A&M University following the
1999 Bonfire Collapse

Sylvia Grider

*Spontaneous shrines at sites of traumatic death and disaster reflect responses
to the grieving process. Shrines and memorials are useful for many to express
feelings of shock and loss, and universities can facilitate the maintaining and
dismantling of them. A university's memorial to the traumatic death of some of
its students provides a tangible example of a community response to its pain.*

Apparently, starting with the unprecedented public response to the Vietnam
Veterans Memorial, the creation of spontaneous shrines at sites of traumatic
death and disaster has emerged as a modern grieving ritual. Although leaving
candles and flowers at death sites, cemeteries, and memorials has long been part
of the traditions of many cultures, visitors to the Vietnam Veterans Memorial
inexplicably began leaving medals, clothing, art works, posters, and other unusual memorabilia along the base of "The Wall." This phenomenon has since
generalized throughout the United States, Australia/New Zealand, England, and
parts of western Europe. Today, the inclusion of idiosyncratic and mundane
secular objects such as teddy bears and t-shirts in shrines marking the sites of
traumatic death and disaster is commonplace and even expected. Perhaps the
most spectacular recent expressions of this new tradition were the shrines constructed throughout New York City, especially at fire stations, following 9/11.

*Sylvia Grider is an Associate Professor in the Department of Anthropology at Texas
A&M University. From 1999 to 2005 she served as Director of Texas A&M University's
Bonfire Memorabilia Project. She has written extensively in the areas of folklore, history,
literature, and material culture.*

Although school shootings, such as at Columbine High School, have frequently resulted in spontaneous shrines, other campus tragedies are marked in this manner as well. In the predawn of November 18, 1999, the huge student-constructed Bonfire on the campus of Texas A&M University suddenly broke apart and collapsed, killing twelve students and injuring scores more. The tradition at A&M is to refer to Bonfire, capitalized and with no article. Students at Texas A&M, known as Aggies, built these bonfires before the annual football game with arch-rival University of Texas. Although there had been injuries and occasional deaths off-campus through the years—generally related to car wrecks and cutting down trees for Bonfire—the total collapse of the 1999 stack and catastrophic degree of death and injury were unexpected and traumatic.

The exact location changed over the years, but Bonfire was always built on the campus, making it accessible to the widest possible range of student participation. The 1999 location was on the vast campus green space known as the Polo Field, bordered by the main intersection in College Station, Texas Avenue, and University Drive, so the stack and subsequent catastrophe were highly visible. American college campuses are often regarded as sanctuaries, where students and faculty are safe from the pressures and dangers of the outside world as they engage in the pursuit of knowledge. That the collapse was on the main campus, within sight of the main administration building, contributed to the shock and disbelief experienced by the community as a whole, as well as by the students, faculty, and staff who lived, studied, and worked on the campus. For many of the students, the collapse of Bonfire was their first direct experience with disaster.

For approximately twenty-four hours after the accident, the site was filled with emergency vehicles, cranes, law-enforcement personnel, media trucks, and hundreds of volunteers (mostly students) helping move the tangled logs as the dead and injured students were pulled from the wreckage. The football team decided to forego their regularly scheduled practice for the upcoming UT game and instead came out to the site and helped move logs. Thousands of stunned students and townspeople stood silently on the Polo Field watching the rescue efforts and grieving together. The students vowed to stay at the site until the last Aggie was taken from the stack. As nighttime grew colder, the local TV station issued a plea for blankets and sweatshirts to be taken out to the site because the students refused to leave, even to go back to their dorms and apartments for warm clothing. This poignant vigil was intensified when word spread among the crowd that twelve students had been killed (not all of the students died at the site; some died in local hospitals).

Twelve is a number with extraordinary symbolic significance to Aggies. One of the most remarkable Aggie traditions is the student body standing throughout football games, symbolizing their willingness to suit up and join the team on the field if needed; the student body is known as The Twelfth Man. This tradition dates back to 1922 when so many Aggie football players were injured during a game that the coach had a student not on the team suit up anyway, just in case he was needed. For days after the bonfire accident, in a show of solidarity and grief, hundreds of students wore t-shirts and jerseys emblazoned with the number twelve. As soon as all the dead and injured students were removed from the stack, a temporary security fence was erected around the site in order to secure it for investigation into the causes of the accident. In a process remarkably similar to the public response to the bombing of the federal building in Oklahoma City, in the days and weeks following the bonfire accident, this fence became the focus of a vast spontaneous shrine composed of thousands of grief offerings brought to the campus by students and the extended Aggie family. A candlelight vigil attended by an estimated 15,000 to 20,000 people was held at the site the night before the game, when Bonfire had been scheduled to burn. Memorabilia from the vigil became part of the shrine. The 1999 A&M versus UT football game was held at Kyle Field on the A&M campus, and after the game fans from both schools went out to the bonfire site; many left memorabilia from the game there, such as football tickets, used and unused.

Smaller shrines developed at other campus sites, among them the flagpole of the near-by Systems Administration Building, but the shrine at the bonfire site attracted the most grieving pilgrims and accumulated the most memorabilia. There is no way to know how many thousands of people visited the shrines, nor the percentage of those visitors who chose to leave memorabilia there. The memorabilia ranged from religious items, such as crosses and rosaries; to children's toys and drawings; to Aggie-related items, the most remarkable of which was an assemblage of Aggie class rings. (All but one of these rings were returned to their owners by the Former Students' Association. The name was deliberately filed out of the ring, which is now part of the Bonfire Memorabilia Collection.)

Memorabilia began accumulating at the shrine almost immediately following the accident, as student workers left behind their "pots" (decorated helmets) and "grodes" (work clothes) and tools as the area was being cleared by emergency personnel. The shrine remained in place until the last of the memorabilia was finally removed the day before the university closed for the Christmas holidays. Throughout the month that the shrines were in place, there was growing concern statewide about preserving this remarkable outpouring of communal grief. Within the context of the importance of traditions in Aggieland and the depth of the emotion surrounding the bonfire collapse, the memorabilia took on enormous symbolic importance. Dozens of people came out to the site independently and systematically photographed all of the memorabilia, trying to create a permanent record. Student leaders discussed various plans for gathering the memorabilia, but all recognized the daunting enormity of such an undertaking.

As a folklorist, for the past few years I had been studying the spontaneous shrine phenomenon, starting with the eccentric and whimsical shrine in Austin, Texas, when the historic Treaty Oak was poisoned there in 1989. I was intrigued by the outpouring of grief exemplified in the spontaneous shrines worldwide following the death of Princess Diana, as well as the shrines in the aftermath of the Oklahoma City bombing and the various school shootings, primarily at Columbine High School in Littleton, Colorado. It was obvious that the Bonfire shrine fit into this modern grief ritual.

The Anthropology Department, of which I am a part, specializes in archaeology and archeological conservation. The weekend after the accident, as I sat in my car at midnight watching the enormous crowds quietly visiting the floodlit bonfire shrine, I realized that as a major research university we had all of the necessary resources—ranging from professional archaeological expertise to volunteers to supplies and equipment—available to gather and preserve the memorabilia from what we later called this "archive of grief" (Grider, 2000). After the Thanksgiving holidays, we mobilized the Bonfire Memorabilia Project, under my direction, and during two collecting periods (December 2-3 and December 20) systematically collected and inventoried all of the memorabilia left at the primary campus shrines. Following the precedent set when the London shrines for Princess Diana were dismantled, the flowers were composted by personnel from the landscape maintenance division of the Physical Plant.

Students have been involved in the Bonfire Memorabilia Project from the very beginning, when student leaders agreed to a faculty-led project. We all worked and grieved together as members of the Aggie family—students, faculty, staff, and administrators. Student dedication to the project was so complete that during the awful last day of the collecting process, when we were all miserable from the wind and driving rain and physical exhaustion, they crawled on their hands and knees around the then-bare fence to make sure that we had gathered absolutely everything so that not one precious memento would be left behind in the mud.

The over 5,000 artifacts and 4,000 photographs, as well as clipping archives of the Bonfire Memorabilia Project, are boxed and temporarily stored in the Anthropology Building. We are in the process of preparing the catalog and final report and will continue working with the conservation and curation of the collection in preparation for possible exhibit at some future date. The artifacts in the collection have a powerful emotional effect on all who work with them, from professional staff to student workers and volunteers. The intensity of the overwhelming communal grief following the accident is embodied in the thousands of notes, posters, artworks, articles of clothing, and other memorabilia contained in the collection.

References

Grider, S. (2000). The archaeology of grief: Texas A&M's Bonfire tragedy is a sad study in modern mourning. *Discovering Archaeology, 2*, 68-74.

14

Dedications, Memorials, and Posthumous Awards

Jerome Weber and Katherine Garlough

University administrators oversee dedications, awards, and memorials for deceased students. Often, the Office of Development or Institutional Advancement can assist in attending to family and student needs in the memorial aspect of institutional response to death. In such a response, universities can provide a lasting act of remembrance for family and friends.

Even for those in the prime of life and in enviable circumstances, catastrophe can strike, bringing promising life to a sudden end through a variety of circumstances. One need only read the newspapers to find examples of college students whose lives have ended tragically, leaving their families and campus communities bereft. One study (Euster, 1991) has indicated that memorials had multiple benefits, including easing the pain of the family and providing financial support for campus programs important to the student. However, a small sample of institutions contacted in preparation for writing this chapter showed that most campuses have relatively little in the way of policies and procedures to offer those inquiring as to how to initiate a memorial. It is hoped that the observations contained in this chapter will help those who are interested in creating a memorial to an enrolled student who has died.

The question of which campus personnel should oversee dedications, awards, and memorials will vary by institution. For most campuses, large or small, the responsibility for dedications and memorials will fall to the institutional officer charged with private fund raising. A large gift to a university averages seven years to realize, thereby conferring a long-term relationship with the bereaved family and enhancing the significance of the personnel involved

Jerome C. Weber, Ph.D., is Regents' Professor at The University of Oklahoma with appointments in the Colleges of Education and Arts and Sciences. He served in central administration for over 20 years. In October 2005 he was inducted into the Oklahoma Higher Education Hall of Fame. Katherine Garlough, Ph.D., is the executive director of International Development for Enterprise and Autonomy, the author of several international grants, and an instructor at Oklahoma City Community College.

(Worth, 1993, p. 135). Whether that individual carries a title such as Vice President for University Development, Vice President for Business, or Vice President for Student Affairs, it is the institution's responsibility to respond quickly, clearly, and with compassion and understanding in the very difficult circumstances that would accompany an inquiry into ways of memorializing a deceased loved one. However, the family desiring to inquire into such a matter may not be aware of the existence of a development office or other institutional personnel familiar with such procedures. Thus, all institutional offices dealing with any aspect of student life or fund raising should know how to direct inquires when they arise.

It is the charge of the development officer to balance the "needs and best interests of the donor and the donor's relatives, with the institution's own needs and best interests" (Elliot, 1995, p. 10). The language of fundraising theory identifies two basic approaches to giving: exchange theory expresses offers in terms of opportunities, while altruism theory expresses the discharge of an obligation. While fund raising is moving more in the direction of exchange theory, in the case of the bereaved family the language of altruism is often more appropriate. According to the theory of altruism, the fundraiser approaches the family with the means and a method to give voice and visibility to the principles and moral convictions of the family they determine to be appropriate in their choice of memorial (Elliot, 1995, p. 46).

Often there is no real institutional policy on memorials for students who die while enrolled. Certainly, there is a special obligation to work with survivors as closely as possible to achieve their memorial wish. As for the Development Office, it may manage such gifts consistent with their usual practices, but sensitivity to the situation must be of paramount importance. Basically, memorials originate from (a) the survivors, which are handled on a case-by-case basis depending on the donation involved and the family's desires, or (b) the institution, which may have a tradition of bestowals, memorials, or awards given in memory of a deceased student. At times, the circumstances of the student's passing are so sympathetically pervasive to the university community that the institution is inspired to take exceptional measures to memorialize.

Donations to the University

The family may have specific ideas about donations, and funeral notifications will often carry a notation to the effect that memorial donation can be made to a particular charity or organization. From the perspective of the potential donor, what is most important to remember is that it is possible to support or create almost any sort of permanent memorial that is consistent with the memory of the individual being memorialized, assuming that such a memorial is also consistent with the principles of the institution.

While scholarship funds and contributions to ongoing campaigns are obvious vehicles, there is little to restrict the possibilities, other than imagination and the resources available for the purpose. Regardless of the field of study of the deceased student, s/he may have had an interest different from their intended profession, which may provide a glimpse into additional opportunities for support. One example might be support of an ongoing lecture series keyed to an area of the student's interests. For example, if the student was interested in literature or film, the institution might have a lecture series named after the student, designed to bring speakers with this interest to campus, either as a one-time event or on a continuing basis. A student who was interested in physical fitness might be remembered best by means of a contribution to the institution's fitness center. An art exhibit or musical performance by a visiting artist could be supported and named for the deceased student.

Those who work in university development and student affairs are probably aware, if only from their reading of *The Chronicle of Higher Education*, if not from their own experience, of instances in which contributions were accepted for particular purposes that were not sufficiently clarified between the donor and the receiving institution, creating confusion and resentment as a result of misunderstandings (Murphy, 1997, p. 60). What are the tenets the family wishes to impose as far as eligibility or use? If it is a scholarship, is the money simply given to the recipient to use as s/he wishes? In some cases the donors may expect control over the use of the funds donated, such as naming the recipient of an endowed chair. In other instances, the donor may expect the dollars to be used in a way that differs from that intended by the institution. As an example, the creation of an endowed chair in Ethnic Studies might be used to support another area of study. While particular restrictions a family may wish to impose on a potential scholarship recipient might be difficult to accept, particularly for a public institution, the fundamental ethical consideration is that "a gift given with restrictions is restricted, and the restrictions must be honored" (Rhodes, 1997, p. xxiii). Funds from a restricted gift demand the highest level of institutional integrity as to their application.

However, a poor fit between donor and institution does not mean that the family's intent may not be appropriately fulfilled; it may be channeled to a more appropriate means. For instance, if it is the family's desire that funding in a student's memory be restricted to students of a particular religion, it may be possible to do so by utilizing a mechanism outside the institution itself to serve as the vehicle for funding. Almost all campuses will have campus clergy who represent a wide variety of faiths and who provide a source of spiritual guidance to students of those faiths. A scholarship for Baptist students could be set up through the Baptist Student Union, for Jewish students through the Hillel Foundation, for Catholic students through the Newman Society, for Methodist students through the Wesley Foundation, etc. For those interested in such an approach, almost any college's student affairs office should be able to offer the names and contact numbers of appropriate personnel. The lesson to be learned is that the receipt of funds, unaccompanied by common understandings and expectations on the part of both the donor and recipient, can result in embarrassment to everyone involved, thus souring what had been intended to be a positive relationship.

Endowed Scholarships

Many families and friends wishing to memorialize a student will consider an endowed scholarship that will help other students. By placing the donation in an endowment and utilizing the interest earned to fund a scholarship, the scholarship becomes self-perpetuating so that every year a student will be honored with a scholarship in the name of the deceased. The emotional authenticity and appropriateness of this option is apparent. A question may arise when considering the restrictions of a new scholarship or adding funds to already-existing scholarships. One advantage to donating to an existing scholarship is that the mechanisms are already in place within the institution for contributions of any size. The existing scholarship can be augmented by donations in memory of the deceased student. Donations to a scholarship fund are not constrained by time, and regardless of how long after the death of the student, these donations will be well received and well utilized.

As in any situation in which the institution must deal with a potential donor, thought must be given to financial considerations. For example, consider a case in which the object is to endow a new scholarship in the deceased student's name. For purposes of illustration, consider a modest scholarship that might provide $500 per semester to a recipient to help with expenses, such as the purchase of books, supplies, tuition, and similar items. Given the costs of college attendance, it would be a modest sum indeed, but it would take a gift of $20,000 to create a permanent scholarship that provides the recipient $1,000 each academic year. A rule of thumb is that private funds can be invested in such a way as to allow the institution to utilize an average of 5% earnings of the fund per year. While this might have seemed like a very low return at a time when annual investment returns were in double digits, the 5% figure recognizes that the market falls as well as rises and is generally seen as a reasonable average return to count on when discussing the creation of an endowed fund to last in perpetuity.

When a family has specific ideas or restrictions about memorizing a student in a particular fashion, the matter can quickly become complicated. Few institutions would have an objection to restricting a scholarship, for example, to a junior or senior student majoring in a particular field of study who has maintained a specified minimum grade-point average. On the other hand, many institutions, particularly public institutions, would have some reservations or restrictions about limiting eligibility to those of a particular race, ethnicity, or gender. Even though the source of these funds is not the federal government, therefore making these restrictions automatically illegal, they might be seen as inappropriate in the overall institutional context. The same restrictions, legal or otherwise, might not exist in a different context. For instance, it might be seen as perfectly appropriate to restrict eligibility for a new scholarship to those of a particular religion in a religiously affiliated institution, which would, by definition, be a private institution. The obvious lesson for institutions would be to have clear guidelines as to exactly what figures are used to calculate the dollars available to the recipient of a newly established scholarship, and within what parameters the eligibility and use of those dollars must lie. Any institution wishing to conduct its business in a responsible manner must, as a matter of policy, look each "gift horse" in the mouth.

Dedications

An alternative choice for the family wishing to memorialize a student may be a contribution to an institution's capital campaign, those fund raising campaigns that are generally designed to help the institution meet non-recurring costs such as building a classroom building or buying computer equipment. Capital campaigns are often of great magnitude, with a number of institutions today conducting billion-dollar, multi-year campaigns. When means are relatively unlimited a sufficient contribution can result in the naming of a college or a building, but this typically requires a contribution of a magnitude beyond most people's means. However, a contribution made in a deceased student's name to his/her institution is a wonderful way to remember that student.

It is always possible for a donor to come to the development office with a certain size donation in mind and inquire as to what such an amount can accomplish. In cases in which an individual, former student or not, is being memorialized, visibility and permanence are often significant considerations in the minds of the potential donors. If available, a contribution to a particular program of study or project with which the student was associated can increase the sense of identity. One obvious advantage of such a mechanism is that funds are given on a one-time basis and can be dedicated to a named memorial. A classroom, a computer laboratory, or a dance studio may display a plaque indicating a donation and dedicating the gift to the memory of a student. These types of opportunities will exist in every institution, regardless of size or type. Again from the perspective of the institution, it is wise to have available a list of such naming opportunities, not only for cases in which a student is to be memorialized, but also for good fund-raising practices in general.

Regardless of the issue of visibility, most potential donors want to have a clear idea of how their funds will be used, even assuming they do not come to the institution with a specific plan for the utilization of those funds. It is the rare donor who gives unrestricted funds to an institution to use as it wishes. Most donors, whether memorializing a student or not, specify how the dollars are to be spent. A campus with a well-planned and sophisticated development program should have many giving opportunities. Opportunities to give should present a wide array of options and costs and provide meaningful and permanent enhancements that serve both the institution's and the donor's purposes. Campus landscape features offer a number of opportunities for the creation of permanent memorials. As an example, a campus might have outdoor benches with plaques attached that provide an attractive landscape feature for the campus, add to the comfort of persons on campus, and also serve as an attractive memorial. Other landscape choices may involve planting trees in memory of individuals or providing an endowment for the cost of maintaining gardens located on the campus.

As noted earlier, one of the responsibilities of the well-prepared institution is to have a variety of such opportunities available for consideration, representing many areas of the institution's activities and allowing for widely varying costs. It would be difficult to overstate how disconcerting it might be to a family or group wanting to memorialize a deceased student, to be faced with a situation in which the relevant institutional personnel seem unprepared to respond with carefully and thoughtfully prepared options for consideration. Likewise, the family or group must be aware of how expensive some of these options may be and should be prepared to consider offering their contribution within the context of ongoing activities.

Case: Institutional Awards

The Aviles case presented here in a series of newspaper quotes exemplifies the circumstance of a student's passing that was so sympathetically pervasive to the community that the institution was inspired to take exceptional measures to memorialize him. In order to fully appreciate the magnitude of the Florida State University bestowal and Aviles' impact on his community, it must be noted that Aviles never attended FSU; he was an outstanding prospective student already accepted by the university community as one of their own. The institutional awards of honorary alumnus, a memorial ceremony, and the full scholarship passing to the sibling are examples of the range and depth of dedications in which the institution may have liberty to apply to special circumstances.

> Andy graduated third in his class at Robinson High School. He postponed a full academic scholarship at Florida State University, where he planned to study business, to serve in the Marine Reserves (Dyer, 2006).

> But Aviles differed from his clique, many of whom got retail jobs instead of college handbooks. Aviles was getting out-bound for Florida State University on a full scholarship after a quick tour in Iraq with the 4th Assault Amphibian Battalion (Wexler, 2003).

> Marine Lance Cpl Andre Aviles of Tampa put off a full academic scholarship at Florida State University because he felt he had a "moral obligation" to serve his country only to be killed in the early stages of the war in Iraq (FSU press release, 2003).

> More than 1,000 people attended Aviles' funeral in Tampa. A hero's burial at Arlington National Cemetery followed. The city and county issued proclamations honoring him. FSU [Florida State University] made him an honorary alumnus and gave a full scholarship to his brother, Matthew, who will start there next fall (Arlington, 2004).

> On Tuesday, FSU President T.K. Wetherell honored Aviles' military service and academic accomplishments by making him an honorary alumnus in a ceremony attended by Aviles' family and friends. "Andrew exemplifies everything that is great about this country and this university," Wetherell

said. "He was a dedicated patriot, an outstanding student, and he excelled in everything he did. FSU would have been a better place if Andrew had come here. I hope that by naming him an honorary alumnus this university can show its appreciation to Andrew and his family" (FSU press release, 2003).

Posthumous Degrees

Among the considerations of institutional awards that should be addressed as a matter of institutional policy is whether it is appropriate to award a degree posthumously. It is likely to have great emotional meaning to a grieving family and may be considered when an institution's policies allow such action. For private institutions, this is often a wholly internal matter. For public institutions, depending on the extent to which such matters are controlled by the state's higher education coordinating agency, judgments external to the institution may be involved. While there clearly is no single, appropriate answer applicable to all institutions, the following are two examples of policy and procedure.

The University of Virginia's policy states:
> Upon the recommendation of the faculty of the appropriate school, the general faculty of the University may make a posthumous award of the degree or degrees the student was pursuing if all requirements were likely to have been completed during the final year for which the student was registered had it not been for the intervention of death or debilitating illness. It shall be the responsibility of the Vice President for Student Affairs to assure that appropriate procedures to implement this policy are established in the various schools of the University. The policy shall be retroactive (University of Virginia).

The University of Oregon's policy states:
> Upon learning that a student has died, the Dean of Students will consult with the Registrar, the major department, and, where appropriate, the Dean of the Graduate School to determine if the student is eligible for a posthumous degree. If the student possessed appropriate academic credentials at the time of death, and the family wishes, the Dean of Students shall recommend that the University President authorize the posthumous issuance of the appropriate degree (University of Oregon).

Regardless of the nature of the institution, the awarding of a posthumous degree should be a policy matter that is not decided on the emotional context of an individual set of circumstances. The need for the institution to appear clear of purpose and consistent in application under such circumstances must remain wholly separate from any issue of gift to the institution. While it would be far more pleasant to assume that the need for policy to respond to a posthumous degree inquiry may never arise, it would seem imprudently optimistic to count on that being the case.

Conclusions

The institution must consider donations that are appropriate in terms of the institutional mission, as well as long-term costs such as maintenance, in addition to initial costs. The acceptance of a donation is not automatic. While these and additional factors are part of the institution's considerations in determining acceptance, it is paramount that college officers communicate clearly and empathically so that survivors and the institution craft mutually satisfying arrangements when such an unfortunate need arises. It would seem wise for this to be clearly set out in institutional policy assuring a clear and consistent response when such a need arises. Thus, while death is not something normally associated with college students, it is important to recognize that it does occur and the wishes of the family and friends of the deceased student must be carefully considered whether in the form of contributions to existing programs or the establishment of new programs. From the perspective of the institution, the humane and wise administration will hope fervently that the need to respond to such circumstances will not arise, but will plan carefully for the possibility that it may, thus allowing the institution's response to be clear, appropriate, consistently applied, and communicated with respect, grace, and sensitivity.

References

Arlington National Cemetery Website. (2006). Andrew Julian Aviles, Lance Corporal, United States Marine Corps. Retrieved: August 27, 2006. Available: http://www.arlingtoncemetery.net/andrew-aviles.htm

Elliot, D. (Ed.). (1995). *Dilemmas in higher education fund raising: The ethics of asking.* Baltimore: John Hopkins.

Euster, G. L. (1991). Memorial contributions: Remembering the elderly deceased and supporting the bereaved. *Omega Journal of Death and Dying, 23,*169-179.

Duke University: Trinity College. (2006). Retrieved April 24, 2006. Available: http://www.aas.duke.edu/trinity/t-reqs/bereavement.html

Dyer, E. (2006, April 8). Vigil honors fallen Marine. *St. Petersburg Times*, pp. 3B. Retrieved: August 27,2006. Available: http://pqasb.pqarchiver.com/sptimes/acess/1017948971.html?dids=1017948971:1017948971&FMT=FT&FMTS=ABS:FT&date=Apr+8%2C+2006&author=ELISABETH+DYER&pub=St.+Petersburg+Times&desc=Vigil+honors+fallen+Marine

Florida State University Press Release. (2003). Retrieved April 24, 2006. *FSU honors marine killed in Iraqi conflict.* Available: http://www.fsu.edu/~unicomm/ pages/releases/2003_07/release_chrono_0307.htm

Murphy, M. K. (Ed.). (1997). *The advancement president and the academy: Profiles in institutional leadership.* Council for Advancement and Support of Education: American Council on Education: Series on Higher Education, Phoenix: Oryx Press.

Rhodes, F. (Ed.). (1997). *Successful fund raising for higher education: The advancement of learning.* Council for Advancement and Support of Education: American Council on Education: Series on Higher Education. Phoenix: Oryx Press.

University of North Carolina, Charlotte. (2006). Retrieved April 24, 2006. Available: http://www.legal.uncc.edu/policies/ps-80.html.

University of Oregon. (2004). University of Oregon Policy Statement: 2.000 Academic and Curricular Procedures. Retrieved April 24, 2006.Available: http://policies.uoregon.edu/ch2a.html

University of Virginia. (2004). University regulations: Posthumous degrees. Retrieved April 24, 2006. Available: http://www.virginia.edu/registrar/records/98ugradrec/chapter5/uchap5-1.22.html

Wexler, K. (2003, April 23). *Iraq: Victim of war is laid to rest.* St. Petersburg Times. Retrieved April 24, 2006. Available: http://www.sptimes.com/2003/04/23/Hillsborough/ Victim _of_war_is_laid.shtml

Worth, M. (Ed.). (1993). *Educational fund raising: Principles and practices.* Council for Advancement and Support of Education: American Council on Education: Series on Higher Education. Phoenix: Oryx Press.

15

Marshall University Plane Crash, A Triumph of Will

Steve Wulf

Reprint permission has been secured from TIME Magazine.
Original printing November 24, 1997.

Even without knowing its significance, a visitor would be mesmerized by the fountain on the campus of Marshall University in Huntington, W.Va. Water flows from the top of 75 strands of steel shaped and forged to look like a gigantic flower. On this particular autumn Saturday morning, the steady trickle is the only sound on a campus that will soon shake with cheers.

They love the Thundering Herd in Huntington. Stand anywhere in this Rust Belt, Bible Belt city of 60,000, twirl around, and you will see at least one green-and-white GO HERD sign. Young and old are wearing shirts and hats with the Heisman Trophy symbol and MARSHALL 99 on them—acknowledging the presence among them of wide receiver and Heisman Trophy candidate Randy Moss. Last year the Herd went 15-0 to win the national championship of 1-AA. This year, in its 100th season of college football, Marshall is playing in Division 1 for the first time in a long, long time, and it has a chance to go 11-2 and win the championship of the Mid-American Conference (MAC), the conference that once expelled it. These are great days to be one with the Herd.

There is a day, however, that Marshall would like to forget. Last week the water in the fountain was turned off until next spring, the football players gathered for a solemn ceremony, three wreaths were placed at the foot of the

Steve Wulf is the coauthor of the bestseller Baseball Anecdotes *(Oxford University Press), as well as the coauthor of* I Was Right On Time, *the autobiography of Negro Leagues legend Buck O'Neil. A founding editor of* ESPN The Magazine, *Wulf has also been on the staff of* Time *and* Sports Illustrated, *and written for* Entertainment Weekly, Life, the Wall Street Journal, *and the* Economist.

fountain, and taps was played one more time. Under a cloudy sky, people close to Marshall recalled Nov. 14, 1970. But then they remember that date on an almost continual basis. As Marshall football coach and former Herd running back Bob Pruett says, "I think I speak for a lot of people when I tell you that on that day, the bottom of my heart fell out."

High above James F. Edwards Field, Keith Morehouse, the play-by-play man for the Thundering Herd Network, and color commentator Ulmo ("Sonny") Randle are calling third-quarter action for viewers of Marshall's game with visiting Eastern Michigan University. Actually, the broadcasters are gently chiding Marshall fans for being too quiet.

"Seems like a fog of lethargy has fallen the crowd, Sonny."

"They might be spoiled by all this success, Keith. Or else they're worried about turning their clocks back tonight."

"First down, Marshall...and there's some polite golf applause...It wasn't that long ago that these fans would cheer louder for a long incomplete pass."

Indeed, Marshall has the winningest football program in America in the '90s. But in the '70s, Marshall's was the worst team in the nation—22 wins in 10 years. The Herd had one 12-game losing streak and two 10-game losing streaks. A petition was even circulated around campus to drop football. Had Marshall done that, though, the tragedy would have deepened. "Seventy-five people would have died in vain," says Morehouse.

On Nov. 14, 1970, Marshall lost a 17-14 heartbreaker at East Carolina—its sixth defeat in nine games. Still, as the players, coaches and boosters boarded the Southern Airways DC-9 in Greenville, N.C., there was the feeling of promise, as well as of escape from the winless seasons of '67 and '68 and a subsequent recruiting scandal that had got Marshall thrown out of the MAC.

It was a rainy, windy night, and none of the crewmembers had ever landed at Tri-State Airport, which is located on a tabletop plateau close to the Kentucky-West Virginia-Ohio border. At 7:42 p.m., as it was about to land, the plane clipped the tops of the trees west of Runway 11 and crashed into an Appalachian hillside with a full load of fuel. Onboard the plane were 37 players, 25 supporters, eight coaches and five crewmembers. None of them survived the fiery crash, the worst ever involving an American sports team. One of the victims was sportscaster Gene Morehouse, who was also the school's sports-information director and the father of six children.

"I was nine years old at the time," says Keith. "All I knew was that I had lost my father. I didn't think about all the doctors and civic leaders and coaches and players, all the other children who lost parents in the crash, all the parents who lost children."

The force of the blow to the city of 60,000 and the college of 9,000 was immeasurable. Among those lost in the crash were head coach Rick Tolley and athletic director Charles Kautz, four physicians, a city councilman, a state legislator, a car dealer and several prominent businessmen. And the pain wasn't confined to Huntington alone. Four of the players—including Ted Shoebridge, the starting quarterback, and Arthur Harris Jr., the team's leading rusher and pass receiver—were from northern New Jersey. As fate would have it, Arthur Harris Sr. was also on the plane because he had been offered a seat by assistant coach Deke Brackett. And as fate would have it, assistant coach William ("Red") Dawson was not on the plane. It had been decided that he, along with graduate assistant Gale Parker, would drive back from North Carolina in the car that Dawson had been using for a recruiting trip.

Parker and Dawson heard about the crash on the car radio. Keith Morehouse was home watching The Newlywed Game with his mother and his twin sister when the bulletin flashed across the screen. "My mother shrieked and started making frantic phone calls," Keith recalls. "People started coming over, and it was a blur after that." Longtime Huntington residents can tell you without hesitation where they were when they first heard the news—at the drive-in movie theater, in a restaurant, at a dance. Jack Hardin, a police reporter for the Huntington Herald-Dispatch, rushed to the airport not knowing what plane had gone down. When a Baptist minister, who had got to the crash site before him, showed him a wallet and asked him if he knew the name Lionel Theodore Shoebridge Jr., Hardin thought, "Oh, my God."

The task of identifying the bodies was both excruciating and excruciatingly slow. A wake was held in Lyndhurst, N.J., for Teddy Shoebridge even before his body was positively identified. Six victims were never identified; today, those six bodies are buried in adjacent graves next to a monument in Spring Hill Cemetery, which overlooks the Marshall campus.

The task of rebuilding the football team fell briefly to Dawson, then to new coach Jack Lengyel. Thankfully, a few of the players from the 1970 squad had not made the East Carolina trip because of injuries, and the NCAA gave Marshall special permission to play freshmen. President Richard Nixon sent Lengyel a letter of encouragement, writing, "Friends across the land will be rooting for you, but whatever the season brings, you have already won your greatest victory by putting the 1971 varsity squad on the field."

The "Young Thundering Herd," as Lengyel labeled it, did win two games that season, the first a miraculous 15-13 win over Xavier in the second game of the year. But Marshall settled into a perfectly understandable futility after that '71 season. Sonny Randle, the great NFL receiver, arrived in 1979 to breathe fire into the program, and while he did lay the foundation for the future, he left Marshall after winning 12 games and losing 42 in five seasons. In 1984 the team had its first winning season in 20 years, and the Herd hasn't had a losing season since. In 1992 host Marshall defeated Youngstown State, 31-28, to win the Division I-AA championship.

Covering that game for WOWK-TV in Huntington was Keith Morehouse. "I don't think I was consciously trying to follow in my father's footsteps," he says, "but that's the way it turned out." He enrolled at Marshall in the fall of '79 as a broadcast-journalism major and covered the football team for the school newspaper. By then, he had already met his future bride. The summer after his senior year in high school, Keith was in Myrtle Beach, S.C., when he ran into

Debbie Hagley, a girl from a different Huntington high school. "I knew immediately who she was because the names of the victims are emblazoned in the minds of all the survivors," says Keith. Her father and mother, Dr. Ray Hagley and Shirley Hagley, were on that plane, and left behind six children. "I didn't have it easy," says Keith, "but she had it much tougher than I did."

Bonded by the tragedy, Keith and Debbie Morehouse were married in 1985. They have a 6-year old son, Lake, who is already an avid Thundering Herd fan. "He's got a football autographed by coach Pruett," says Keith, "and one of those big foam No. 1 hands. Debbie also decorated his room in green-and-white wallpaper."

Over lunch at a steak house outside Huntington, some men are talking about Randy Moss, the wonderfully gifted wide receiver whom Marshall inherited after 1) Notre Dame turned him away because of a battery charge, and 2) Florida State kicked him out when he admitted to having smoked marijuana. In the eyes of Marshall boosters, however, Moss's biggest crime is insensitivity. It seems he was quoted earlier this fall as having said the plane crash was "nothing big" to him.

"Give him a break," says the tall, impressive-looking man in work clothes. "I'm sure he didn't know what he was saying. People around here don't like the way he wears his hair in braids or the rap music he plays. Heck, I used to get kidded for wearing a crew cut and listening to Hank Williams. 'Course, I wasn't as good a receiver as he was."

Red Dawson—the speaker—was pretty good though. And like Moss, he was a blessing to Marshall from Florida State. Dawson arrived in Huntington in 1968 after a brief stint as a tight end for the Boston Patriots. He was an All-American at Florida State, the "other end" down the line from legend Fred Biletnikoff. "Freddy used to say one of the hardest times he was ever hit was when I ran the wrong route and collided with him," says Dawson. "I'm here to tell you, it was Freddy who ran the wrong route."

Dawson is president of the successful Red Dawson Construction Co. in Huntington. He loves his work, he loves his family, he loves his golf, and he loves West Virginia. "The Old Master's blessed me real good," he says.

Some people might disagree. Dawson was handed an almost unbearable burden the night of Nov. 14, 1970. The assistant coach, all of 27 years old, had been with those 75 people that day. But when they boarded the plane, he got into his car. He might have been with them. He might have been spared the pain and the guilt.

Red doesn't like to talk about that night. Who would? But he remembers. Here is a man, after all, who casually mentions that the play he called from the press box to beat Xavier in the second game of the '71 season was a "2-13 bootleg screen" from quarterback Reggie Oliver, clear across the field to Terry Gardner.

Dawson left the Marshall football program after that season, partly because he could sense that he was reminding others of the tragedy, partly because he wanted to get away from football. "I love this area, so I never thought about moving," he says. "I just got a job with a friend's construction company as a trainee. Basically, it was hard labor, and it was the best thing for me. Took my mind off things."

Dawson is not a morose man or one given to introspection. But in an unguarded moment, Red does reveal a little of his anguish. "The worst part," he says, "was trying to tell the parents of players I recruited, people who had welcomed me into their living rooms, how sorry I was that their sons were on that plane." When he says that, his eyes seem to want to cry, but can't. It's as if they're tapped out.

From his distant vantage point, Dawson has watched over the 1970 Marshall football family. When the son of one of the crash victims got himself into some trouble a few years back, Dawson became his unofficial guardian. When the parents of Ted Shoebridge came down from Lyndhurst for the induction of their son into the Marshall Hall of Fame in 1990, Dawson was there to meet them at the airport.

The last two Marshall coaches, Jim Donnan and Bob Pruett, have made it a point to make Dawson feel welcome. Red was on the sidelines when the Herd won its national championship in '92, and this year Pruett invited him to be the honorary assistant coach for the season opener against West Virginia—the first time the two schools had met since 1923.

"We lost 42-31, even though we had the lead after three quarters," says Dawson. "Coach Pruett later said that he let me coach the fourth quarter. But I had a great old time on the sidelines. I was yelling so loud that I thought the referees might penalize me. Never thought I'd be yelling on the sidelines of a Marshall game ever again."

At a kitchen table in Lyndhurst, Yolanda Shoebridge presents a pile of newspaper clippings, programs and magazines to a visitor. They all sing the praises of quarterback Ted Shoebridge Jr. "He is a bright, intelligent young man and an excellent playmaker," the 1970 Marshall football program said of the junior quarterback. Indeed, Shoebridge set 18 passing records at Marshall, and his stats compared favorably with other start college quarterbacks at the time— Terry Bradshaw, Joe Theisman, Jim Plunkett, and Dan Pastorini. His path seemed headed for the NFL.

"He was a great kid," she says. "We'd drive down to Huntington for his games, and he would always be looking for us to arrive. And when we did, he'd run over to us, pick each of us up in his arms and twirl us around. I once said, "Teddy, aren't you afraid of showing affection in front of your teammates?' and he said, 'Nah, I'm the starting quarterback.'"

The Shoebridges didn't travel down to Greenville for the East Carolina game. They watched their second son Thomas play for Lyndhurst High that day, then came home to scan the TV for the Marshall result. "We couldn't figure out why there was no score." Yolanda remembers. "Then came the knock at our door. It was our parish priest." Somebody at Marshall, knowing the Shoebridges were devout Catholics, had asked the priest to deliver the news

Yolanda and Ted Sr., an auto mechanic, had their two other sons to raise: Tom, who became a teacher and track and football coach at Lyndhurst High, and Terry, a former Milwaukee Brewer minor leaguer who is now an accountant. But the loss of Teddy took so much out of them. "People say it gets better over time," says Yolanda, "but it only gets worse. My husband stopped going to church, and for years he refused to go with me to Teddy's gravesite. He bought all of Teddy's game films for $1,200 but then couldn't bear to watch them. The films are still in the basement, unopened." When Marshall decided to induct Ted. Jr. into its Hall of Fame in 1990, Yolanda and Ted Sr. flew to Huntington—but only at the urging of their sons. "It was a good thing to do," she says. "Seeing Red Dawson again, talking to people who knew Teddy eased the pain a little."

Ted Sr. died last year, and now Yolanda lives with Tom. Their living room is filled with pictures of the whole family, but the most prominent keepsakes are Teddy's old Marshall helmet and an oil painting of a handsome young man in a green No. 14 jersey.

During Saturday home games at Lyndhurst High, Yolanda sits under the scoreboard dedicated to her son and watches a quarterback who could have been his son. She goes home and looks for the Marshall score on TV; these days she usually smiles at the result. At bedtime she performs her nightly ritual of reading a Mother's Day card that Ted Jr. once sent her.

Hers is a fountain that flows every day, keeping the memory alive.

Part V

Administrative Concerns

16

From Crisis to Community:
The Oklahoma State University Plane Crash

Lee E. Bird, Suzanne Burks, and Cindy Washington

The Oklahoma State University response to a plane crash that killed a group of students provides a case that highlights critical issues and actions taken by a university in response to tragedy. The narration focuses on the decisions made and tasks accomplished in the days, weeks, and months following the crash. The authors hope that telling the story may benefit others facing multiple deaths, in providing a human and real-life example of a university's responses to dilemmas posed by traumatic student death.

On January 27, 2001, three planes associated with the Oklahoma State University (OSU) basketball program left Jefferson County Airport in Colorado. Only two arrived home safely. The third plane, a Beechcraft King Air, lay in ruin in a snow-covered field east of Strasburg, Colorado. All ten men aboard were killed. That tragic night, Oklahoma State University lost two student athletes, a student manager, the sports information coordinator, an athletic trainer, a basketball staff member, two media personnel, and two pilots. Upon learning of the tragedy, OSU began mobilizing to deal with the unfolding crisis.

Lee Bird is the Vice President for Student Affairs at Oklahoma State University and has served in similar capacities at St. Cloud State University in St. Cloud, Minnesota, and Lycoming College in Williamsport, Pennsylvania. She often speaks at the regional and national level on issues of campus First Amendment and judicial affairs. Suzanne Burks is the director of University Counseling Services at the Oklahoma State University and has extensive experience with individual, group, and crisis intervention modalities. She serves on various community boards of directors in areas related to domestic violence and sexual assault. Cindy Washington received her Master's of Science in Counseling and Student Personnel from Oklahoma State University where she now serves as a clinical counselor. She has been a bereavement caseworker and has volunteered at a hospice and among the Stillwater AIDS community.

Teammates, coaches, athletic personnel, and others gathered at the basketball office on the campus. Dr. Lee Bird, Vice President of Student Affairs, and Dr. Suzanne Burks, Director of University Counseling Services, went to the basketball office. Cindy Washington, Clinical Counselor, and other counseling personnel reported to the athletes' residence hall to assess the situation there and offer support where needed.

The Concentric Circle Crisis Management Model:
A Conceptual Framework

Imagine a stone being thrown into a pond. The size of the rock (in this case, the magnitude of the incident) dictates the size and number of ripples that develop. The number of people involved, the mechanism of death, the event's perceived media importance, and the probability of litigation dictate to some degree the level of crisis. The ripples emanating from the center help identify the most immediate needs. In this incident, the needs of the family members, teammates, coaching staff, and close friends were our first priority, followed by associates, classmates, staff, faculty, and many total strangers moved by the magnitude of the loss. First, keeping in mind the emerging needs of those closest to the epicenter helped us focus resources where they were needed most.

Initial Response: Saturday Night

Counseling Director Burks and Vice President Bird arrived on campus within minutes of the initial television news brief. Drs. Bird and Burks initially went to the basketball office, where Coach Eddie Sutton was making phone calls to families of the deceased, a task that he insisted on handling personally. OSU President James Halligan, with key OSU administrators and athletic staff, were with Sutton. Outside the building, the OSU Police and Public Information Office staff were attempting to engage and to some degree "corral" the growing number of media.

Although the presence of the media was at times aggravating because of our desire to protect the privacy of grieving teammates and staff, we had to consider that they were doing their jobs. Although those of us closest to the incident knew that there were no survivors, this information was not immediately available to the public.

It was important to identify spokespersons who could inform the media of what we knew at that early stage. Although, speculation about the crash was to be expected, all OSU staff were instructed not to hypothesize about the situation. Only facts known at the time (and there were very few) were to be discussed, and then only by OSU Public Information Office staff. It is important to note that with an event of such magnitude and the media's responsibility to report, some family members first learned of the crash on the ten p.m. news, despite dauntless efforts by Coach Sutton to make first contact.

Athletic departments tend to be closed "family" systems. The presence of Dr. Burks at the basketball office that first night paid dividends later, as the opportunity for formal, informal, individual, and small group counseling emerged. The bond and trust initiated that evening was critical.

Once the basketball office began to clear, Drs. Bird and Burks checked in with staff assigned to the halls. Most students were doing exactly what they needed to, talking with friends and supporting each other. Counseling staff was visible and mainly supported residence hall staff and students as needed. Private meetings with residence hall staff and counselors clarified roles, identified possible warning signs to look for in their residents as the grieving process began, and provided information on how to contact UCS for assistance.

Sunday Morning

At approximately two o'clock Sunday morning, members of the University's executive group and athletic department staff met at an off-campus location to discuss initial plans for the memorial service set for Wednesday, January 31, 2001 and how OSU could best monitor recovery efforts in Colorado. Three staff members selected for their unique personal and professional backgrounds, Associate Vice President and Controller, Dr. David Bosserman; OSU Police Sergeant, Leon Jones; and Assistant to the Athletic Director, Carter Mattson would fly to Colorado later that day to serve as the "eyes and ears" of Oklahoma State, on behalf of the family members. Their presence would aid communication and provide OSU the assurance that recovery efforts would be conducted in a respectful and dignified manner. The on-site team would coordinate efforts with the National Transportation Safety Board (NTSB) and local Colorado law enforcement.

Assignments for the memorial service were made consistent with our responsibilities on campus. The list included possible speakers, music, and seating arrangements for family members, as well as lodging, transportation needs, and volunteers to help with parking and at the service. Before the service, it would be necessary to collect photos of the deceased and information about their lives. The meeting adjourned shortly after four a.m.

It was decided that an athletic department staff member would be assigned to each family to assist with any needs, answer questions, and provide information about the planned memorial service. This effort was further enhanced when the Counseling Center assigned a counselor to work with each of the families of the deceased, to provide information about the memorial service, and offer support throughout the difficult time.

Later that morning, Drs. Bird and Burks began making family visits to the local area homes of the deceased. During these visits, we were better able to determine the needs of family members and/or make referrals for assistance. During one visit, one of the newly widowed women asked for advice on how to tell her three-year-old daughter that daddy would not be coming home. A call was made to a local therapist who specialized in working with children, and she agreed to meet with the mother at home and offer suggestions.

Beginning with the first family contact, Dr. Burks began compiling a notebook with information on each of the families. It contained the names of family members (immediate and extended), close friends and their roles, phone numbers, birth dates, anniversary dates, and even the names of family pets. Ideas they wanted to introduce into the memorial service were recorded and shared with appropriate staff members. This information was extremely helpful for us and for the president and others who would make additional home visits. At each home, business cards were left with our home and cell phone numbers and the invitation to call us at any time night or day.

By day two, when individual counselor assignments were made, we had a better idea of the families who were struggling and those who needed less support. Assignments were made based on counselors' prior acquaintance with families and the level of training and experience of each counselor in dealing with trauma and grief issues.

Pre-memorial Activities

The campus was eerily quiet Monday morning. As preparations for the memorial service continued, the Counseling Center prepared and distributed printed material dealing with grief and loss to key offices on campus. Counseling center staff cleared schedules as much as possible to allow for the expected higher than average walk-in traffic. Freedom from regularly scheduled appointments also allowed the director and counselors to continue meeting with members of the basketball team, other athletic teams, coaches, individuals, and family members, as requested. The meetings did not take place in the Counseling Center, but in residence halls, athletic department offices, hotel rooms, homes, and at any location requested.

As members of the basketball team prepared to give their first news conference, Dr. Burks attended their team meeting. By asking them to tell her about the friends they lost and their favorite memories, a dialogue was opened and team members were able to express themselves as is necessary in the grieving process. Business cards were distributed with each contact.

Thousands of flower arrangements, cards, and letters began to arrive on campus. The president's office staff, faculty wives, and other volunteers noted each expression of sympathy and filled Gallagher-Iba Arena and the arena lobby with the floral arrangements. University staff acknowledged every letter and gift of flowers. A large signing wall was set up in the arena lobby so those attending the memorial service could express their feelings. The messages were heartfelt and moving.

The Memorial Service

Families were gathered in the practice gym at Gallagher-Iba Arena prior to the memorial service. Athletic department and counseling center liaisons met with the families, and the counseling staff distributed OSU angel teddy bears to the mothers, widows, and children of the deceased. Family, friends, and team members were escorted into Gallagher-Iba Arena accompanied by counseling and athletic department liaisons. University Counseling Services staff wore purple armbands so they were easily identified. More than 100 community counselors and ministers volunteered their services and flanked the arena, also wearing purple armbands for identification. As the families entered the arena, music selected by family and friends of the deceased was playing. As if on cue, more than 13,000 people in the arena rose to their feet and stood in silence while the families were escorted to their seats. In front of the stage, large pictures of the deceased were displayed. Families were given the opportunity to place mementos by their loved ones' pictures prior to the service.

Each family provided memories about their loved one to be shared with the audience by specially selected local newscasters who were close associates of many of the crash victims. One of the men who died in the crash had worked with these newscasters as sports director at an Oklahoma City television station. A particularly moving moment was when President Halligan spoke, promising that the children of the deceased were assured a free education at OSU. He also committed to the families to provide two memorials to their loved ones, one at the crash site in Colorado and another in Gallagher-Iba Arena. Promises made that day would be honored.

The memorial service was broadcast live on all television stations in Oklahoma City and Tulsa. The service was also broadcast on the OSU campus cable system. Television sets in various locations on campus accommodated overflow from the arena.

More than 200 student volunteers assisted with delivering floral arrangements to Gallagher-Iba Arena, parking, directing people in the arena, and seating them. The Governor and Lt. Governor of Oklahoma both spoke at the memorial service, and OSU Police provided security for dignitaries.

Following the service, a meal was served for family members and attending dignitaries. The OSU Student Union dining services catered the meal. Counselors attended and were able to interact with families and friends, building bonds and rapport. UCS counselors found that this informal time gave families the opportunity to ask questions and seek advice regarding their specific issues.

Each of the ten families involved in the plane crash responded differently to the loss. Some reached out to the counseling office for support, while others declined that offer and relied on the support of family members and friends. Overall, campus athletes had a difficult time accepting that their friends and peers were gone. Many college students have never dealt with a significant loss and are therefore unprepared for the magnitude of emotion. It brings to light their own sense of mortality and increases feelings of anxiety and fear. Many experienced difficulty concentrating on school and sports for months to come.

Concerned coaches and athletic trainers often contacted the counseling office to ask for a counselor to come talk with their team or with specific team members. Each outreach request was responded to promptly. Counselors often provided handouts explaining the process of grieving, normalized feelings, and contact information for further assistance.

In the days that followed, individual funerals were held. Dr. Bird, Dr. Burks, or Cindy Washington and other key university personnel attended all the funerals. It was essential to keep notes so names and relationships could be remembered later, when communicating with family. With the exception of one service in Detroit, Michigan, OSU President, James Halligan and his wife attended all the services.

The three-person team dispatched to the crash site did not return from Colorado until all the deceased had been positively identified and released to their next of kin. No team member wanted to leave Colorado until his or her fallen fellow Cowboys had gone home. After eight days in Colorado, working with the NTSB and Adams County Sheriff's Department and Coroner, the on-site team returned to Stillwater. The team was supported daily in Colorado with phone calls from Dr. Burks and other university administrators. All three team members participated in critical incident debriefing with Dr. Burks upon their return to Stillwater.

Over the next few months, communication with the families continued. Counseling and athletic liaisons sent cards and made phone calls on a regular basis. A local publishing company donated a four-series booklet on the grieving process, which was mailed to families at regular intervals throughout the first year following the crash. In December 2001, Cindy Washington obtained commemorative Christmas ornaments from the local hospice, which were mailed to each family with a framed poem, "Christmas in Heaven." This was a personal way to support families through their first holiday season without their loved one. Further, Dr. and Mrs. Halligan sent commemorative ornaments to families and many OSU staff, reflecting the "kneeling cowboy" that would become symbolic at the Gallagher-Iba memorial.

In March, Oklahoma State invited the families and other representatives to a dinner on campus, to view and give input on the Colorado memorial design. Family members were asked to provide photos and a memorial statement to be engraved on the granite memorial. It was determined that an essentially flat decagon design would better survive the harsh weather conditions and not attract vandalism. An iron fence would be placed around the granite memorial. The dedication of the Colorado memorial was set for August 25, 2001.

The Colorado Memorial Dedication Service

Oklahoma State University acquired the land for the memorial through a gift from the landowner. The memorial was constructed 1,032 feet west of the crash site. University staff members made many trips to Colorado to oversee and evaluate progress on the memorial. The logistics of constructing a memorial and planning a second memorial service in Colorado were daunting. Everything needed for the memorial service would be brought from Oklahoma to Colorado. Many safeguards were put in place to assure a meaningful, appropriate, and error-free service. The university arranged to fly four members of each family to Colorado for the memorial dedication service. Transportation and housing needs were carefully coordinated for the families. Many other family members and friends made the trip to Colorado on their own. A diverse team of staff members from Oklahoma State was hand picked to attend and help with the memorial dedication. Two professional counselors, Burks and Washington, and Vice President Bird, who also has a counseling degree, were among those selected. A master list of tasks was created and reviewed by the team several times daily.

One week prior to the memorial dedication, Dr. Burks or Ms. Washington called all of the families, discussed the schedule in Colorado, and answered any questions about the event. Each family had specific questions (i.e., How should they dress? Could they visit the crash site prior to the service?). In the course of these calls, families were informed that although every effort had been made to clear the site, there might still be remaining debris from the airplane. Most would be visiting the site for the first time, and we wanted to forewarn them of this possibility.

Two days prior to the service, the OSU team and representatives from the Adams County Sheriff Department and Strasberg Fire Department walked the area of the crash and retrieved ten large garbage bags full of small pieces of debris, to assure that family members would not be faced with finding pieces of the airplane or its contents. Weeks before, the ground had been turned, and fuel-saturated soil had been removed, but many small pieces of metal and plastic remained until the crew canvassed the area.

The day before the memorial dedication, briefings took place with the university team and the Adams County Sheriff's Department. Staff from the Department's victim advocacy program volunteered to assist with counseling needs, and our staff would continue to take the primary role. Following the briefing, members of the counseling staff and others went to the memorial and crash sites in anticipation of early family visits. All but one family made its way to the site, most seeing for the first time the place where their loved ones died. Temperatures were in the 90s that day. We were concerned that visitors might become overheated and made arrangements for water to be available during the service. Medical personnel, including area doctors, nurses, and emergency medical technicians, also volunteered to be on site both the day before and the day of the service. OSU hosted a dinner for family members the night before the dedication service, and the schedule for the following day was reviewed. OSU staff cell phone numbers were provided for family members and guests for easy access to information and assistance.

The university team wore OSU shirts the day of the service. Nametag lanyards were given to family members, their guests, and OSU staff, making them easily identifiable to security personnel. Only those with lanyards were permitted to walk from the memorial site to the crash site. University staff members remained with those who chose not to walk there. Media staff remained at the memorial, showing a measure of privacy for family members. Local law enforcement officers helped buffer family members from the media as they left the buses.

The day of the memorial dedication, Saturday, August 25, 2001, we were surprised to wake to cold, windy, rainy weather. Buses arrived at the hotel to transport the somber crowd on the 30-minute ride to the site. OSU Police and Adams County Sheriff Department vehicles escorted the buses for the entire trip, blocking freeway entry ramps to speed our travel.

An unexpected miracle that day was the effort of local medical and law enforcement personnel to provide blankets and rain gear for family members and guests. Families sat under a tent, huddled together to stay warm. The dedication service was meaningful and brief. At the conclusion of the service, family members were offered the opportunity to lay a rose on the memorial.

Finally, the sun emerged from behind the clouds as staff and family members walked to the crash site. Family members spoke with the NTSB representative and the Adams County coroner and had the opportunity to ask questions of the experts who investigated the crash. First responders to the crash were also available to speak with family members. As difficult as the information must have been to hear, it was extremely important and valuable to family members. They wandered the area alone and in small groups, absorbing the information they had heard.

Following the family time at the crash site, we were taken by bus to the Strasburg Elementary School where school staff had prepared a meal for Strasburg community members and all those who attended the memorial service. This signaled a change in mood for many. The luncheon was lively, stories were shared, laughter was plentiful, and smiles replaced the sad faces of the memorial service. It seemed the pressure of facing the service was over, and people were rebounding. Members of the Strasburg Fire and Rescue, Adams County Sheriff Department, and others had an opportunity to meet family and friends of the deceased. The NTSB representative and the coroner continued to answer questions through lunch.

President Halligan thanked the community of Strasburg for their assistance that day and in the preceding months. The healing process began that day for many of us. We were all overwhelmed with the connection to and kindness of this small community. We returned to the hotel and were available to help with any needs of the family members as they left Colorado. The majority of the OSU team was to fly back to Oklahoma the day after the memorial service.

The Continuing Journey of Grief
To assist the bereaved family members, Cindy Washington prepared the following document about understanding the process of grief.

Many people assume that six months after a significant loss, a person should be "getting over" it. Friends may stop asking how they are doing (this could be a relief, too), and they may talk about loved one less often. In many instances people who are grieving say that six to twelve months after the loss they feel worse and may wonder if something is wrong with them. Nothing is wrong if they feel this way. Here are some of the reasons:

1. They may feel guilty that for brief periods of time, they "forget" about the loved one and go on with everyday life. This is normal and is a sign of adapting to a new life without the loved one.
2. As time passes, they recall more things that they miss about the loved one. Birthdays, anniversaries, holidays, and even the changing of the seasons can spark memories and be painful reminders of loss.
3. When a loss is sudden and unexpected, they need to know everything they can about how and why it happened. When the answers are not forthcoming, it becomes more difficult to "move on" and grieve the loss. They may find that until a final report gives them the "answers" they are looking for, it will be challenging to come to closure.
4. When a loss is highly publicized and media reports are regular, it becomes more difficult to resume a normal routine. They may find it irritating to watch the news, knowing that their personal loss may be casually discussed in a news report by strangers who never met their loved one.

Grief is a journey. The loss will be with them for the rest of their life, but it won't always hurt this badly. Advise them to continue to take it one day at time, knowing some days will be better than others, continue to talk about their loss with those who are patient enough to listen, and continue to cry when they need to, laugh when they can, and honor their loved one's memory by living life to its fullest.

The First Anniversary

Oklahoma State University, in keeping with the desires of family members, made the decision not to plan a formal remembrance on the first anniversary of the plane crash. Planning for the memorial in Gallagher-Iba Arena was already well underway. It would, in some ways, mirror the Colorado memorial, with pictures of the men who died and a message written by family members engraved in a granite wall, which serves as the backdrop for a sculpture depicting a kneeling cowboy (the mascot of Oklahoma State University).

The Gallagher-Iba Arena Memorial Dedication Service

Space constraints and privacy issues limited attendance at the GIA memorial dedication service. It too was dignified and brief. Family members representing multiple generations of survivors were asked to remove the drape covering the sculpture. At a luncheon following the service, each family was given a replica of the kneeling cowboy sculpture. What had been promised so many months before had now been accomplished.

Saying Thank You

OSU created an opportunity to say thank you to Strasberg individuals, including members of the Adams County Sheriff's Department and Strasburg Fire and Rescue Department, with a visit to the OSU campus for a basketball game in the spring of 2002. On the OSU campus, representatives from Colorado planted columbine flowers (the Colorado state flower), symbolic of the shared experience of our two communities.

Equally important was the need to say thank you to the OSU team members, who had helped throughout the entire ordeal. President Halligan hosted a luncheon to express his appreciation and give each person a commemorative piece made from the same granite as both memorials as a reminder of our journey together.

The Chinese symbol for crisis is the combination of two words, disaster and opportunity. Our shared experience was precisely that. We joined together to help the families of those killed in a tragic plane crash and as a consequence, grew as a community and gained new found respect for one another and our various roles at Oklahoma State University.

Recommendations

1. Develop a response plan. Include a phone list in your planning with home and cell numbers of all key personnel. Know that if you have to implement the plan, the specifics of the event will dictate modifications. However, planning will greatly enhance your efforts, as well as help avoid duplication of efforts.
2. With the assistance of the public information office, establish a protocol for dealing with the media. Expect the counseling office to receive requests for interviews. Identify one or two trained spokespersons to field all media calls. Keep the public information office informed of media contacts and requests.
3. Have plans in place at memorial services/funerals to shield family/survivors from the media.
4. A tragedy of such magnitude and the presence of the media often attract emotionally disturbed people. Such individuals interrupted the OSU memorial service and one of the private services. Have police/security in attendance at any memorial or funeral service to handle any disturbances.
5. Screen all volunteers (counselors, ministers, etc.) to assure that they are equipped to deal with the event.
6. Know your staff and their individual strengths, and delegate tasks accordingly.
7. Build relationships with resource persons such as residential life, police, and community.
8. Such relationships should be solid before a tragedy occurs.
9. Pay attention to detail and take copious notes. In the midst of trauma and tragedy, our memories often fail!

10. If you are not on the "front lines," do what you can. Answer phones, run errands, and provide food.
11. Keep a survivor notebook with names, dates, and all other information you acquire. This is especially important when there are many survivors and a great deal of information to remember.
12. Only promise what you are certain you can provide, and keep all promises you make without fail.
13. Have materials on grief and trauma readily available for quick production and distribution.
14. Have plenty of business cards on hand.
15. Cell phones are invaluable tools to keep staff connected. Don't forget to carry chargers and/or extra battery packs.
16. Take care of yourself and your staff. Rest whenever you can, at home or at the office. Be aware of staff members who may need a time out (this includes you!), and insist that it is taken!
17. Keep an ongoing list of all those you need to thank, and be sure to express your appreciation in writing as soon as feasible.
18. It is said that laughter is the best medicine.

How true this was for those of us intimately involved in dealing with the trauma and aftermath of the OSU plane crash. A wink, a hug, or a brief smile got us through the long days, weeks, and months of helping the OSU family deal with this tragedy. When we had time alone together, we shared stories to debrief, we laughed to ease the pain, and we made sure each of us had our creature comforts (a soft drink or a glass of brewed ice tea). We slept in when we could and left work a little early when possible. We made phone calls home to our loved ones to check in. New bonds were formed during this time among university departments that previously hardly knew the other existed. These bonds remain today. The opportunity that presented itself was for us to grow as a community, and we did that.

In Retrospect

Thankfully, facing an incident of such magnitude is rare. It is difficult to tell this story because in reality it involves hundreds of stories. Family members, friends, and staff members involved have their own memories and stories about the crash, the aftermath, the funerals, and memorials. Lives were changed in an instant. All the hopes and dreams, not only of the men who died, but of those left behind, including wives, children, parents, family members, and friends, were irrevocably changed.

As seasoned professionals, we all knew we could help guide some individuals through the initial shock and early grieving process. We also knew from the beginning that we couldn't give what the survivors wanted most: to have their loved ones return home safely. We felt overwhelmed with the magnitude of the tragedy and could only imagine how our lives would change.

There were so many tender and intimate moments with students, staff, and family members, so many minor miracles that took place all around us following the crash, and so many relationships built from this tragedy. Volumes could be written telling these stories. Instead, we have focused on the decisions made and tasks accomplished in the days, weeks, and months following the crash. It is our hope that telling our collective story may benefit others facing a major campus tragedy. This is our perspective, and these were our recollections. Many others were involved in the incident, and their stories are equally as vivid and valid.

17

Legal Aspects of Coping with Death on Campus

Joseph Beckham, Douglas Pearson, and K. B. Melear

In the legal relationship between students and university institutions, there is an obligation of the agents of the administration to act in good faith and to deal fairly with students in times of crisis. Universities must develop and execute an institutional plan that demonstrates sensitivity and addresses the key aspects of potential legal liability in dealing with loss in an organizational context.

Because the grieving process takes many forms and is an intensely personal emotion, it is often difficult to frame institutional responses that allow people to come to terms with loss and the resulting change in their lives. While many within a college or university community may experience numbness, disbelief, anger, or denial, there are legal and administrative responsibilities associated with the death of a student that must be addressed by institutional leaders. When viewed from the perspective of the evolving legal relationship between a higher education institution and its students, developing and executing an institutional plan that demonstrates sensitivity and addresses key aspects of potential legal liability is an essential component of avoiding liability and dealing with loss in an organizational context.

In some cases, addressing legal responsibilities can be part of an organizational effort that contributes to the recovery process. For institutional representatives, the initial responsibility is to investigate and inform authorities, family, and key members of the campus community about the death. This should be followed by a plan to assist members of the campus community and others affected by the death to cope with the loss. Ultimately, it is the responsibility of the institution's leadership to insure that, to the extent reasonably possible, the events or activities that led to loss are critically examined, evaluated, and subjected to a risk assessment that will influence future policy at the institution.

Joseph Beckham is the Allan Tucker Professor of Educational Leadership at Florida State University and has written extensively in the area of educational law. Douglas Pearson is the Associate Vice-President for Student Affairs at the University of West Florida. K.B. Melear is an Assistant Professor of Higher Education at the University of Mississippi. His research areas include university law, public policy, and finance.

The Legal Relationship Between Students and Institution

Although colleges no longer stand *in loco parentis* in their legal relationship to students, a number of legal theories apply in defining an institution's responsibilities to students (Buchter, 1973). Fiduciary, constitutional, and contract theories have emerged in case law as perspectives that illustrate the legal relationship between college and student (Stamatakos, 1990). Taken together, these legal theories impose an obligation on the agents of an institution to act in good faith, to deal fairly with students, and to avoid deliberate indifference or callous disregard for the welfare of students in the aftermath of a campus tragedy.

A fiduciary relationship is created when one party reasonably entrusts and reposes confidence in another party to act on his or her behalf. Weeks and Haglund (2002) contend that although universities no longer stand in the place of the parent, when students reasonably rely on faculty and administrators in pursuing their education, colleges and universities may acquire fiduciary obligations toward those students. The authors concluded that fiduciary theory has received increased application in recent years, as student-plaintiffs' estate representatives assert claims that the institution owed a duty to provide for the safety and security of the student. Finally, the authors observed that the concept of fiduciary duty is an amalgam of both contract and trust law, imposing a duty on institutions to treat the student as if he or she was the beneficiary in a trust relationship defined by implied rights and obligations that relate to insuring well-being.

More prevalent than trust or fiduciary theories, and a catalyst for the proliferation of contemporary contract cases filed against postsecondary institutions, is the constitutional theory of the relationship between college and student. Dixon v. Alabama State Board of Education (1961) is often considered the genesis of the constitutional theory (Grossi & Edwards, 1991). Constitutional theory advances the philosophy that students in public institutions of higher education possess rights under the United States Constitution, particularly under the Fourteenth Amendment's due process guarantees. Predicated on these due process protections, a federal appeals court in Dixon held that students at state-supported institutions had the right to procedural and substantive due process in a disciplinary action that might result in dismissal. Following Dixon, substantive due process protections in public institutions have been extended, in limited circumstances, to the duty to act reasonably and to avoid callous disregard or deliberate indifference to the welfare of students. This constitutional theory, applied most often in cases involving severe sexual harassment of students, is not applicable to private higher education institutions because independent institutions are not government agents, and thus not bound to federal constitutional protections.

A contractual relationship is predicated on an express or implied agreement between student and institution that defines mutual obligations of the parties and includes valid consideration. When students pay tuition and fees, they are considered by judges to have entered into an implied contract with the institution in which the institution is obligated to provide services congruent with an agreement to educate. This relationship has been affirmed by judges in decisions interpreting the institution's bulletin as a contract for services on which a student might reasonably rely. In a more limited range of cases, an implied contract may be judicially recognized when institutional representatives make statements about services that induce a student to enroll and pay tuition.

Contract theory provides students a means to seek reparation of their disagreements with colleges and universities, and courts embraced the contractual relationship in an effort to frame the reciprocity of rights and obligations between student and institution. Beh (2000) has argued that implied contractual obligations of good faith and fair dealing hold the potential to define and to police the student-university relationship. However, judges have cautioned against the rigid application of classic contract principles in the higher education setting. As one state appeals court expressed this caution:

> The judicial inquiry should be directed toward the bona fides of the decision making and the fairness of its implementation: whether the institution acted in good faith and dealt fairly with its student body should be the polestar of the judicial inquiry. This approach will give courts broader authority for examining university decision making in the administrative area than would a modified standard of judicial deference and will produce a more legally cohesive body of law than will application of classic contract doctrine with its many judicially created exceptions, varying as they must from jurisdiction to jurisdiction (Beukas v. Farliegh Dickinson University, 1991, p. 784).

Therefore, colleges and universities have the task of reconciling their desire to provide a supportive relationship with the student, with their need to maintain a legal responsibility to the obligations of university administration.

Undertaking Risk assessment and Risk Management

It is essential that, in the aftermath of a student's death, the institution's agents review the circumstances that led to the loss and undertake a risk assessment. This is the first step in designing and implementing a risk management policy intended to reduce the risk of a future incident that may result in the death or injury of a student. Risk management policies are intended to eliminate or substantially reduce foreseeable risks by increasing precautions commensurate with the degree of risk involved in the activity.

The principal source of legal liability for serious injury or death on a campus or in sponsored activities is negligence. Since the landmark decision of Bradshaw v. Rawlings (1979), the question of how and to what extent institutions of higher education could be held liable for negligence involving the serious injury or death of a student has been evolving in state and federal courts (Bickel & Lake, 1997). In general, institutional liability for negligence in the death of a student must be predicated on a showing that the institution owed a special duty of care to the student and breached that duty in a manner that proximately caused the student's death. It is essential for a plaintiff claiming institutional negligence to establish that a special duty was owed and a foreseeable risk existed.

If risks are foreseeable, that is, if they are known to institutional agents, there is an increased potential for negligent liability when injury or death occurs. To counter the known foreseeable risks, institutional agents must take affirmative steps to eliminate or reduce risks. Risk management may take the form of eliminating an activity or enforcing rules or regulations that are intended to prohibit or reduce the likelihood of certain conduct. Other risk management policies may involve informing students about the known dangers of an activity so that they understand and accept the risk of participation or providing training and invoking safety procedures that reduce foreseeable risks to manageable proportions.

Special Duty Relationship

While higher education institutions are not legally regarded as insurers of a student's safety, institutions can be held to have created a "special duty" relationship that may be a basis for negligent liability in certain circumstances, particularly when a foreseeable risk is recognized. For example, judges have long recognized that higher education institutions owe a legal duty to students to provide proper instruction and adequate supervision in classroom contexts that involve high risks, foreseeable harm, and the instructor's special expertise (Fu v. State, 2002, involving an explosion in a chemistry laboratory; Garrett v. Northwest Mississippi Junior College, 1996, student injury in using milling machine, and Delbridge v. Maricopa County Community College, 1994, student injury in fall from utility pole during training classes).

Because of the degree of supervision and control exercised over school sponsored intercollegiate athletic programs, several courts have imposed a special duty relationship in this particular context of student-institutional relationships. For example, in Kleinknecht v. Gettysburg College (1993), a federal appeals court upheld liability specifically predicated on a special duty relationship. After a student who had been recruited to play lacrosse suffered a fatal heart attack during practice, the parents of the student brought a negligence action against the college, arguing that a special relationship existed between the student and the college by virtue of the student's status as a member of the intercollegiate athletic team. A federal appeals court agreed, reasoning that because the student was recruited to play lacrosse and, at the time of his heart attack he was participating in a scheduled athletic practice for a college-sponsored intercollegiate team, a special relationship existed that was sufficient to impose a duty of reasonable care.

Having determined that a special relationship existed, the court then reviewed the record to evaluate whether the incident was foreseeable and to assess whether a duty of care was owed. The court determined that it was foreseeable that a member of the college's interscholastic lacrosse team could suffer a serious injury during an athletic event, and concluded the college owed a duty to the student to take precautions against the risks of injury. In making its determination, the federal court clearly intended to set limits on the class of students to which this decision would apply, emphasizing the difference between a student injured while participating as an inter-collegiate athlete in a sport for which he was recruited and a student injured at a college while pursuing his private interests, scholastic or otherwise. This distinction serves to limit the class of students to whom a college owes the duty of care that arises here. Had the student been participating in a fraternity football game, for example, the college might not have owed him the same duty.

Klienknecht is a unique circumstance because of the degree of control an institution exercises over intercollegiate athletes, but it reflects the principle that a university or college may be liable for a death or an injury when it is clear that institutional officials did not exercise reasonable care in the context of a special duty relationship involving a clear risk of foreseeable dangers. (See Wallace v. Broyles, 1998, for a case in which the Supreme Court of Arkansas determined that genuine issues of material fact precluded summary judgment in a case in which an athlete's suicide was alleged to have been proximately caused by the illegal and uncontrolled dispensing of controlled drugs by institutional employees.) To be foreseeable, the injury does not have to be specifically foreseen by the university, but need only fall into a general category of injuries likely to occur during participation in an athletic activity. (See Howell v. Clavert, 2000, in which the Supreme Court of Kansas affirmed institutional liability in a case in which two student-athletes were struck from behind by a truck during a mandatory early morning conditioning run.) To reduce the risk of liability in future cases of this type, colleges and universities must assess the known risks involved in the activity and adopt a risk management plan that, at a minimum, provides periodic warning to students of the risk inherent in the activities and proper training and supervision commensurate with the risks involved in the activity.

Foreseeable Risk in Third-Party Attacks on Students

Foreseeable risks may be based on a previous instance of injury or death, a generalized awareness of risk, or the institution's violation of a rule or policy designed to reduce risk. The death of a student or students requires investigation and risk assessment so that the institution can adopt policies and practices that reduce the likelihood of a similar incident and parse the institution's risk of liability for any future death or serious injury that may involve circumstances similar to that of the initial loss. By way of illustration, the evolution of institutional liability for third party attacks on students provides an example of the principle of foreseeable risk and the importance of continuous risk assessment and risk management.

In the 1960s and 70s, the weight of judicial opinion, congruent with the Restatement (Second) of Torts (1964) emphasized that there was no duty to control the conduct of a third person or to prevent him or her from causing harm unless a special relationship existed that imposes such a duty. However, the general rule was that there was no duty to protect a student from a third party attack (Hall v. Board of Supervisors, 1983). Throughout the 1980s and 1990s, as reports of third party attacks on students in campus residence halls grew, judges began to couple the evidence of a foreseeable risk with the principle that the institution's role as a landlord in maintaining residence halls created a special duty to protect student-tenants residing in those residence halls (Cutler v. Board of Regents of State of Florida, 1984; Miller v. State, 1983; & Nero v. Kansas State University, 1993). The heightened risk of liability led institutions to adopt security and surveillance policies in residence halls and to inform students of their obligation to avail themselves of the security system by locking doors, reporting unknown persons in hallways, and conforming to security checks at entrance doors.

Third party attacks on students that occur on the campus, but outside of residence halls, continue to present substantial challenges for plaintiffs because the landlord-tenant relationship applicable to residence halls is untenable. However, if there is substantial evidence of a known foreseeable risk, judges have been willing to impose institutional liability based on the recognition of a special duty relationship. Two cases with dramatically different outcomes serve to illustrate this evolving legal principle. In Klobuchar v. Purdue University (1990), a university student who was injured after her husband kidnapped her from campus brought an action against the university for failing to provide adequate security. An Indiana appeals court affirmed summary judgment in favor of the university after determining that there was no material fact that gave rise to a special duty to protect the plaintiff. In its decision, the court emphasized that even in light of a duty to the plaintiff that would be the same general duty afforded to the public, there was nothing that would have alerted the university that the student's husband constituted a foreseeable danger.

In contrast, in the case of Sharkey v. Board of Regents (2000), a state university was held to owe a duty of care to a husband and wife, both of whom were students, in an instance in which the husband was stabbed during a confrontation with another student. The confrontation arose from the third student's alleged harassment of the wife while on the campus, which had been reported to campus security. When campus security took no steps to address the harassment, the husband intervened and was stabbed in an attack. The Supreme Court of Nebraska concluded that the university owed a duty of care to the students as invitees and reasoned that the institution's police force had been made aware of the harassing student's specific behavior on more than one occasion prior to the stabbing. It found that it was reasonable to foresee that the harassing behavior would escalate into violence and held that the institution had a duty to take reasonable precautionary measures to protect the students.

Judges are reluctant to impose liabilityon an institution for a third party attack on a student when the student is involved in an off-campus activity supervised or sponsored by the institution. The general weight of authority conforms to the decision in Bloss v. University of Minnesota (1999), in which a student participating in an international study abroad program was sexually assaulted by a taxi cab driver. Despite contentions that the sponsoring institution was negligent in failing to secure housing closer to the program site, failing to provide safe transportation for students, failing to inform students of the risks, and failing to protect students from a foreseeable harm, a state appeals court rejected the student's negligence claim and affirmed summary judgment for the institution. The court reasoned that the suit arose out of discretionary functions performed by state officials in planning and implementing the international program and the risk involved could not have been foreseen. However, in Nova Southeastern University v. Gross (2000) the Supreme Court of Florida ruled that a university could be found negligent if it assigned a student to a mandatory off-campus internship site that institutional officials knew to be unreasonably dangerous. In this case, the graduate student was abducted from the parking lot of her assigned internship site, robbed, and assaulted. University officials had been made aware of a number of criminal assaults that had occurred at or near the internship site, but provided the student with no warning of the danger. While refusing to adopt a general duty of supervision for the safety of students, the court found that the institution had a duty to use ordinary care in providing educational services and programs. Noting that the case was not based on premises liability, the court emphasized that the "special relationship" in this case was limited to the foreseeable risk involved, the institution's knowledge of that risk, and the failure to warn the student of the known danger.

Similarly, student injuries caused by hazing have departed from the presumption that institutions owe no duty to students in the context of third party attacks. In Furek v. University of Delaware (1991) the Supreme Court of Delaware determined that the magnitude of the foreseeable risk and the institution's policies towards hazing imposed a duty of reasonable care for the safety of students. Furek involved a student injured in a hazing-related accident at a fraternity on the University of Delaware campus. In its decision, the court emphasized that judges have been reluctant to impose institutional liability because higher education institutions are not insurers of students' safety. However, the Furek court reasoned that the university's policies against hazing (which reflected state law mandates), the commitment to provide security on its campus, and the university's knowledge of previous hazing incidents in fraternities created such a duty.

In Furek, the court concluded that changing societal attitudes toward hazing suggest that institutions are not free from all obligations to protect their students. On balance, the court found the likelihood of injury during hazing activities occurring on university campuses to be greater than the utility of university inaction. Imposing liability on the institution was based on the belief that the university had a degree of control over its premises, including the fraternity house, which was supported by its involvement in the regulation of fraternity life. This control, combined with the cumulative evidence that the incident was foreseeable, created a duty to protect the student from harm.

The Supreme Court of Nebraska used reasoning that paralleled the Furek decision in Knoll v. Board of Regents (1999). In this case, a student who was injured in a hazing activity filed suit against the university, alleging that it acted negligently in failing to enforce prohibitions against hazing, consumption of alcohol, and physically abusive behavior. The state supreme court reversed a grant of summary judgment to the university, finding that the hazing activities were foreseeable by the university, which had knowledge of previous instances of hazing by other fraternities and of specific instances of possession of alcohol, alcohol abuse, and assaults involving the fraternity that had subjected the student to hazing. The court paired the concepts of special duty and foreseeable risk and adopted the view that it is the risk reasonably to be perceived that is the determinant of whether a duty is owed.

The examples presented in this section are meant to illustrate that institutions must conscientiously investigate the death of a student in order to develop and implement risk management plans to reduce future risks. Effective risk management requires the application of a risk assessment plan in which investigation enables the institution's agents to appreciate the foreseeable risks related to and identify the conditions associated with an injury or death. Once the risk assessment concludes, the institution must develop and implement policies to reduce risks, instruct participants in safety procedures and equipment use, and develop, audit, and evaluate procedures to insure conformance with appropriate risk management standards.

Conclusions

Framing an institutional response to death and loss can be informed by our knowledge of the legal relationship between higher education institutions and their students. While the law does not compel heightened sensitivity to individual needs, it does sanction callous disregard and deliberate indifference on the part of institutional representatives. The evolving legal relationship between a higher education institution and its students requires an institution to develop and execute an institutional plan that harmonizes the needs of the organization and the individual. That plan must insure that appropriate staff take responsibility for the initial investigation of a death or deaths on campus and inform authorities, family of the deceased, and key members of the campus community. The plan should assist members of the campus community and others affected by the death or deaths to cope with the loss. Finally, the plan should incorporate risk assessment and risk management tools effectively designed to reduce the likelihood of future incidents that could result in death or injury.

In an age of international terrorism, a scenario in which multiple deaths occur is not beyond possibility. As a consequence, institutional leaders and employees should develop an action plan for dealing with the death of a student or students and undertake training and simulations that provide staff with opportunities to develop competence and lead to coordinated activities between local community agencies and institutional representatives. These staff members are better prepared for the range of possible conditions that could result in the loss of life and are more likely to take actions that ameliorate potential loss.

Staff members should also be educated in the range of emotions individuals are likely to experience in the aftermath of tragedy. If effectively prepared, they are able recognize that suppressing or denying feelings of loss may create an additional risk for those who are grieving. These staff members are more likely to be cognizant of the possibility that those who feel an acute sense of loss may also express a desire to harm themselves. Staff so educated will also recognize that even those who appear to be coping effectively may be overwhelmed by emotional exertion at some point.

Institutions should use the process of inquiring, informing, and assessing risk as a dimension of an institutional healing process that helps others in the adjustment to life without the deceased. Ultimately, this process will lead to the identification of what affirmative steps might be required to reduce future risks and the adoption of risk management and risk avoidance practices that will remain subject to continuous review and revision as circumstances warrant. Application of these practices reduces the risk of loss and improves conditions of safety and security on a campus. That application also constitutes the most defensible basis for avoiding any future institutional liability for negligence.

References

Beh, H. (2000). Student versus university: The university's implied obligations of good faith and fair dealing. *Maryland Law Review, 59,* 175-193.

Bickel, R. & Lake, P. F. (1997). Emergence of new paradigms in a student-university relations: From *in loco parentis* to bystander to facilitator. *Journal of College and University Law, 223,* 755-73.

Buchter, J. (1973) Contract law and the student-university relationship. *Indiana Law Journal, 48,* 253-268.

Grossi, L. & Edwards, T. (1997). Student misconduct: Historical trends in legislative and judicial decision-making in American universities. *Journal of College and University Law, 23,* 829-852.

Stamatakos, T. (1990). The doctrine of *in loco parentis*: Tort liability and the student-college relationship. *Indiana Law Journal, 65,* 471-490.

Weeks, K. & Haglund, R. (2002). Fiduciary duties of college and university faculty and administrators. *Journal of College and University Law, 29,* 154-172.

Case Citations

Beukas v. Farliegh Dickinson University, 605 A.2d 776 (N.J. Super.L. 1991)

Bloss v. University of Minnesota, 590 N.W.2d 661 (Minn. App. 1999)

Bradshaw v. Rawlings, 612 F.2d 135 (3rd Cir. 1979)

Cutler v. Board of Regents of State of Florida, 459 So.2d 413 (Fla. App.1984)

Delbridge v. Maricopa County Community College, 893 P.2d 55 (Ariz. App. 1994)

Dixon v. Alabama State Board of Education, 294 F.2d 150 (5th Cir. 1961

Fu v. State, 643 N.W.2d 659 (Neb. 2002)

Furek v. University of Delaware, 594 A.2d 506 (Del.1991)

Garrett v. Northwest Mississippi Junior College, 674 S.2d 1 (Miss. 1996)

Hall v. Board of Supervisors, Southern University, 405 So. 2d 1125 (La. App. 1981)

Houck v. University of Washington, 803 P.2d 47 (Wash. App. 1991)

Howell v. Clavert, 1 P.3d 310 (Kan. 2000)

Kleinknecht v. Gettysburg College, 989 F.2d 1360 (3rd Cir. 1993)

Klobuchar v. Purdue University, 553 N.E.2D 169 (Ind. App. 1990)

Knoll v. Board of Regents, 601 N.E.2d 757 (Neb. 1999)

Miller v. State, 478 N.Y.S.2d 829 (App. Div. 1984)

Mullins v. Pine Manor College, 389 Mass. 47, 449 N.E.2d 331 (Mass.1983)

Nero v. Kansas State University, 861 P.2d 768 (Kan. 1993)

Nova Southeastern University v. Gross, 758 S.2d 86 (Fla. 2000)

Sharkey v. Board of Regents, 615 N.W.2d 889 (Neb. 2000)

Wallace v. Broyles, 961 W.S.2d 712 (Ark. 1998)

18

Image Repair Strategies: A University in Crisis

Kathleen Donohue Rennie

Media coverage of higher educational institutions has become more investigative and aggressive. The intensity of the coverage of the university has amplified calls for universities to be accountable to internal and external publics during crises in an effort to address questions of image and image repair.

In the last two decades, media coverage of colleges and universities has changed significantly. News organizations have devoted less space to higher education, diminishing its treatment as a hot topic. In his analysis of the media, Footlick (1997) tracked coverage of higher education from the 1960s through the late 1990s. He noted that while past coverage was serious and extensive, in recent years many education reporters have been re-assigned. Other news organizations now emphasize brevity in educational reporting. As an example, he noted that "editors of one of the country's leading newspapers told their top education reporter that the paper would not run stories on higher education longer than 1,500 words" (Footlick, 1997, p. 4). In addition, "many news organizations now often report [higher education's] difficulties argumentatively, as if increasing tuition were an administrative conspiracy against parents, or if professors who didn't teach three classes a semester were deliberately cheating students" (Footlock, 1997, p. 4). In short, coverage of higher education has become more investigative, aggressive, and similar to coverage of corporations, politicians, and the entertainment industry (Maeroff, 1998).

Kathleen Donohue Rennie, Ph.D., senior faculty associate, is an accredited public relations professional. She supervises Seton Hall's public relations and advertising undergraduate sequence and teaches undergraduate and graduate communication courses. Rennie manages her integrated marketing company and has served as president of the New Jersey chapter of the Public Relations Society of America.

In Ratcliff's (1995) study of how the press covers higher education and how public research universities work with the press to advance their agendas, reporters and editors provided a long list of reasons for "policing" public universities. Quite simply, the media have joined the growing chorus of constituents (among them parents, legislators, government officials, alumni, faculty, and community members) seeking greater accountability from higher education institutions. Editors note that "newspapers' goals of policing universities are no different from their goals in policing other institutions—universities have just [in the past] had a free ride" (Ratcliff, 1995, pp. 16-17).

The intensity of media coverage of the university and amplified calls for universities to be accountable to internal and external publics are, perhaps, most evident during crises—low probability/high consequence

> situations in which an organization is faced with a critical problem, experiences both sharp external pressure and bitter internal tensions, and is then brutally and for an extended period of time thrust to center stage...with the certainty of being at the top of the news on radio, television and in the press for a long time. (Lagadex, 1984, as cited in Ogrizek & Guillery, 1997, p. xvi)

As opposed to a mere "hot topic" such as spiraling tuition costs, affirmative action, star professors who rarely enter classrooms, and over-crowded lecture halls, crises form a point in an organization's history that irreversibly changes its culture and business (Murphy, 1996). Crises at a university may include accidents, crimes, racial tensions, financial issues, personnel concerns, questions about the integrity of research results, sports program conflicts/abuses, and more. The elements of a crisis common across most definitions include a threat to the organization, the factor of surprise, and a short decision time (Massey, 2001). A university campus is typically a focal point of a city, and its crises could affect the entire community, including faculty, alumni, employees, students, parents, and potential students (Kennedy, 1999a).

Over the past five years, the media have given comprehensive/investigative national coverage to major campus crisis events. To determine the scope of such coverage and to identify a potential focus for a case study, a Lexis- Nexis search was conducted using search terms *die(s), students(s), campus,* and *college* or *university* of national newspapers including the *Los Angeles Times, New York Times, USA Today, Wall Street Journal, Washington Post,* and Associated Press. Three national magazines were also searched. These included *Newsweek, Time,* and *U.S. News & World Report.* The search was confined to the time period of January 1, 1998, through January 1, 2002, and explored coverage of crises in which one or more students died.

Regional coverage of off-campus apartment fires and abundant coverage of alcohol-related student deaths appeared throughout the national press. During the time period examined, numerous stories focused on the binge-drinking trend on college campuses, particularly the death of Scott Krueger at the Massachusetts Institute of Technology in September 1997 in what *Newsweek* dubbed the most famous example of the troubling national trend of binge drinking. (Although the incident took place in 1997, it continued to receive considerable attention during the time period examined.) Heavy coverage was also devoted to the savage beating and death of University of Wyoming student Matthew Shepard in 1998. Shepard, an openly gay man, was lashed to a fence post and left to die by two men (non-students) who espoused anti-gay sentiments.

By far, the November 18, 1999, Texas A&M collapse of a bonfire structure, which left 12 people dead and 27 injured, received the greatest amount of national media attention during the time period analyzed, appearing in all of the outlets searched. A Seton Hall University residence hall fire in January 2000 that took the lives of three students and injured nearly 60 also received significant national attention, with extensive coverage from the *New York Times*, *USA Today*, *Wall Street Journal*, *Washington Post*, *Newsweek*, and Associated Press.

Coverage by the Associated Press deserves special attention. Whereas a story in a daily newspaper or monthly news magazine appears in that particular publication (and potentially, on its Web site), it may be recirculated by the Associated Press and can then appear in various and numerous media outlets. Campus, local, regional, state, and national print media download and publish Associated Press stories to complement reports written by their own staff reporters. Once a story is reported on by the Associated Press, it can be "picked up" by any member publication. A majority of the 4,115 fire-related Seton Hall University stories that appeared in newspapers across the nation during the height of that crisis, from late January 2000 through April 2000, were Associated Press stories. In short, Associated Press coverage of a campus crisis has the potential to communicate to people across the nation in their state, local, or campus newspapers.

"Organizations earn legitimacy when their activities reflect the values held" (Perrow, 1972; Sellnow, Ulmer, & Snider, 1998, p. 65). In the media glare of a crisis, the expectations for universities to justify their reactions and responses in terms of prevailing norms are particularly intense. During these times, legitimacy management—the process whereby organizations attempt to gain, regain, or maintain stakeholder support for an organization's actions—is critical (Massey, 2001). Often, however, universities are unprepared for the public scrutiny a crisis provokes, and their communications can violate established social norms. The price paid for lack of proper crisis communication includes decreased organizational credibility, a weakened reputation, and renewed efforts by the press to more aggressively investigate campus issues/actions. If not handled correctly, crises can stick to a university in media reports long after crises events. Noted Zelizer (Zelizer, 1993; Ratcliff, 1995), "Even though incidents took place a few years ago, reporters and editors [can] recount their occurrences to uphold their professional ideology and affirm their practices of policing universities" (p. 16).

To maintain or regain legitimacy during and after a crisis, "organizations must engage in a discourse with their public(s) that provides adequate justification for whatever actions are under scrutiny" (Strauss, 1982; Turket, 1982; Sellnow, Ulmer, & Snider, 1998, p. 62). This discourse may be suggested via a crisis communication plan, a document that provides a practical framework for communication when a crisis occurs and that incorporates the tactical "lessons learned" from similar institutions/organizations that have faced crisis events in the past. Such plans are developed prior to crisis events and in anticipation of the emergency, organizational, and communication-related responsibilities of an organization in crises. A typical campus crises communication plan provides policies and procedures for the coordination of communication within the university, and among the university, the media, and the institution's publics in the event of an emergency or controversial issue.

The value of a crisis communication plan to corporations is well established in the communication literature (Cutlip, Center, & Broom, 1995; Hendrix, 1998; Newson, Turk, & Kruckeberg, 2000; Seitel, 2001; Wilcox, Cameron, Ault, & Agee, 2003). Several researchers (Seeger & Barton, 2001; Seeger, Barton, Heyart, & Bultnyck, 2001) have explored crisis communication planning at elementary and high schools. Although some writers (Wilson, 1992; Kennedy, 1999) note the need for colleges and universities to develop crisis communication plans, just how many institutions have such plans in place is not known. Little additional insight on university crisis planning is gained from today's leading crisis communication professionals. Larry Smith, president of the Institute for Crisis Management, noted that the Institute "had not formally studied the issue, but [that] based on calls from colleges and universities, very few have a crisis communication plan...and most haven't even thought about it" (personal communication, September 27, 2001). According to Hill and Knowlton's Crisis Team (personal communication, August 14, 2001), "public relations and communication planning at most colleges remains focused on fund raising...even recent, major campus tragedies have not sent a wake-up call." While little has been examined regarding crisis communication planning in higher education, even less analysis has been conducted regarding universities' actual communication during and after a crisis event—or what in the crisis communication literature is referred to as image restoration discourse, the theoretical foundation for crisis communication (Coombs, 2000).

Image Restoration Discourse Theory centers on what an organization says and what information it disseminates during a crisis. Image restoration discourse speaks to the understanding that "every crisis is also a crisis of information ... and that failure to control the crisis of information results in failure to control the crisis, including its directly operational aspects" (Scanlon, 1975; Ogrizek & Guillery, 1999). The theory organizes image repair strategies into five broad categories: denial, evading responsibility, reducing offensiveness, corrective action, and mortification.

Denial

When a wrongful act occurs, the accused organization can deny that it occurred or that the organization performed it. A subset of denial is shifting the blame, a tactic used in an attempt to refocus attention elsewhere (Brinson & Benoit, 1996). In theory, if the denial is accepted, the organization's image is repaired. Brinson and Benoit (1996) discussed Dow Corning's use of denial through much of its crisis regarding silicone breast implants. Although Dow Corning eventually switched to more effective image restoration tactics, it continually asserted that its product was safe.

Shifting the blame is evident in Exxon's response to the 1989 Valdez disaster, in which a 987-foot oil tanker ran aground, spilling 260,000 barrels of crude oil in the waters of Prince William Sound. After the spill, Lawrence G. Rawl, chairman and chief executive of the Exxon Corporation, attempted to shift responsibility for a slow response and clean-up to state officials and the Coast Guard (Benoit, 1997).

Brinson and Benoit (1994) noted that some evidence suggests that "denial and shifting the blame are not considered by those who are injured by the [corporation's or individual's] actions to be as appropriate or effective as other potential image restoration strategies" in restoring social legitimacy (p. 87). Sellnow, Ulmer, and Snider (1998) offered a comprehensive explanation for why avoiding or delaying the acceptance of responsibility results in such a hard hit to an organization's ability to repair its social legitimacy. The researchers note that Dow Corning's initial denial of responsibility extended its image crisis and it was only after the company altered its approach that social legitimacy began to return. "An unwillingness to accept responsibility or to engage in significant corrective action during critical period of crises serves to intensify damage done to public image" (Sellnow, Ulmer, & Snider, 1998, p. 61).

A denial of wrongdoing and/or responsibility for a crisis situation is, of course, often a strategy preferred by corporate lawyers. Fear that statements of responsibility will return to haunt corporations in court battles can prevent organizations from moving past denial. The damage to social legitimacy that results from denial, however, and the benefits of corrective action, which expresses regret rather than guilt, is why denial is not frequently a preferred image restoration strategy.

Evading responsibility
Rather than denial, an organization may attempt to restore its image by evading responsibility for a crisis or developing excuses for the occurrence. Brinson and Benoit (1999) described four subcategories of evasion of responsibility—provocation, defeasibility, accidents, and good intentions:

Provocation suggests that the wrongdoing was a response to previous wrongful acts that provoked the offender. Defeasibility argues that lack of information or control over events caused the wrongful act. The strategy called accidents points to unforeseeable circumstances as a self-defense strategy. Finally, the accused could use good intentions as an evasion strategy. This option presents the rhetor's praiseworthy motives as a way to reduce responsibility for a wrongful act. (p. 3)

Reducing offensiveness

A third option in response to crisis is attempting to reduce the offensiveness of the act. This strategy includes six variations. The first, bolstering, uses positive comments in the hope of strengthening the public's opinion about the organization. Corporations and universities are bolstering when they describe offensive acts/crises scenarios as "unacceptable" or "never tolerated here." This kind of image repair strategy is used frequently to defend an institution's image in light of charges of racism or sexism. Texaco repeatedly used bolstering in its initial response to accusations that management was racist (Brinson & Benoit, 1999). The company explained that "discriminatory behavior is prohibited by Texaco's 'clear and vigorously-enforced policies against discrimination' and discriminatory behavior violates the 'company's core values and principles" (Brinson & Benoit, 1999, p. 4). Bolstering is most effective in restoring social legitimacy when messages emphasize the values held by and cultural expectations of the publics and shared by the institution.

A second subcategory of reducing offensiveness is minimization, an attempt to reduce the offensiveness of the act/crisis by downplaying negative outcomes of the crisis. Organizations can also use differentiation to reduce offensiveness. This tactic requires institutions to present examples of similar issues but those that feature more severe harm. Although not discussed in the literature, this researcher suggests that universities and colleges engage in a type of differentiation when they cite a "growing trend" as the root of a crisis situation. An alcohol-related death may, for instance, be positioned as an example of a greater/nationwide alcohol or drug problem. When a University of Michigan engineering student died in November 2000 after trying to drink 20 shots of Scotch whiskey in 10 minutes, for instance, the school provost noted, "This could happen to any student. This is not a student who was normally drinking to excess this way." Placing further emphasis on a national/growing trend, the university's vice president of student affairs, E. Royster Harper said, "The 21st birthday celebration that has developed on other campuses has come to our own" (Enders, 2000, paragraph 10). Clearly, university use of differentiation by citing a larger national trend deserves further investigation.

A fourth way to reduce offensiveness is through the transcendence, or highlighting the greater good that comes from the organization's actions. Lastly, an organization in crisis can attack the accuser or offer/give compensation—striking back or making up (Benoit, 1997).

Mortification

The fourth major category of image repair discourse is mortification, or admitting to the act, asking forgiveness, and apologizing. As noted by Benoit and Brinson (1994) in their analysis of AT&T's response to long distance service interruption in New York in 1991, the act of mortification helps to restore social legitimacy by conveying a "strong sense of security. It is neither easy nor pleasant to confess responsibility for the suffering of others" (p. 83). Doing so makes the communicator appear honest and trustworthy. Society holds people and organizations responsible for their actions. A sincere apology shows acceptance of this responsibility. "Burke discusses the purgative-guilt cycle, in which humans inevitably violate the social order, requiring redemption" (Beniot & Brinson, 1994, p. 87). Mortification is a primary means of symbolically killing the guilt. Although usually explicit, mortification/regret can be implied from corrective action taken after a crisis (Sellnow, Ulmer, & Snider, 1998).

Corrective Action

The final category of Image Restoration Theory is identified in the literature as corrective action, which "attempts to repair existing damages and/or to prevent future recurrence of the wrongful act" (Brinson & Benoit, 1999, p. 3). Sellnow, Ulmer, & Snider (1998) examined corrective action as an initial and primary means of restoring an organization's public image, finding that "taking some degree of responsibility for the crisis during critical periods and providing corrective action can expedite the organization's efforts to rebuild its legitimacy" (p. 61). Companies that fail to accept responsibility can intensify their image problems. Benoit and Czerwinski (1997) explained that "unlike compensation, which seeks to pay for a problem, corrective action seeks to prevent or correct" (p. 45). Corrective action means making real, long-term changes within an organization. The image restoration discourse literature clearly highlights the assumption that organizations facing crises must take some degree of responsibility if they hope to restore their social legitimacy. Corrective action speeds up this process (Sellnow, Ulmer, & Snider, 1998).

Corrective action taken and publicized shows publics that a significant change has been made, that measures have been taken so that a similar crisis does not occur in the future. It is not compensation (which may imply guilt); it is a voluntary remedial response. Such a response—one that addresses the core concerns brought to light by the crisis and moves to deter similar events—can "enhance a perception of preventive, long-term change and renewed social legitimacy " (Sellnow & Seeger, 1989, p. 17). Sellnow, Ulmer, and Snider (1998) note that corrective action is an appropriate and effective response even when the organization is not considered responsible for the crisis. As evidence of this, the researchers point to the success of the Johnson and Johnson Company during its Tylenol poisoning crisis. Although Johnson and Johnson did not take responsibility for the poisoning, it voluntarily took the corrective actions of removing the product from store shelves and later of changing the product design and product packaging.

Consideration of corrective action must, of course, include recognition of legal consequences. Ultimately, wrote Benoit (1997), organizations "must decide whether it is more important to restore image or avoid litigation" (p. 183). Another consideration is resources. Corrective action will not be effective and, in fact, should not be considered if the organization does not have the financial resources to pay for corrective measures.

A final consideration focuses on the impact of the crisis. If the impact is contained (i.e., a fire that results in a certain number of injuries), well known (i.e., salmonella is identified in a product, but the infection is understood and treatable), or avoidable (i.e., a syringe in a can of cola can be avoided by pouring the liquid into a glass), corrective action can contribute to the restoration of social legitimacy. If, as in Corning's case, the full impact of the crisis will not be known for many years, "immediate correction action has little impact" (Sellnow & Seeger, 1989, p. 69).

Several crisis communication "morals" are evident from the exploration of image restoration strategies. Some of the advice is applicable to persuasion in general: "avoid false claims, provide adequate support for claims, develop themes throughout the campaign, and avoid arguments that backfire" (Benoit, 1997, p. 183). Benoit (1997) provided others, including admitting fault when at fault and reporting plans to correct and/or prevent recurrence of the problem.

Other strategies such as shifting the blame and defeasibility can also be constructive if well planned. After an investigation of its poisoned capsules, Tylenol successfully shifted blame to an unknown person. (It followed with voluntary corrective action) "Related to this is the strategy of defeasibility. Exxon, for example, could have done a better job of stressing poor ocean conditions for problems with its [oil spill] clean-up." These factors beyond Exxon's control "could have alleviated responsibility and helped restore a tarnished image" (Benoit, 1997, p. 184).

Clearly, image restoration strategies must be carefully matched to the specific crisis situation and audiences affected. They must also be used with an understanding that powers of persuasion are limited. No one strategy or combination of strategies is best in all situations. What is important, however, is that communicators consider Image Restoration Discourse Theory in their communication crisis plans. Without an understanding of how others have applied these strategies to publicly recover from crisis situations, communicators and their organizations risk considerable damage to their image.

Case: Seton Hall University

Less than one hour after an intense, early morning fire broke out in the third-floor common area of Boland Hall, a six-story freshman residence hall housing 640 students on the campus of Seton Hall University, local and national news helicopters hovered over the school, broadcasting live from the scene. Hundreds of print reporters, broadcast journalists, photographers, camera crews, and news vans followed. Although the fire was extinguished quickly, it left three male 18-year-old freshmen dead, five critically injured, and more than 60 hospitalized with injuries ranging from burns to smoke inhalation. The tragedy ignited a public relations crisis unprecedented in the university's 144-year history and focused national attention on the school's crisis communications and image.

Public relations professionals have long recognized one essential truth about communication: If a vacuum develops in popular opinion, speculation will fill it. No time should be lost in providing accurate facts (Cutlip, Center, & Bloom, 1995). Seton Hall is located in one of the world's most intense media markets. The information vacuum enveloping the university on the morning of January

19 began to fill immediately. At daybreak, "chopper" coverage of the fire scene was broadcast, and journalists and anchors speculated about the fire's origins. By 7 a.m., the fire had been attributed to everything from careless smoking and space heaters to criminal activity and over-exuberant partying after a Seton Hall basketball game. Seton Hall worked to provide facts and a consistent message.

At 7 a.m., New Jersey's local News 12 television station broadcast the university's first statement from Lisa Grider, Seton Hall's Assistant Vice President of Alumni and University Relations and Chief Spokesperson. Grider announced that the university was in the process of creating toll-free number for parents and a phone bank for students to call home. Parents wishing to come to campus were encouraged to come to the university's reaction center. By 8 a.m., News 12 and one New York metropolitan area station were broadcasting more from Grider, including confirmation of three fatalities, a hotline for parents to call for information, and the cancellation of classes. All other local and national news programs broadcast information about the fatalities, injured students, the hotline, and class cancellations without the on-camera statement from Grider. Although Seton Hall's first official statements featured no clear signs of an image restoration strategy, a central and bolstering message of "community" was evident from the beginning. Throughout the crisis, the "we are a special community" message was evident in Seton Hall's discourse.

At the university's noon press conference on January 19, Seton Hall issued its first written briefing. The document (literally) spelled out the issues discussed at the press conference. It is in this initial briefing that the university made its first attempts to restore legitimacy using defeasibility. A subset of evading responsibility, defeasibility is used to communicate minimal control over events or a lack of information/correct information about a potential harm (Benoit, 1999). Seton Hall used defeasibility when it explained that Boland Hall had received recent and complete authorization from fire and safety officials as a safe resident hall.

By 11 a.m. on January 20, the focus of broadcast reports had moved from "what" had occurred on the campus of Seton Hall University to "how" and "why" it had occurred—or more specifically, "who was responsible." Another information vacuum was occurring. New Jersey law requires the County Prosecutor's Office to lead investigations of incidents involving deaths. Although Essex County Prosecutor Don Campolo could provide explanations of what had happened at Boland Hall, reporters' questions about "why" were typically answered with "this is part of the ongoing investigation." When Seton Hall officials were asked similar questions, they referred reporters back to the prosecutor's office. In order to get their stories, therefore, reporters turned to students for their thoughts on the possible *hows* and *whys*. Three central themes emerged in all afternoon local and national newscasts. The first was that fire hoses in Boland Hall had recently been disconnected. The second was that Boland Hall did not feature sprinklers. The third was that residents of Boland Hall had endured 18 false alarms since the start of the school year.

The number of false alarms, frigid temperatures, and the early morning hour of the January 19 alarms made many students slow to evacuate Boland Hall. At the noon press conference on January 19, reporters' questions centered around these three issues. Essex County Prosecutor Campolo responded to each. The disconnected cloth hoses were recently detached to be readied for the trash. The old hoses were antiquated and would not have been used by firefighters. The residence hall was built in 1952, with all construction predating a 1984 state requirement for installation of sprinkler systems. Although four Seton Hall dormitories built in the 1980s did have sprinkler systems, two did not (Boland being one of them). Finally, Boland Hall residents had indeed had 18 false alarms since September.

As the prosecutor responded to questions about the investigation, Seton Hall (through spokesperson Grider) continued to use defeasibility as well as elements of good intentions as restoration strategies during press conferences, focusing on the university's compliance with existing fire regulations. No sprinklers were in the building because they were not required. All pull stations, fire alarms, and extinguishers were in working order. University officials said that evacuations caused by frequent alarms at Boland Hall trained students for evacuations—adding to the number of alarms (more than two per week) with staged evacuations would not, the university claimed, have been helpful. The university stated that no alarms are considered false at Seton Hall. The university also continued to focus its comments on community, with statements about what was being done for its community, including counseling, information hotlines, immediate loans, temporary bedding, an evening prayer vigil, and later, the planning of a memorial service. During the last press conference of the day, Grider discussed some of the heroic acts of Boland Hall students, emotionally describing how one student re-entered the building four times to bring other residents to safety. The university's discourse at this time took the form of bolstering, a subcategory of reducing offensiveness using positive comments in the hope of strengthening the public's opinion about an organization.

After being centrally featured during the first 48 hours of the Seton Hall crisis, the disconnected hoses in Boland Hall became a non-issue with the press. In his statements, Essex County Prosecutor Campolo dismissed the hoses as old and unusable. Grider called the hoses obsolete. Another hot issue that cooled after the initial 48 hours was the danger of false alarms and the prevalence of "boy who cried wolf" scenarios at Seton Hall and across college campuses nationwide. Although colleges and universities often initiate the "citing a national trend" strategy during a crisis, Seton Hall did not publicly note the growing trend of false alarms on college campuses. Doing so, according to Image Restoration Discourse Theory, may have reduced the offensiveness of the crisis by presenting a similar issue of a potentially more severe harm. In fact, this image restoration strategy was not necessary on Seton Hall's part. Reporters themselves both recognized and isolated "pranks" as a local and national problem. An Associated Press story ran in dozens of papers on January 20 that focused on concerns about false alarms. Accompanying this Associated Press story was a report from an Associated Press National Writer with commentary from experts that indifference to alarms is common both on campus and off.

What did remain an intensely covered topic was the lack of a sprinkler system in Boland Hall. Although Seton Hall continued to note its full compliance with existing fire regulations and its recent fire safety inspections (defeasibility), headlines and reports were largely critical of the university for not having sprinklers. An Associated Press piece on sprinklers and alarms ran on January 20 in dozens of newspapers across the nation. The same theme was highlighted in New Jersey's daily newspapers. The focus on Seton Hall's lack of sprinklers prompted the university to commission a report from Lipman Hearne, an independent public relations firm with whom the university had an 18-month relationship, to determine what dormitories in New Jersey did/did not have sprinkler systems. Results of the study, top university administrators hoped, could potentially reframe the media focus on "no sprinklers at Seton Hall" to "no sprinklers in a majority of college/university residence halls across the nation." Seton Hall asked Lipman Hearne to use existing data to determine how many college residence halls in New Jersey were equipped with sprinkler systems. Because no data existed, the firm conducted its own primary research of state universities, finding that more than 65 percent of all residence halls in New Jersey lacked sprinklers. The results were released to the media. *The Star-Ledger* subsequently conducted its own study with similar findings.

Seton Hall's release of the report, in terms of Image Restoration Discourse Theory, can be seen as differentiation—or presentation of similar issues that feature more severe harm in order to reduce offensiveness. Seton Hall presented the facts about sprinklers as proof of its compliance with accepted procedures (defeasibility) and of the bigger issue (and more severe harm) of residence hall safety across the state to shift media focus off the university. When New Jersey's state newspaper, *The Star-Ledger*, published its story on the report, however, its focus was on image repair itself rather than on any "bigger picture" message. An Associated Press story based on *The Star-Ledger*'s coverage ran in dozens of papers across the nation with the headline: School's Image a Concern after Fire.

The media's critical analysis of Seton Hall's public relations strategies in the midst of the Boland Hall crisis supports Footlick's (1997) contention that news coverage of colleges and universities has become more argumentative, investigative, and aggressive. Seton Hall's request that its public relations firm conduct research and report on the overall status of sprinkler systems in New Jersey colleges is, in practical terms, sound public relations. The findings help reframe the issue, turning the media focus to the bigger picture. The media's scrutiny of the university's image restoration strategy and its negative portrayal of a college's concern about image are intriguing and deserve further investigation.

Although Seton Hall's use of differentiation did not have its intended impact in the press, local, state, and national legislators got the message that most college and university residence hall rooms lacked sprinklers. Within days of the fire, New Jersey Governor Christine Todd Whitman said she would consider legislation requiring sprinklers in all college residence halls. Legislators in New Jersey, New York, and several other states reviewed requirements and discussed amendments. *The New York Times* reported that by February 1 in New York State alone, 10 lawmakers had introduced 10 fire safety bills (Jacobs, February 3, 2000).

At Seton Hall, the image restoration strategy of defeasibility and differentiation began to give way to hints of corrective action. In fact, on February 2, two weeks after the tragic fire, Seton Hall called a press conference to announce that sprinklers would be installed in Boland and Aquinas Halls and upgraded in all other dorms on campus—immediately and even though it was not required by law.

As the University announced corrective action, it continued to include signs of defeasibility and differentiation in its image restoration discourse. The corrective action, however, dominated headlines and leading broadcast stories. It also eased the critical tone of media coverage. Although the *hows* of the tragic fire were still under investigation, the university was moving forward in its efforts to prevent a recurrence. The corrective action strategy gained momentum when the university changed its fire drill policy by scheduling surprise drills. The positive impact of Seton Hall's corrective action is perhaps most evident in the media's March 1 coverage of a New Jersey Fire Safety Report on the university. Although more than 800 violations (among all of the school's 35 buildings) were cited, the coverage was more balanced than any previous coverage of fire-related events/communications.

After the university took corrective action, this more balanced coverage continued through two potentially very damaging fire-related stories in March and April. In March, a small fire that started in a dryer in Seton Hall's Recreation Center received attention from state print media and state and network broadcast media. While most every report mentioned "memories of January 19," coverage was free from the aggressive, negative speculation and finger pointing experienced during the Boland fire. In April, when the lawyers for the families of two deceased students and three injured students held a press conference to announce intent to sue the university, coverage remained balanced, with all media outlets prominently featuring one particularly strong portion of a statement from the university's president. When corrective action was already taken, this bolstering statement served to reduce the offensiveness of the crisis (Beniot, 1997).

Conclusion

Important lessons can be learned from this investigation into Seton Hall University's public relations tactics and communication discourse during and immediately after its crisis. The first, and perhaps most obvious, is that an analysis of communication discourse during a crisis yields important insight not evident from an investigation of public relations tactics. If public relations professionals on college campuses really want to dissect the success of their crisis response, they must consider their discourse.

The analysis also highlights the importance of corrective action when a crisis occurs at an institution that considers itself (and promotes itself as) a "community." Corrective action "attempts to repair existing damages and/or to prevent future recurrence of the wrongful act" (Brinson & Benoit, 1999, p. 3). Sellnow, Ulmer, and Snider (1998) called corrective action an initial and primary means to restore an organization's public image, finding that "taking some degree of responsibility for the crisis during critical periods and providing corrective action can expedite the organization's efforts to rebuild its legitimacy" (p. 61).

Further investigation is also needed to determine if defeasibility is a widely used and useful strategy for universities. Although Seton Hall was able to reframe its message with this approach, the university was also negatively portrayed in the media for attending to its image by pointing out the bigger picture, the lack of sprinkler systems in all college residence halls. A key question about this approach to communication discourse is whether it is useful in today's media environment, where coverage of higher education is becoming more investigative, aggressive, and similar to coverage of corporations, politicians, and the entertainment industry. The outcome of the Seton Hall fire and the university's ability to restore its image is as much about what it said as about what it did during and after the Boland Hall crisis. Words, in this case, spoke as loudly as actions.

References

Benoit, W. L. (1997). Image repair discourse and crisis communication. *Public Relations Review, 23*, 177-186.

Benoit, W. L., & Brinson, S. L. (1994). AT&T: Apologies are not enough. *Communication Quarterly, 42*, 75-88.

Benoit, W. L., & Brinson, S. L. (1999). Queen Elizabeth's image repair discourse: Insensitive royal or compassionate queen? *Public Relations Review, 25*, 145-156.

Benoit, W. L. & Czerwinski, A. (1997). A critical analysis of USAir's image repair discourse. *Business Communication Quarterly, 60*, 38-57.

Brinson, S. L. & Benoit, W.L. (1996) Dow Corning's image repair strategies in the breast impact crisis. *Communication Quarterly, 44*, 29-41.

Coombs, W. T. (2000). *Reasoned action in crisis communication: Moving toward a symbolic crisis communication theory.* Paper presented at the Annual Convention of the National Communication Association, Seattle.

Cutlip, S., Center, A. & Broom, G. (1995). *Effective public relations.* Upper Saddle River, NJ: Prentice Hall.

Enders, D. (November 14, 2000). *Michigan Daily* via U-Wire.

Footlick, J. K. (1997). *Truth and consequences: How colleges and universities meet public crises.* Phoenix: American Council on Education and The Oryx Press.

Hendrix, J. (1998). *Public relations cases.* Belmont, CA: Wadsworth Publishing.

Jacobs, A. (2000, February 3). Seton Hall will install sprinklers in dormitories. *The New York Times*, B5.

Kennedy, M. (1999a). Crisis Management: Every school needs a plan. *American School & University*, S25-S26.

Kennedy, M. (1999b). Surviving a crisis. *American School & University*, 42b-42e.

Massey, J. E. (2001). Managing organizational legitimacy: Communication strategies for organizations in crisis. *The Journal of Business Communication, 38,* 153-182.

Maeroff, G. I. (1998). *Imaging education: The media and school in America.* New York: Teachers College.

Murphy, P. (1996). Chaos Theory as a model for managing issues and crises. *Public Relations Review 22,* 95-113.

Newson, D., Turk, J. V., & Kruckberg, D. (2000). *This is PR: The realities of public relations.* Belmont, CA: Wadsworth Publishing.

Ogrizek, M., & Guillery, J. M. (1999). *Communicating in crisis: A theoretical and practical guide to crisis management.* New York: Aldine DeGruyter.

Ratcliff, G. R. (1995). *The press as a policy actor and agent of social control and the efforts of universities to negotiate.* ASHE Annual Meeting Paper.

Seeger, M. W. & Barton, E. A. (2001, May). *Crisis in the public schools: An examination of school crisis plans.* Poster session presented at the International Communication Association Convention for the Public Relations Division, Washington, DC.

Seeger M. W., Barton, E. A., Heyart, B. & Bultnyck, S. (2001). Crisis planning and crisis communication in the public schools: Assessing post-Columbine responses. *Communication Research Reports, 18,* 375-383.

Seitel, F. P. (2001). *The practice of public relations.* Upper Saddle River, NJ: Prentice Hall.

Sellnow, T. L. & Seeger, M. W. (1989). Crisis messages: Wall Street and the Reagan administration after Black Monday. *Speaker and Gavel, 26,* 9-18.

Sellnow, T. L., Ulmer, R. R. & Snider, M. (1998). The compatibility of corrective action in organizational crisis communication. *Communication Quarterly, 41,* 60-74.

Wilcox, D. L., Cameron, G. T., Ault, P. H., & Agree, W. K. (2003). *Public relations: Strategies and tactics.* Boston: Allyn and Bacon.

Wilson, B. G. (1992). *Crisis management: A case study of three American universities.* Unpublished doctoral dissertation, University of Pittsburgh.

19

Instructional Scenarios for
Critical Incident Response Team Training

Stephanie Griffith and Erin Taylor Weathers

*Readers can use these instructional scenarios to practice prioritizing and re-
sponding to concerns arising from a student's death. The section concludes
with seven questions to guide discussion and evaluation of current practices.
These scenarios and questions can strengthen current practices while also allowing staff members to test their abilities to respond to campus crises.*

In an effort to integrate theory and practice, we have developed several
training scenarios. While each of the students in the scenarios is fictitious, the
nature of his or her deaths is the amalgam of actual events.

A Critical Incident Response Team (CIRT) can only be as prepared as it has
been trained to be. Appropriate CIRT training gives student affairs staff the resources they need to respond quickly and proactively to a student's death. Training can help diminish a university's fear of responding fully because of potential
litigation. Ideally, CIRT training asks participants to examine their own cultural
beliefs about dying, death, and the afterlife while encouraging them to explore
alternative perspectives. Another important facet of this training is discovering if
certain university policies actually compound rather than facilitate an appropriate university response. Finally, effective CIRT training "walks" staff members
through hypothetical student deaths, allowing for reflective staff discussion and
CIRT procedure revision. It is pointless to maintain policies and guidelines if
those responsible for the provision of direct services to students are not in

*Stephanie Griffith is completing her Ph.D. in Adult and Higher Education at the Univer-
sity of Oklahoma. She is an adjunct instructor for Freshmen Programs at the University
of Oklahoma working with students as they transition from high school to college. Erin
Taylor Weathers completed her Ph.D. in Adult and Higher Education at the University of
Oklahoma in 2006. She has served in numerous student affairs capacities working with
adult students, universities abroad, and marginalized female populations.*

positions to test them. This is the function of scenario work. By placing staff in hypothetical "death scenes," they must implement the protocol of their Critical Incident Response Team as well as exercise their own critical evaluation of the situation. Many times, the loopholes in an organization's critical incident response come to light in these training sessions.

Scenario training works best in a team setting after staff members have been taught university response procedures and have received bereavement and death notification education. Training participants should be given minimal time to develop their response to the scenario because students' deaths are always untimely and almost always unanticipated.

Encourage staff members to serve as the university liaison in a scenario. Having two staff members role play as dual responders to the event can enrich this experience. Ask staff members to consider what issues must be addressed first and which community agencies will be involved in the death event. Finally, all members of the response team should follow all scenario work with an evaluation of the response.

Case 1: Adrienne Salinas

Adrienne Salinas, a junior, was killed driving home last night when she crossed a country road median and struck an oncoming vehicle. She died immediately as did the man driving the other car, a husband and father of two. It appears Adrienne was driving under the influence of alcohol. Friends who last saw her at an off-campus party last night have disclosed to Adrienne's resident advisor that she was "pretty drunk."

The 8 a.m. local news reported on the accident including mention that this was likely a drunken driving accident.

It is now 10 a.m. and you know the local police have already contacted Adrienne's mother. She will be arriving (along with Adrienne's fourteen year-old brother) on a 1 p.m. flight. Adrienne's father lives in Barcelona. He and Adrienne's mother have been divorced several years and no longer speak to one another. Adrienne's mother declined to be the one who informed her ex-husband of their daughter's death. As far as you know, he has yet to be notified.

Adrienne's roommate contacted her resident advisor after a local news reporter knocked directly on her door this morning to speak to her about "Adrienne's drinking problem."

The news of Adrienne's death is quickly making its way around campus. At the accident site, fellow students are beginning to leave cards, stuffed animals, and flowers. Also present are mourners for the man who was killed. You are still unaware of the man's name.

Case 2: Malcolm Oliver

Malcolm Oliver was a "big man on campus." As student body vice-president, an Omega, and senior honor student, Malcolm was popular with students, student life staff, and faculty. He was also well known as the mayor's son in your community.

On the Saturday evening before finals week, Malcolm drowned while jet skiing at a nearby lake. The police report says no alcohol or illegal substances were involved. Malcolm was not wearing a life jacket, and several of his fraternity brothers tried to swim out to him before he sank below the lake's surface.

The story has been reported on that night's 10 p.m. news, and most of the campus knows of Malcolm's death by Sunday evening.

The Omega house, where Malcolm lived, is being inundated with calls from reporters and directives from the Mayor's Office. The Mayor and her husband have asked that the Monday evening student-led memorial service be a non-media event.

Case 3: Angela Ashford and Robert Velmont, Jr.

Angela and Robert began dating the third week of their freshman year. Angela was a first generation student from a rural community 400 miles away. While she won a full scholarship, she has been on academic probation this second semester. She confided to her resident advisor how much harder college was than high school, how discouraged and homesick she felt, and how her dad thought Robert was the cause of her academic struggles. Angela's father urged her to withdraw and return home after this semester.

Robert's background was different. While his high school grades were only mediocre, his parents convinced him to attend this college because of its strong MBA program. Robert seemed more interested in writing. His residence hall neighbors are aware of his illegal drug use. Robert was caught with marijuana in his room early in the fall semester but talked his resident advisor out of reporting the incident.

Angela and Robert had become increasingly close, speaking openly of their love for each other. They had begun to shun friends, cut classes and "hole up" in one another's room.

This background information is relevant because Angela and Robert have just completed a suicide pact. After each swallowed approximately fifteen sleeping sedatives, that were prescribed to Angela by a campus doctor, they injected one another with a massive dose of heroin.

When Robert's roommate returned to his room at 1:40 a.m. Sunday morning, he found their seemingly lifeless bodies curled up together on Robert's bed. Taped to the wall next to them was a three-page suicide note written by Robert but signed by both. The roommate immediately called 911 and then raced to the resident director's suite.

Angela was pronounced dead at the scene. Robert was rushed to the hospital where his life was saved by extraordinary measures. The hospital staff contacted Robert's parents, who live in a nearby city. They arrived at the hospital at 4 a.m. By 8 a.m., doctors listed him in "guarded condition." You assumed campus or local police would contact Angela's family, but, at 9 a.m., the campus chief of security calls to ask you when you intend to notify them.

Case 4: Callie Barnett

Callie was a senior psychology major at your religiously affiliated college. She was active in a campus ministry program. For spring break, Callie had flown to Costa Rica on a mission trip as a part of this organization. While traveling on the Atlantic coast, her vehicle was car jacked. Callie and two other students attempted to stop the robbery, and gunfire ensued from the attackers. One student was seriously wounded but is expected to survive; another student had no injuries. Callie was shot and died within the hour. The nearest hospital was two hours away, and it was unlikely the facility was capable of treating her due to the severity of her injuries.

The story is picked up by international news agencies, and this is how your staff hears about Callie's death. Immediately after, Callie's father calls your office, distraught: Had Callie been in that car? Was she okay? You are unsure if the campus ministry program knows of the incident, but hope they maintain an itinerary for the mission trip and a list of Costa Rican contacts.

Case 5: John Tran

John is dying of pneumonia. It is common knowledge that the pneumonia was brought on due to a weakened immune system from AIDS. John is an extremely gifted architecture graduate student, having returned to school after working for fifteen years. He has won numerous awards. In two weeks, the campus childcare center that John designed is slated to open. John has also been active in campus and community gay advocacy groups as well as his church. He is often requested to speak on behalf of gay issues, including spirituality.

John's hospital room is flooded with cards, flowers, and peers. John's partner Adam, himself a medical student, rarely leaves his bedside. John's family, however, is absent. Not only do they live thousands of miles away, they also have severed ties with John when he disclosed to them that he was gay.

John's pneumonia is so advanced that doctors feel he will die in a matter of hours. John is rarely conscious, but when he is, he knows he is dying.

Further Considerations

The following questions are meant to stimulate discussion and encourage the evaluation of current practices and policies.

1. There are instances where a student commits a homicide against another student before completing his or her own suicide. Consider how you work with both grieving families. How might this affect your response to Case #3?

2. Imagine an older student dies, for example, a divorced father whose twelve year-old daughter lives with him. How would you respond to a case like this?

3. Many college students die far from campus, on road trips, during spring break, or in their hometown. What is expected of your crisis response team then?

4. Some families may want your feedback on developing a memorial scholarship or pursuing a posthumous degree. What can you tell them, and which referrals need to be made?

5. Some suicidologists argue that memorials for students who complete suicides may "glamorize" the act and encourage "copycat" events. How do you feel about this? How might this affect how you respond to Case #2?

6. What can legal counsel teach you? Are there situations in which you would include university counsel when working with the grieving family?

7. What are your personal experiences of death and grieving? Have you ever felt helpless when those you care about lost loved ones of their own? What did you do that seemed particularly helpful?

Suggested Readings

Allen, P. (1792). *An oration on the death of Roger Williams Howell: a member of the senior class of Rhode-Island College, who died October 7, 1792, aetat.20: pronounced in the college-chapel, November 22, 1792.* Providence, R.I.: J. Carter.

Archer, J. Jr. (1992). Campus in crisis: Coping with fear and panic related to serial murders. *Journal of Counseling & Development, 71,* 96-100.

Bailley, S. E. (1999) *Personality and grieving in a university student population.* Doctoral dissertation, University of Windsor, Ontario, Canada.

Balk, D. E. (1990). *The many faces of bereavement on the college campus.* Paper presented at Annual Convention of American Psychological Association, Boston, MA. ERIC accession# ED326794.

Balk, D. E. (1997). Death, bereavement, and college students: A descriptive analysis. *Mortality, 2*(3), 207-220.

Balk, D. E. (2001). College student bereavement, scholarship, and the university: A call for university engagement. *Death Studies, 25*(1), 67-84.

Balk, D. E. Tyson-Rawson, K., & Colletti-Wetzel, J. (1993). Social support as an intervention with bereaved college students. *Death Studies, 17*(5), 427-50.

Barry, D., & Jacobs, A. (2000, January 23). Fire, prayer and a loss of innocence at Seton Hall. *New York Times, 149,* p. 1.

Baxter, G., & Stuart, W. (1999). *Death and the adolescent.* Toronto: University of Toronto.

Bernard, J. L., & Bernard, M. L. (1982). Factors related to suicidal behavior among college students and the impact of institutional response. *Journal of College Student Development, 23*(5), 409-413.

Brown, L. M. (2001, February 15). Student deaths shake up college campuses. *Black Issues in Higher Education,* p. 7.

Buelow, G., & Range, L. M. (2001). No-suicide contracts among college students. *Death Studies, 25*(7), 583-592.

Campus PR Director's messages suggest he tried to "spin" news of student's death. (2001). *Chronicle of Higher Education, 47,* p. A48.

Charles, K. E. & Eddy, J. M. (1987). In-service training on dying and death for residence hall staff. *NASPA Journal 25,* 126 29.

Corazzini, J. G., & May, T. M. (1985). The role of the Counseling Center in responding to student deaths. In E. S. Zinner (Ed.), *Coping with death on campus* (pp. 39-50). San Francisco: Jossey-Bass.

Crafts, R. (1985). Student affairs response to student death. In E. S. Zinner (Ed.). *Coping with death on campus* (pp. 29-38). San Francisco: Jossey-Bass.

Cushing, D. D. (1849). *A eulogy, delivered in the chapel of Williams College, November 6, 1823; on account of the lamented death of Orren Ware: a member of the sophomore class, who departed this life October 9, 1823, in 19th year of his age.* Williamstown: Ridley Bannister.

Domino, G. (1988). Attitudes toward suicide among highly creative college students. *Creativity Research Journal, 1*, 92-105.

Donohue, W. R. (1977). Student death: What do we do? *NASPA Journal 14*(4), 29-32.

Halberg, L. J. (1986). Death of a college student: Response by student services professionals on one campus. *Journal of Counseling & Development, 64*(6), 411-413.

Hardin, C., & Weast, P. G. (1989). *Campus suicide: The role of college personnel from intervention to postvention.* Paper presented at the Annual Meeting of the American College Personnel Association. Washington, D.C.

Hendrickson, S. & Cameron, C. A. (1975). Student suicide and college administrators: A perceptual gap. *Journal of Higher Education 46*(3), 349-354.

Hipple, J., Cimbolic, P., & Peterson, J. (1980). Student services response to suicide. *Journal of College Student Personnel, 21*, 457-458.

Jacobs, B., & Towns, J. E. (1984). What residence hall staff need to know about dealing with death. *NASPA Journal, 22*(2), 32-36.

Knott, J. E., & Crafts, R. (1980). The realities of college student death. *NASPA Journal, 18*(2), 29-34.

LaGrand, L. E. (1985). College student loss and response. In E. S. Zinner (Ed.), *Coping with death on campus* (pp. 15-28). San Francisco: Jossey-Bass.

Lévy, J. J., Sansfacon, D., Samson, J., & Champagne, L. (1993). Death, grief, and solidarity: The Polytechnique case. *Omega: Journal of Death & Dying 27*(1), 67-74.

Manning, K., Ed., (1999). *Giving voice to critical campus issues: Qualitative research in student affairs.* Lanham, MD: American College Personnel Association: University Press of America.

Maxcy, J. (1819). *A funeral sermon occasioned by the death of Mr. John Sampson Bobo a member of the Junior Class in the South-Carolina College, who was unfortunately drowned in the Congaree River, near Columbia. Delivered in the college chapel on Lord's Day, Oct. 10, 1819.* Columbia, S.C.: Daniel Faust.

Mishara, B., Baker, A. H., & Mishara, T. T. (1976). The frequency of suicide attempts: A retrospective approach applied to college students. *American Journal of Psychiatry, 133*(7), 841-844.

Mitchell, S. L., Elmore, K., & Fygetakis, L. M. (1996). A coordinated campus response to student suicide. *Journal of College Student Development 37*(6), 698-699.

Oltjenbruns, K. A. (1998). Ethnicity and the grief response: Mexican-American versus Anglo-American college students. *Death Studies 22*(2), 141-155.

Reisberg, L. (2000). MIT pays $6-million to settle lawsuit over a student's death. *Chronicle of Higher Education*, p. A49.

Rickgarn, R. L. V. (1987). The death response team: Responding to the forgotten grievers. *Journal of Counseling and Development, 66*(4), 197-99.

Scheibel, D (1999). *If your roommate dies, you get a 4.0*: Reclaiming rumor with Burke and organizational culture. *Western Journal of Communication, 63*(2), 168-192.

Schuh, J. H. & Shipton, W. C. (1985). The residence hall resource team: Collaboration in counseling activities. *Journal of Counseling and Development, 63*(6), 380-381.

Scott, J. E., Fukuyama, M. A., Dunkel, N. W. & Griffin, W. D. (1992). The trauma response team: Preparing staff to respond to student death. *NASPA Journal, 29*(3), 230-37.

Seymour, C. P. (1828). *A eulogy, delivered in the chapel of Williams College, on account of the lamented death of Harry Ware, a member of the freshmen class, who departed this life November 19, 1827, in the 22d year of his age.* Williamstown, MA: Ridley Bannister.

Streufert, B. J. (2004). Death on campuses: Common postvention strategies in higher education. *Death Studies, 28*(2), 151-172.

Swenson, D. X., & Ginsberg, M. H. (1996). A comprehensive model for campus death postvention. *Journal of College Student Development, 37*(5), 543-549.

The Riot at New Haven Between the Students and Town Boys, on the night of March 17, 1854, which resulted in the death of Patrick O'Neil, and the wounding of several persons &c., &c. together with the coroner's investigation and the verdict. (1854). New Haven, CT: Richardson's Book, Magazine, and Newspaper Depot.

Tuttle, J. F. (2000). South African student killed at tuition protest. *Chronicle of Higher Education,* p. A61.

Index

About the Editors

Rosa Cintrón is an Associate Professor at the University of Central Florida. At the beginning of this book project she was a faculty member in Adult and Higher Education and Dean of The University College at the University of Oklahoma. She received her doctorate at Florida State University and her master's in Clinical Psychology from the University of Puerto Rico. Her current research interests focus on the first year experience and issues of diversity and social justice. Her husband is also a professor at the University of Central Florida. They have one daughter, Sara. She and her husband still miss their little Daniel who died in infancy.

Erin Taylor Weathers is a 1993 graduate of Texas A&M University and completed her Ph.D. in Adult and Higher Education at the University of Oklahoma in 2006. She has served in numerous student affairs capacities working with adult students, universities abroad, and marginalized female populations. Raised in Costa Rica, Erin is married and a mother to three young children. Her experiences when her sister, a college sophomore, died set in motion the development of this book.

Katherine Garlough received her doctorate at The University of Oklahoma in Adult and Higher Education. She is the executive director of International Development for Enterprise and Autonomy and the author of several international grants. She teaches college freshmen and has taught at the graduate level. The major thrust of her efforts continues to be in supporting higher education in the Middle East. Her husband's sudden death occurred the semester she re-entered college to complete her bachelor's degree.